Praise for *A Place to Stand:*

"*A Place to Stand* is about place in the largest, most flexible sense of the term: as home, but also as the soil of one's roots and as the literary pantheon into which one fits. In that sense the book belongs to the subgenre of prison tales for which the twentieth century was fertile ground . . . from *The Autobiography of Malcolm X* to Vaclav Havel's diaries. . . . [Baca is a poet who] travels outward and inward as a Chicano in America, with all the complications that the identity entails . . . a poet in control of his craft . . . whose voice, brutal yet tender, is unique in America . . . one worth paying attention to. [*A Place to Stand*] is a luminous book that is at once brave and heartbreaking . . . a thunderous artifact."—*The Nation*

"Baca chronicles his brutal experiences with riveting exactitude and remarkable evenhandedness. An unwilling participant in the horrific warfare that rages within prison walls and a rebel who refused to be broken by a vicious and corrupt system, Baca taught himself to read and write, awoke to the voice of the soul, and converted 'doing time' into a profoundly spiritual pursuit. Poetry became a lifeline, and Baca's harrowing story will stand among the world's most moving testimonies to the profound value of literature."

—*Booklist*

"As brawny and brilliant as its author, *A Place to Stand* is a triumph."

—*Tucson Weekly*

"*A Place to Stand* is an astonishing narrative that affirms the triumph of the human spirit and for that reason alone it is an important story. . . . Executed in broad strokes and startling colors . . . [Baca's memoir] is destined to become a benchmark of Southwestern prose."

—*Arizona Daily Star*

"A family history, a personal voyage and a searing critique of America's penal system, *A Place to Stand* is one of the most gripping memoirs in recent memory." —*Alibi*

"Baca enters [prison] rootless and illiterate, a child of abject poverty in southern New Mexico, having lived through an inexorable path of loss, abandonment, and violence. How he survived and became an internationally regarded poet and social activist is a gritty story unflinchingly told in *A Place to Stand*."
—*The Santa Fe New Mexican*

"Poet Baca's unflinching account of his incarceration, with its brutality and occasional benevolence, reveals the paradox of prison life. Ironically, his time in solitary confinement redeemed him, prompting lifesaving memories of his rural New Mexico childhood, which ignited his ability to use language to elevate himself above his immediate surroundings. The rustic imagery is beautiful, but beautiful too is the sun's path down the dark prison corridor. . . . [*A Place to Stand*] is worth reading from both a literary and social perspective." —*Library Journal*

A PLACE TO STAND

PREVIOUS WORKS BY THE AUTHOR:

Black Mesa Poems

Martin & Meditations on the South Valley

Immigrants in Our Own Land and Selected Early Poems

Working in the Dark: Reflections of a Poet of the Barrio

A PLACE TO STAND

The Making of a Poet

◆

Jimmy Santiago Baca

Grove Press *New York*

Copyright © 2001 by Jimmy Santiago Baca

All rights reserved. No part of this book may be reproduced in any form or by any electronic or mechanical means, including information storage and retrieval systems, without permission in writing from the publisher, except by a reviewer, who may quote brief passages in a review. Any members of educational institutions wishing to photocopy part or all of the work for classroom use, or publishers who would like to obtain permission to include the work in an anthology, should send their inquiries to Grove/Atlantic, Inc., 841 Broadway, New York, NY 10003.

Special thanks go to Anton Mueller for his effort in making this book a reality.
Names have been changed to protect the privacy of certain individuals.

Published simultaneously in Canada
Printed in the United States of America

Library of Congress Cataloging-in-Publication Data

Baca, Jimmy Santiago, 1952-
A place to stand: the making of a poet / Jimmy Santiago Baca.
p. cm.
ISBN 0-8021-3908-6 (pbk.)
1. Baca, Jimmy Santiago, 1952- 2. Poets, American—20th century—Biography. 3. Ex-convicts—United States—Biography. 4. Solitary confinement—United States. 5. Mexican American poets—Biography. 6. Prisons—United States. I. Title.

PS3552.A254 Z473 2001
811'.54—dc21
[B] 00-051400

DESIGN BY LAURA HAMMOND HOUGH

Grove Press
841 Broadway
New York, NY 10003

05 10 9 8 7 6 5

For Tones and Gabe

◆

PROLOGUE

◆

I was five years old the first time I ever set foot in prison. A policeman came to the door one night and told Mom she was needed at jail. She took me with her. When we arrived at the booking desk the captain asked, "You married to Damacio Baca?"

"Yes."

"He was arrested for drunk driving. His bail's a hundred. Sign here and make sure he appears for court."

"What are they?"

"His release papers."

The captain studied her hesitation.

"He stays till his appearance then." The captain shrugged, surprised at her, and led us past holding cells to the drunk tank.

It smelled like urine and whiskey vomit. I held tightly to Mother's hand. The corridors were dark and gloomy, and the slightest sound echoed ominously in the hall. We stopped in front of a cell where men sat and stared at the wall in front of them. Some were crumpled on the floor where they had passed out.

"*¡Oye, Damacio, despierta!*" the captain cried, and banged the bars with his baton.

The inmates glanced at us with hung-over disinterest, and one shook my father awake. He rose in a groggy stupor. Cautiously stepping over bodies, losing and regaining his footing, he approached the bars. He rubbed his face and blinked his red eyes.

"Did you have to bring *him*?" he asked accusingly. Then he added, clearly hurt that I was there, "I don't want him seeing me like this. Get me out of here."

"No," Mom said.

He stared at her. "Listen, you, don't—" Shaking with rage, he looked at me and made an effort to control himself.

We stood in silence for a few seconds. Then Mom cried, "Stay away from us!"

He reached his hand through the bars to me but Mom yanked me away, her hand painfully gripping mine. I wanted to tell her not to leave Father in there. I feared he might be hurt or be swallowed up by the darkness, and we would never see him again. The green painted bars, the guards with guns and keys and surly attitudes, the caked grime on the walls and floor, the unshaven men with no teeth and swollen red eyes and scratched faces—these filled me with terror. I tried to free my hand from Mother's to go back to him, but she squeezed harder and dragged me along.

"Get back here!" My father's voice was strained by both aggression and self-pity, but Mom opened the door and we left. I wanted to tell him I was sorry. I didn't want to keep him in jail. Only when he was drinking did he threaten to beat Mom up, wreck the car, lose his paycheck gambling, or sometimes not show up for days. He was not drinking now. We should have let him come home with us. When he would stagger in drunk, Mieyo and Martina would hide under the bed or in the closet, but I wasn't afraid of him. I would hold his hand and guide him to his chair, and he'd put me on his lap and moan drunkenly about how sorry he was for drinking and not being a better father. Even as scared as I was by the jail, I wanted to sit on the floor outside the cell bars and hold his hand because he needed me.

For weeks afterward my father's voice from behind bars echoed in my head as I moped around our yard or slept at my mother's side in our narrow bed. I had nightmares of violent forces hurling my father through the air; I tossed and turned but could never reach him. When I woke and lay still in bed, smelling my mother's skin, putting my face against my brother's hair, clutching my sister's hand, I curled in closer, fearing that a strange official-looking person would come and take my sister and brother and me away. There had been conspiratorial whispers between aunts and uncles in Grandma's kitchen. With Father in jail, I thought maybe Mother might be thinking of moving us. I no longer trusted that my brother and sister and I were safe.

Outside the thin walls of our shack, howling winds swept the New Mexico prairie with violent moans that reminded me of the misery of the jail, its dark gloom and the faces that stared at me from behind the bars. Again and again I recalled the wasted features of the prisoners, the faraway eyes, pleading to be let out, gazing at me as if from a distant place.

In time I would become all too familiar with such places, not only with those very same cells down on Garcia Street but with a long string of others as well, on different if equally dusty streets, with different but similar jailers, different but similar men. That initial encounter, however, never left me. It remained a fixed, haunting reference point to which I would return to time and again. Whether I was approaching it or seeking escape from it, jail always defined in some way the measure of my life.

As I grew up, my own eyes came to reflect those of these drunks, addicts, and beggars, those grieving men, women, and children and their stories. It was the same despair I had seen through the bars in my father's eyes, the same story. Over the years, I encountered all of them: eyes filled with raging despair, with weary despair, with insane despair; eyes with the despair of an old man who can no longer fight injustice; eyes filled with the dark despair of terror or mental illness; the anguished eyes of a child weeping in a corner. In time, my own eyes would show all these emotions. My own voice, calling through another set of bars, would merge with distant echoes of my father's voice and permit some final but forever insufficient understanding, love, and forgiveness to pass between us.

The last time I was in prison it was for five years. It was serious time in a serious place—Florence, a maximum-security state prison in Arizona. I landed there as I had landed in the others, by being a poor kid with too much anger and the wrong skin color and by fucking up again, though this time I was innocent of the specific charges against me. I was only twenty-one years old, still young, but by then I had already served a long apprenticeship in jail time. Some men measure their lives in terms of basketball games, fishing trips, school friends, movies, sleep-overs; these things, if they happened to me at all, were brief moments compared to the times I sat staring at cell walls for hours, days, and months at a stretch.

No, prison was not new to me when I arrived at Florence; I had been preparing for it from an early age. I had visited it a thousand times in the screams of my father and my drunken uncles, in the tight-lipped scolding of my mother, in the shrill reprimands of the nuns at Saint Anthony's orphanage; in all the finger-pointing adults who told me I didn't belong, I didn't fit in, I was a deviant. Security guards and managers followed me in store aisles; Anglo housewives walking toward me clutched their purses as I passed. I felt socially censured whenever I was in public, prohibited from entering certain neighborhoods or restaurants, mistrusted by government officials, treated as a flunky by schoolteachers, profiled by counselors as a troublemaker, taunted by police, and disdained by judges, because I had a Spanish accent and my skin was brown. Feeling inferior in a white world, alien and ashamed, I longed for another place to live, outside of society. By the time I arrived at Florence, a part of me felt I belonged there.

But if prison was the place of my downfall, a place where my humanity was cloaked by the rough fabric of the most primitive manhood, it was also the place of my ascent. I became a different man, not because prison was good for me, but in spite of its destructive forces. In prison I learned to believe in myself and to dream for a better life.

You make use of what is available and near at hand, no matter what your circumstances. I did what I had to do to survive. But I was also determined not to become what in my heart I knew I was not: I was not going to let them make me into a ward of the state. I was lucky, too. For in that place where life and death are waging war every day and the right choice is often the most difficult one, I was able to reach out and find a finger hold on the fragile ledge of hope. Hope didn't support me all the time, and wouldn't have supported others in quite the same way, but it served well enough for me to slowly pull myself up. Very simply, I learned to read and write.

Language gave me a way to keep the chaos of prison at bay and prevent it from devouring me; it was a resource that allowed me to confront and understand my past, even to wring from it some compelling truths, and it opened the way toward a future that was based not on fear or bitterness or apathy but on compassionate involvement and a belief that I belonged.

I have been a writer ever since, a poet. Poetry became something to aspire to, to live up to. It informed how I saw the world and my purpose in it. It was never the answer to everything and could not become so. At times, I had to put my pen down and fight with my fists, and sometimes when I yearned for answers to allay the excruciating pain of merely surviving, there were none. But poetry helped make me the person I am today, awakening creative elements that had long lain dormant in me, opening my mind to ideas, and enabling my intellect to nourish itself on alternative ways of being. Poetry enhanced my self-respect. It provided me with a path for exploring possibilities for my life's enrichment that I follow to this day.

The person I have become, who sits writing in this chair at this desk, has been forged by enormous struggle and unexpected blessings, despite the dehumanizing environment of a prison intended to destroy me. Prison was the most frightening nightmare I ever experienced. It stripped me down to nothing, until I huddled in the dark corner of a cell, sometimes shivering with fear, other times filled with so much anger and self-loathing that it would have been better to die. I have never told the full story of my transformation, a story I now believe is important, especially for my sons, playing in their room. I want them to know my heart and not be confused by conflicting rumors and gossip, wondering which ones are true. When I asked my father about his history, he would never answer. When I asked my grandmother about her history, she didn't want to talk about it. My sons won't have to ask. I want them to know their father's story, good parts and bad. I want to share with them what I have gone through, so they can make wiser choices where I did not and be invigorated with the courage and honor to live better lives.

It is also important for my father, who was never blessed with the good fortune I had in discovering a new path. I believe his death was hastened from the heartbreak of knowing I was in prison. But his failure as a father gave me a determined strength in my struggle for a better life that helped me be a better human being, even in a place like Florence. This maximum-security prison was a frightening and pain-racked place, but perhaps not as painful as other prisons I visited on my way there. I must tell you about them as well.

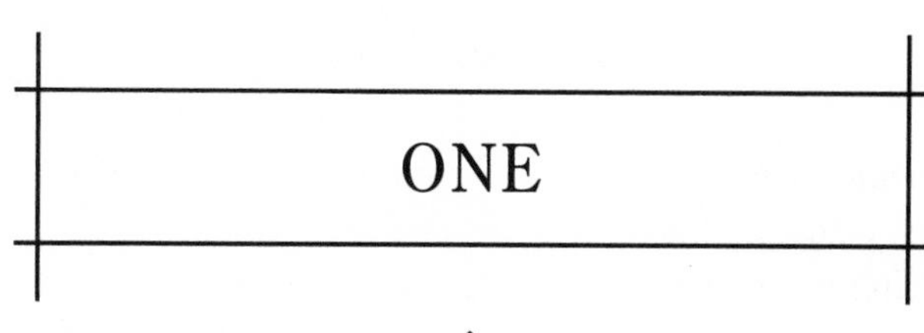

ONE

◆

When I was a boy, my father always wore a pained expression and kept his head down, as if he couldn't shake what was bothering him. He snapped irritably at the slightest infraction of his rules and argued continuously with Mother. He drank every day and she sank deeper into sadness and anger. To escape their fighting, and the gossiping of villagers in my Grandma Baca's kitchen, I often bellied into the crawl space under our shack to be alone in my own world. I felt safe in this peaceful refuge. The air was moist and smelled like apples withering in a gunnysack in the cellar at my Uncle Max's ranch in Willard. A stray dog might be waiting when I entered. Happy to see me, he would roll on the cool earth, panting, his tail wagging, and lick my face. After playing with him, I'd lie on the dirt and close my eyes and float out of my skin into stories my grandfather, Pedro Baca, told me—about those of our people who rode horses across the night prairie on raiding parties, wearing cloth over their heads, as they burned outsiders' barns, cut fences, and poisoned wells, trying to expel the gringo intruders and recover the land stolen from our people. This happened on prairie ranches all over New Mexico, from the late 1800s to the 1940s, when my grandfather was a young man herding sheep on the range.

I don't remember much before the age of five; my memories are of Grandma and Grandpa Baca in the kitchen, whispering sleepily as the coffee pot percolates on the woodstove; at night, their voices become guarded, talking about Father's drinking, concerned by Mother's absence, and worried that there's never enough money. People come and go; behind their conversations, a Motorola radio under the cupboards by the sink drones Mexican *corridos* or mass rosaries. Then tensions rupture in a night of rebukes. Uncle Santiago cuffs his younger brother, Uncle Refugio, for coming home drunk again, and Grandpa scolds Father for *his* drunkenness. I remember wondering if those fights had something to do with what I saw one hot summer afternoon.

I was six years old, in my crawl space under the shack—or La Casita, as we called it—where it was cool and quiet. I was drifting in a reverie when I was jolted back to the present by a door creaking open above me. I scooted to a dark corner and peeked up through a crack in the floorboards. A strange man entered La Casita and sat on the bed. Mother came in behind him, and he embraced her. His shiny wingtip shoes scraped grit into my eyes. They watered painfully, but I forced myself to watch as he raised her skirt and ran his hands along her thighs.

She protested, wrenching to one side and then to the other, pushing him away. But the bedsprings creaked as he pinned her and said, "I love you."

They made love with their clothes on.

She cried, struggling.

His voice trembled.

I wanted to race into the shack and seize him but fear disabled me. I scratched at the ground with my fingers and shook my head to blur what was happening. Dizzy and terrified, all I could do was brace my knees to my chest and hug myself in fear as their bodies bucked back and forth and the iron legs of the bed scratched on the wood floor. She shrieked and he groaned, and then all of a sudden they stopped, gasping for air and sighing.

After he departed, she waited awhile and then left too. I lay in the dark, shaking uncontrollably. The ground trembled. In the distance, a train was braking into the railyard, either to load up sacks of beans or deposit milled lumber or field equipment. An hour or so later, feeling vibrations as it pulled out, I wished it could have taken all our family problems away with it. I didn't know what this affair meant at the time, except I knew it was wrong, and I carried the secret of it like a fresh wound in my heart.

Days passed in anguish. I never told Father and I never let on to my mother that I knew. I feared Father would find out what Mother had done and was glad he hadn't been home for a week.

Mother and I were napping one afternoon when I heard his car pull up outside, tires crunching gravel. She ran out to the car. "Where've you been?"

"You m'jailer?" he countered sarcastically. He'd been drinking again.

"Just stay away!" She had tried many times to avoid fights by ignoring his carousing, but when I looked out at her I saw no trace of the vulnerable bride. Her face reddening, she screamed, "You're a drunk!"

He scoffed. "You love to use the past against me, don't you? It's your weapon; you stab and turn and dig it in!" His bloodshot eyes glared with resentment. "I never wanted to marry you!"

"You raped me," she said, and seemed stifled by her words.

"Liar," he growled. "From the very first day you chased after me. Waiting at school, at the dance, at my house! You trapped me, you wanted it! You can't make love or cook! The whole town's laughing behind my back!"

She turned and came into the house, speaking to herself. "You were so drunk you don't even remember." Tears streamed down her cheeks.

◆

My mother grew up in Willard, New Mexico, with four sisters and three brothers on a forty-acre ranch with no water. Her father, Leopoldo, a Spanish Comanchero, was a renowned cabinetmaker whom I never met, because he died of alcoholism before I was born. His wife, whom I called Grandma Weaver, raised my mother and her seven siblings. They were poor cowboys and cowgirls. When they weren't competing in regional rodeos, they worked long hours outside in the unbearably cold winters and hot sand-blowing summers, milking cows, feeding pigs and horses, filing ax blades, and chopping wood.

Being the youngest and prettiest, my mother, Cecilia, was shielded from much of the harsh work; she stayed indoors with her mother and cooked, canned fruits and vegetables, darned old clothes, and did housework. Her older sisters planned on marrying railroad workers, diesel mechanics, or cowboys, but Cecilia had set her sights above such a mean life. Although her family was Spanish and poor, she was fair-skinned, green-eyed, and black-haired. Her family expected her to marry a well-off gringo with a big ranch, but her heart was set on Damacio Baca, a Mexican from a neighboring village, Estancia, whose parents were landless peasants. When she first saw him in his new car passing her school bus on her way to school, she knew they were going to get married. At fifteen, he wore store-bought clothes and was already working part-time in the local grocery and feed store as stocker and cashier.

Her opportunity to meet him came when he made the high school basketball team and she joined the cheerleading squad. He was the team star and she the head cheerleader. It was the perfect match. Cecilia didn't mind his stopping at Francisco's pool hall to hustle hicks or play poker with older guys in the back room. After school, he usually gave her a ride home, and they would often park in an isolated field, hidden by windrow trees, to drink Seagram's and make out. They went steady for several months; she got pregnant, and they dropped out of school to get married.

Despite the early marriage, most people in Estancia were happy for them and pitched in to make their wedding a memorable one. Grandma and Grandpa Weaver, though indignant and against the marriage, gave them La Casita, which they trucked from Willard to Estancia and set up on blocks in the lot beside his parents' house.

The first few months my parents lived in La Casita next to Grandma Baca's house, but after my sister, Martina, was born, in 1950, Father took a job in Santa Fe, about an hour's drive north. They rented a house in Santa Fe, where they lived during the week, and then on weekends they'd stay in La Casita at Estancia. People liked my father and urged him to work his way into politics and one day run for office. A year later my brother, Mieyo, was born, and when Father was not on the road—he was employed by the DMV to deliver license plates to rural villages—he was with politicos in Santa Fe, drinking at the Toro cantina.

One year after that, in 1952, I was born, and it was about this time that Father's drinking and his absences first became an issue. He was having trouble getting the jobs that the politicians promised him. Also, unlike his village, where everyone respected him, in the urban cities of Santa Fe and Albuquerque, the whites looked down on Mexicans. Mother's frustration began to show. La Casita, with its two tar-papered cardboard rooms, one bed where we all slept, woodstove, and cold water spigot, wasn't the white picket-fenced house in a tree-lined city suburb she'd dreamed of. We had no furniture or dishes; we ate at Grandma's—Martina, Mieyo, and me tugging at Mother's skirt, fighting and crying. Mother tried to care for us, but she didn't know how. She and Damacio were only sixteen when they got married, and with him gone most of the time she had her hands full. Grandma Weaver kept after Mother to divorce him, claiming Father was nothing but a drunk and a womanizer. Her brothers swore they'd shoot him if they ever caught him and blamed her for dishonoring the family by marrying a "damn Mexican."

I remember him being two men. When sober, he looked boyish in pressed trousers, dress jacket, and white shirt, his appearance giving no trace of alcoholism. When he was drunk, he became vulgar and abusive, reducing himself to a pitiful phantom of the man he was when sober. When he was supposed to show up on Friday night, Mother made herself all pretty, and we'd go to the park pond and she'd push me on the swing. She'd chase us across the grass, wrestling us down with hugs, laughing and enchanting us with her girlish enthusiasm. We'd picnic on the grass, her green eyes sparkling with happiness as she told us how we were going to buy a nice house, toys and clothes. But later, waiting for Father, when he didn't arrive, her disappointment would deepen into surly pouting and when I did something wrong, she'd yell, saying she wished I was never born. I thought her sadness was my fault and I'd curl up on the floor in a corner and cry. Later, though, in bed, I'd weave her fingers around mine, kissing and tasting them as she caressed my face, apologized, whispered that everything was going to be fine.

We went back and forth between Santa Fe and Estancia more often once Martina and Mieyo started school in Estancia. I didn't want to go, and they didn't insist, so I played at home. In Santa Fe, although times were hard and we didn't have any money, neighbors sometimes came with canned staples and flour for tortillas. To show her gratitude for their kindness, Mother made me sit as they preached. "What is written in the Bible will come to pass!" they cried, as they stood above me in the middle of the room. "Infidels and sinners! The Lord will dash every idol and take upon himself proud ones and crush them!" I didn't say anything, but I thought they were strange and I was glad their visits were rare.

Not all Christians were the same. Sometimes, when a man named Richard took Mother out, she left me with a kind lady, Señora Valdez. Richard had sneaky ways and I didn't trust him. He was always whispering to my mother. When I asked what he had said, Mother told me I wasn't supposed to ask questions, and I didn't want to cause problems so I was quiet. Anyway, being with Señora Valdez allayed my anxiety about Richard. I often walked with her to the butcher shop for scraps to give stray dogs. At a small stream at the park by the plaza, we'd stand and toss bones to the starving creatures. She'd croon in an archaic voice, *"Bendice El Señor; El Señor perdona tus pecados, y cura tus enfermedades."* Her voice was warm and reassuring. I believed God listened to her prayers and made the dust storms stop, so I asked her to pray for my parents.

Whether we were in Estancia or Santa Fe, Dad would still come in late at night, smelling of whiskey and perfume. When I was six or seven, I was usually in bed right after sundown, but I stayed awake, waiting for him to come home. I would brace myself for a fight, as anything could happen when he was drunk. Many times I hid under my covers. my body tense, as he threatened my mother, hurling a spindle-back chair at her and roaring.

Mom would scream at him to get out. I often wept with fear, hoping he would not hurt her. Some nights he rushed drunkenly into my room and yanked me out of bed. I always looked desperately at my sister and brother as he carried me out, but they couldn't help me. Mom usually hid, afraid for her own safety. He would toss me into the car and drive away. I never knew where we were going. We usually drove for hours on country roads. I looked at the stars, I listened to the Mexican music on the radio, I glanced at him swigging from his whiskey bottle, and I tried to pretend that none of this was happening. I snuggled deep into the suit coat that covered me. The hum of the engine, the drone of the heater, and the wind blowing past his open window made me drowsy, and eventually I would fall asleep, helpless and sad.

On good days he tried to be conciliatory, promising to stay home more and not drink or womanize. On such days he always had surprises to show that life was going to get better. Once, to make us proud of him, he showed us a creased photograph of the governor of New Mexico shaking his hand on the capitol steps. He was excited, saying the governor was going to hire him soon. Often, after sharing good news with us, he'd say he had to run errands and would be right back. And just when I thought he might be sincere, he would return hours later, drooling drunk and crying with remorse. I pretended to ignore his repulsive drunkenness but was deeply disappointed. He always returned, and after slobbering all over me, saying what a good boy I was, how I was his favorite and someday I would be a great boxer, he would then stagger out for the night and not return until the bars were closing.

I didn't know which was worse, eagerly expecting him, but never knowing when he might barge drunkenly through the door late at night to fight with Mom, or fearing he would never come home again at all.

◆

Because father almost never came around, and when he did he was drunk, Mother had taken a job as a cashier at a Piggly Wiggly grocery store. We almost never saw her. I was too young to have understood, when we were living in Santa Fe, what it meant when this guy Richard kept coming over. I knew, though, the night we went to visit his parents, that something was up. I'd always distrusted this thin pimply-faced man from the "other world" who would drive up to our barrio shack in a shiny car and new suit, bearing chocolates and flowers, dresses, blouses, and other presents for Mom. I pretended to be indifferent to the candy he placed on the table and waited until they'd left before I tore it open and stuffed myself. I was only a child, but I understood in the way children do that Mother enjoyed the new standard of living that Richard was giving her. She'd bleached her hair, wore jewelry he'd given her, and always had money. She'd been changing in other ways too. She quit speaking Spanish and told us not to speak it around Richard.

Riding around in the car Richard had given her, she'd point to white-skinned, blue-eyed children and say I should be like them. When she dressed us, she mentioned that we should look like normal American kids. I had no idea how to do this. She would get mad at me for getting dirty playing in the dusty yard; when Richard was around, we had to stay clean and behave and sit quietly in a chair and say nothing. Richard would get mad when I asked for beans, chile, and tortilla, saying, "It's time you started eating American food." I knew Mom was trying to impress him with her "white ways," but it made her look silly.

It wasn't so with my father; he spoke Spanish and used English only when he had to. He listened to Mexican music, and all his friends were Mexicans. I never saw him with an Anglo. He never said anything bad about them, but he made a point to stay away from them. I remember riding around with him and saying, "No, don't want to go in there, too many gringos." I sensed that if he was around them, he'd be placing himself in harm's way. Ever since I could remember, my Baca grandparents mistrusted whites. When they came to Grandma's with official papers, we hid in the back rooms. Grandma said to be polite but warned me not to talk to them more than necessary. Uncle Santiago said they cheated Uncle Refugio out of his pay. When Grandpa was under the tree by the fence with his friends, I'd hear them talk about whites who used lawyers to pass laws to steal land or intimidated poor folks with their money.

That was why I was nervous the afternoon Richard took us to meet his rich parents. We were going into their world. Mom sat up front all made up, wearing a pretty pink dress and red high heels. Mieyo, Martina, and I huddled in the back. When we were almost there, Richard turned to Mom and explained that, since his parents were old-fashioned, it would be best if she said she was Anglo and that she was just babysitting us for a girlfriend. From where I sat I could see Mother bite her bottom lip as she stared straight ahead. I expected her to say something back to him, but instead she said to us, "You better be on your best behavior." And we were, for the whole boring afternoon; all we did was sit on big soft chairs in the living room as still as we had been in the car, afraid to touch the fancy food on small plates on the table unless it was offered, afraid to speak unless asked to speak, afraid to do anything but sit there and pick our fingernails. When we finally said our good-byes and pulled the car door closed, she turned to Richard and asked, "How'd I do?"

"A-plus," he replied, pleased with her. I remember looking at Mother again and noticing that a bit of lipstick that had smudged her bright teeth when she bit her lip was still there. I felt an odd satisfaction.

The next day, driving out of Santa Fe, Mother forced a smile and told us we were going to Estancia. Her voice was tight. She lit cigarette after cigarette, the lighter in her hand trembling. I could feel a mounting tension in Richard. He would press the gas pedal, making the engine hum higher, and then he would release it, and a few minutes later he would press down on the pedal again. I watched his eyes in the rearview mirror. They were hiding something. I felt Richard was going to do something bad to us, and all I could do was sit and wait for it to happen. I wanted to hit him and take control of the situation somehow, but how does a seven-year-old do that? I fidgeted instead, feeling my pulse throbbing in my fingertips, the seat springs against my butt. I looked up and caught Richard's eyes darting in and out of the mirror, looking at me. I picked my cuticles until they were bleeding. I was thinking of grabbing the steering wheel and begging Mother to stop the car and take us back to Santa Fe; or to leave Richard and just let the four of us live together. I looked out the window at endless miles of cactus and sage. In the window was my sister's reflection, her hand running a hair ribbon through her nervous palm, and Mieyo fingering a roll of caps.

"It's your fault," Martina hissed.

I turned and saw her and Mieyo looking at me. Mieyo's face was white, his neck artery engorged, dark eyes full of fear. "Told you," he said, pinching me. I sucked my breath back to hold my tears in but they came anyway. Maybe they were blaming me because I cried too much. "Crybaby," Mieyo said, and then the engine slowed and Richard backhanded him across the face.

"Stop that or I'll throw you out!" he yelled, and the car swayed forward again, picking up speed. "Do something with them, they're your kids," he told Mom.

"I hate you!" I screamed at Richard. Mieyo grabbed the door handle and flung it open. Richard braked, and we lunged forward as the car skidded in the roadside gravel.

Mom turned and slammed the door shut. "What is the matter with you! Don't ever do that again!" I'd peed in my pants, my blood drumming in my head and my heart beating wildly. I kept my head down to hide my tears.

Richard kept mumbling, "I'll be so happy . . . so happy." Why was he going to be so happy? Maybe we were going to picnic at the park pond. Maybe we were going to eat some good beans and hot buttered tortillas at Grandma's. Maybe he was dropping Mom and us off. Maybe he was going away.

After a while, we drove down Main Street. Trucks brimming with potatoes were parked by the track warehouses. There were men working in a big hole, standing around in that easy manner of small-town workers, talking and laughing. We turned off down a dirt road and pulled into Grandma's yard. She came outside and stood in the yard, her long gray hair braided, her apron splotched with flour. Mother brought us to her and kissed us briskly on the cheeks and said she'd be back. As I watched her leave, hearing the tires whir away on pavement, I felt weightless, sucked into a lifeless, paralyzing emptiness. I couldn't breathe and my legs were shaking. An intensely bright, luminous ball of fire was streaming into my eyes and blinding me. I tried to pull free of Grandma's hand, and I heard her say, *"Mañana sera mejor con el favor de Dios."* Tomorrow will be a better day with God's help. But as she led us into the house, I knew tomorrow would never be better. Something in my life had changed forever.

◆

We lived with Grandma and Grandpa Baca. Grandpa said it was only temporary and reassured us that our parents would return to pick us up once they settled into our new home. I looked forward to that day, fantasizing about how happy we'd all be. Little did I know that my mother had eloped to San Francisco with Richard, fleeing into a white world as "Sheila," where she could deny her past, hide her identity, and lie about her cultural heritage. I was also ignorant of my father's alcoholic oblivion, in which he pawned every last possession to get a bus ticket to San Francisco to try and find her.

We were resilient, as most children tend to be, and while we awaited their return, my Uncle Santiago took Mieyo and me everywhere with him—to milk his cows, ride his horses, feed the pigs, gather wood in the mountains, and hunt deer. I started to enjoy living with my grandparents again in Estancia. With my friend Mocoso, who came over when his mother Juanoveva visited Grandma, I spent the whole day roaming the village. We crossed fields, played in trees, tracked coyotes, built mud forts in ditch banks, and watched giant frogs crush our dirt village; we spent days in the barn teasing spiders out of webs, trapping mice, climbing up in the loft and making towns out of gunnysacks and tool crates; spying out of wood cracks at people who visited Grandma. When

Mocoso wasn't around, I went over to the high school and hung out with Grandpa, who was a janitor. I followed him everywhere through the halls, pushing the dust mop; later we went to irrigate a farmer's bean fields; and I walked home with him in the dusk.

Then, suddenly, Grandpa died. Except for my immediate family, I had loved him the most. When my parents left, it was Grandpa who kept life stable as possible for us. He was always reassuring me that things would turn out fine. Grandpa ordered my father and Uncle Carlos to stop arguing, and they did. Grandpa had often come over to La Casita and brought us candy, food, or other surprises. He was a gentle man, and my mother trusted him.

Before I could come to terms with Grandpa's unexpected death, Mieyo and I were taken to St. Anthony's Boys' Home in Albuquerque. Martina stayed in Estancia to help Grandma. It was June 1959.

At seven years old, I could never accept that my parents had abandoned us. What a shock! Thinking we were going to join them, Mieyo and I were driven instead to an orphanage and dropped off. Nuns escorted us up a flight of stairs into a dark, creaky third-floor dorm with kids in cots lined up on each side of the long room. I was scared and confused, weeping and clinging to Mieyo, begging to be taken back to my grandparents' in Estancia because my parents were coming to get us. No matter how hard the nuns tried to explain, not a day passed that I didn't expect my parents to come.

We were not coddled or given any special treatment at the orphanage, nor did anyone tell us anything about our parents. In the snap of a finger I found myself in a different world, among hundreds of strangers, with each minute planned out for me. The first few months, we slept on the condemned third floor. It rained almost every night, and the roof was leaking everywhere, soaking the bedsheets hanging between the bunks. Thunder roared and lightning revealed me weeping on my bunk at night. Mieyo would come and cradle me, and I clung to him as if we were one person.

At 4:30 A.M. we marched in columns to the chapel for mass on the second floor. After mass we went downstairs to the ground-floor dining room for breakfast. After eating, the older kids scattered out to do their chores and then go to school, and at noon we had lunch. The younger kids went to the playroom most of the morning, then napped or played on the playground. After supper the older kids did evening chores and us young kids got to watch TV for an hour; then we washed up and got ready for bed at 6:30 P.M. Six months after our arrival, new dorms had been completed and we moved into them. Groups were divided into age groups. I was in the 200s, the five-, six-, and seven-year-olds; Mieyo was in the 300s, the group of eight-, nine-, and ten-year-olds. I saw him in the dining room and at mass, but after that he went with older kids to do different chores and sit in different classrooms.

I'd always looked up to Mieyo, since he knew how to read people. At the orphanage he soon had the keys to the soda storeroom and the pantry, stocked with fresh-baked sweet rolls; he had a milk can full of marbles; he had the best clothes; and he worked as a barn boy, which gave him a lot more freedom to come and go as he wished. He knew the answers to things. He had comforted me when Mom and Dad fought.

When I asked the nuns if my parents were coming back, I was told the matter was in God's hands and children shouldn't ask such questions. God knew what he was doing. I should consider myself blessed, because God had something special in store for me. I felt lost and confused around grown-ups. They never told the truth. They were always hiding something that would eventually hurt me. I stayed in the field, away from them, playing with other boys—in the wind or on the teeter-totter with Big Noodle, dizzying myself on the merry-go-round with Peanut Head, shooting marbles or spinning tops with Coo-Coo Clock. Those blissful afternoons made me forget my circumstances. I was the happiest when I was by myself playing in the dirt under an elm tree. I'd notice big rigs and cars on I-40 in the distance, running parallel to the back boundary fence, and wonder if any of them might be carrying my parents. I felt a painful longing for Estancia. In the back of my mind, I always hoped that my parents would come for Mieyo and me.

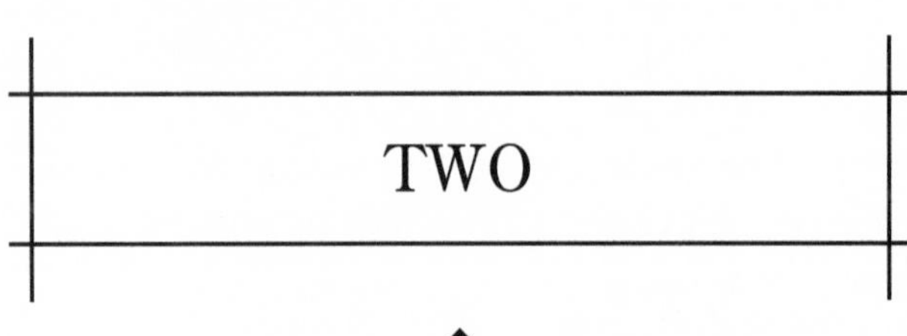

TWO

◆

My parents never did come, and at thirteen years old I found myself behind bars for the first time, in a detention center for boys. The bars weren't there to keep us in so much as to remind us that we weren't really wanted anywhere else. I must have run away from the orphanage a dozen times, and each time an aunt or an uncle would take me back. The last time, however, instead of calling Saint Anthony's, as they had in the past, they notified the police, who took me to the detention center. When we arrived, my Aunt Charlotte, my mother's sister, was there. The receptionist slid the official papers to her and asked her to sign them, "Here and here," relinquishing custody. I knew she didn't know what the words *relinquishing custody* meant, but I felt her relief at getting rid of me when she hurriedly put pen to paper and signed. Perhaps she was ashamed to do what in her heart she knew wasn't right, because she walked away without even a good-bye.

I sat on the bench until a tall lean man came out and greeted me.

"Hello, I'm Nestor." He was tall and thin, soft-spoken, in a brown sports jacket and brown slacks, with black hair meticulously combed and parted on one side. "Let's get some information on you, son. Remember, you're not here because you did something wrong. It's only because you don't have a home."

"How long do I have to stay?"

"Until we contact your father and arrange for you to live with him."

I celled with six other Chicanos. The fluorescent lighting made the apprehension in their faces obvious, but they concealed their curiosity about who I was, where I came from, and what I was here for with a hard-faced indifference. I wasn't prepared for their stony silence. Estancia kids like Mocoso had a kindheartedness that invited spontaneous participation in play or idle talk. Even the kids at the orphanage generously included you in games and asked you to play; they hadn't lost hope. These boys worried about revealing any information that others might take as a weakness or use against them. Suspicion helped them to survive, as did denying their feelings, especially fear. At night, a heaviness lay over the cells; the kids, perhaps sensing their lives falling apart, were distressed and withdrawn.

Hardly anyone blinked the next morning when a kid in the dining room leaped across one of the long stainless-steel tables with a fork and stabbed another kid in the neck. Even as blood ran through the wounded kid's fingers and down his arm, his eyes announced that it didn't hurt, it was nothing, he had no feelings. Everyone looked, but after the two kids had been removed by guards, the rest went on eating their oatmeal. I was too alarmed to eat, unsettled by the victim's nonchalance. If I stayed here long enough, I too would be trained to feel nothing. After being stripped of everything, all these kids had left was pride—a pride that was distorted, maimed, twisted, and turned against them, a defiant pride that did not allow them to admit that they were human beings and had been hurt.

They reminded me of my brother, Mieyo. After Mother's sudden departure he'd become inaccessible and distant. He had started on a process of change, often beating me up for nothing. I let him because I didn't want him leaving me; he was all I had left. One thing for sure: He wasn't the same brother I'd once had. Instead of his usual candor and curiosity, he became cagey and manipulative. I think he learned to dislike himself. He did things at the orphanage that all kids do—pilfer food from the kitchen cart, cheat in class, fudge at marbles— but he didn't get caught. Determined not to be a victim, he'd lie, deceive, and steal. But having spent six years in the orphanage, he was afraid of the outside world and decided against running away. He stayed at the orphanage, while I landed in the detention center.

He was right, of course; it was worse outside the orphanage. But wherever we were, I believed in my naive way that he was figuring a way to rescue me, because he knew how to do stuff like that—he could lie with such pious sincerity anybody would believe him, and he always knew how to get what he wanted. I pictured him pulling off my escape and embracing me after I was free. I knew he'd be waiting one day at the front office, a nod of the head to welcome me back.

During the day, at the D-Home, we mostly lounged in cells, playing dominoes, checkers, chess, or cards; some kids went into the mat room to box and work out on the speed and body bags, while others went outside to stroll or relax in the sun against the fence or play basketball. I joined those against the fence and we talked about girls or our barrios, falling to the ground in between and pumping off push-ups and sit-ups. I was from the orphanage, which drew their sympathy. The fact that I was alone in the world had some significance to them. It took real guts to be out in the world at thirteen. We'd lie on our backs staring up at the clouds and talk without looking at each other. It was better not to look into each other's eyes.

Low-Blow was one of the guys in my cell, a big muscled Chicano whose fighting abilities were renowned. He took me under his wing. Strutting down the halls or in the rec room, he told me, "Never talk to guards. If anybody looks at you wrong, tries to touch you, mess him up. What's a wrong look?" he asked and answered his own question. "It's when they stare at you like you owe money. Like you did 'em wrong and they're holding a grudge against you. The way starved dogs look at each other over a piece of meat and none of 'em wanna share." During chores one day, Low-Blow decked a guy and was put in isolation. With my partner gone, I had to assume an attitude of fearlessness, walk the walk, even though I desperately wanted Mieyo to come. I waited as the days blurred into boring weeks, planning that when my father and brother and I finally got together, I'd work at a gas station or as a laborer and make money. Without Mother or Martina it wouldn't be the same, but at least I'd have Mieyo and my father. As the warm, sunny days passed, I kept myself busy, hoping for the best. I made my bunk every morning and swept the cell, and when Low-Blow came out, he bunked next to me and we both mopped the halls, washed windows, and exercised. It wasn't that bad, except during the night when I worried about my brother and father, fearing something might have happened to them. I prayed to God to help them, as the halls echoed with the ominous reports of the guard's boots as he checked to see if we were all in our bunks and counted. I felt sorry for the kids in for murder, grand theft auto, or drug possession, because they were headed for Springer, a prison for teenagers. Low-Blow was going there for assault with a deadly weapon, and even though he said he wasn't afraid, I knew he was.

With no word from my brother or my father, the director decided it was time for me to go to school. Since the detention center had no educational facility, I was enrolled at Harrison Junior High. It was still dark and cold when he unlocked the main door one morning and led me out into the cold dawn to the street curb. He told me to wait for a woman to pick me up and offered a brief pep talk about doing my best and the virtues of education. After he left, I was afraid but excited. Snuggled in my jacket, under the streetlamp, I waited for my ride. I could hear the crickets and frogs on the ditch bank across the street. I glanced at every car and truck passing, but the drivers kept moving. I jumped, trying to catch a moth fluttering above me, and when a stray dog came over from the ditch, I gave it my peanut-butter-and-jelly sandwich from my sack lunch. It followed me to the ditch, where I threw mud clods at the water. Here I was, with no restraints, legally free, for the first time in a long while. No cops, nuns, aunts, or uncles looking for me to tell me what I'd done wrong. It felt great being on the ditch as the sun was rising, but just as I was wondering whether I should head for the orphanage to find my brother, a lady drove up under the streetlamp and waved to me. I went toward her running, eager to warm my hands and feet by the car heater. The dog followed, but since I couldn't take it, I gave it my other sandwich, which it gobbled up before we had even turned and pulled away onto the street.

School wasn't anything like I expected. Within a week I faked being sick in order to stay out. The real reason was I was ashamed, not only of my old patched clothes but also because I didn't know anything the teachers were talking about. I couldn't talk to the kids because they were so much smarter than I was. They were the kind of kids my mother pointed to, saying I should be like them. I already half believed that I was a sinner and they were not; at least the nuns had told me so. And because of all the trouble in my family, having no parents, the alcoholism and fights, I also believed there was something basically wrong with me. I didn't think anyone else had the kind of problems I had. So it seemed that everything that happened to me justified their view.

I was trying to redeem myself, but my stint at Harrison only seemed to complicate and confuse my efforts. I was more interested in my cell life and my homeboys and what we talked about—doing time, stealing stuff, recalling things that people had done to us and what we were going to do to pay them back. My homeboys wanted me to get addresses of the girls from school, but I was too shy. They didn't understand how crazy it was. After Mrs. Sanchez let me out, I'd get lost in the riotous commotion of buses and parents dropping off kids. Freedom intimidated me. The ease with which the other kids laughed and roughhoused intimidated me. They'd group behind the gym and I'd be by myself, staring at the dusty track and football field. I dreaded going back into class when the bell rang because I'd have to sit in the back and hope the teacher didn't call my name. I hated every hour, restraining my impulse to flee from the classroom. When I was going through the cafeteria line, unable to make up my mind about what I wanted because there was too much to choose from, kids behind me said things to embarrass me and smirked at my social awkwardness. They wouldn't dare if they were back at the D-Home, because I'd bust them up, but I couldn't do anything to them here.

When Mrs. Sanchez asked why I wasn't bringing my schoolbooks, I told her I'd forgotten. She seemed to understand what I was really feeling, so she led me one morning to the gym and told Coach Tracy who I was and where I lived. He was a good guy—outgoing, square-jawed, buzz-cut, and tough as a marine drill sergeant.

Later that day, when I was behind the gym during lunch, sitting on the dirt eating my sandwich, someone called me. When I turned, it was Coach Tracy. He squatted on his toes and slapped my knee, smiling. "You oughta be out there playing football for us! Just look at those shoulders and arms!" I felt embarrassed. "Come on out this afternoon," he continued. "I'll be waiting for you." He looked at my bologna sandwich and said, "Don't blame you, not eating in the cafeteria. Food'll make you gag. Meet me in the locker room after classes."

I asked him, "What about Mrs. Sanchez? I'll get in trouble if I'm not there."

He patted my shoulder. "I talked to her and the director. I'll take you back after practice." He was the nicest man I ever met, I thought, as he walked away, slightly hunched in the shoulders, wearing gray khakis and black-and-white Converse sneakers, his body hard and rugged.

He assigned me my own locker, piled my arms with pants and jersey, shoulder pads, helmet, cleats, and mouthpiece, and after I dressed I trailed the team out to the field in a slow trot. Coach slapped me on the butt and clapped his hands, rousing me to do my best. I felt thankful but uncomfortable with his considerable kindness, but once on the field, my discomfiture evaporated as I tackled and crushed my teammates into the grass. Coach kept smacking my pads, saying to the others, "You see that! That's how I want you to hit! Get over here, Rudy, on all fours—Jimmy, show them how it's done." I got down, and when Coach blew the whistle I hit Rudy so hard he went backwards and groaned over on his belly. I'd forearmed his face mask and given him a bloody nose. "That's how you linemen should be hitting!"

I felt proud of myself because the rest of the guys were looking at me impressed, and some were saying, "Wow, we're going to win some games now," their admiration mixed with trepidation. They studied me with the curiosity of someone viewing a strange oddity. Who is he? Where did he come from? And while I felt satisfied with myself and equal to them on the field, the difference between us became apparent in the locker room, where they put on nice clothes, watches, rings, new shoes. I lied when they asked where I lived and if I needed a ride home, telling them my mother was picking me up and I lived close by. They talked about going to movies on dates with girlfriends, and they tried to be friendly, inviting me to hang out with them, to go for sodas and burgers after practice, but I didn't have any money. On the insides of their lockers they had family photos, cars they were fixing up with their dads and friends, team pennants, posters of rock heroes. I kept to myself, being quiet as I could so as not to invite questions or attention.

Primarily to please the coach and Mrs. Sanchez, I started playing the part of a student by bringing my books. I'd sit in the last row of each class and look at the pictures, to which I added illustrations of my own: a mustache to the moon, penciled flowers on Nebraska cornfields, a sinister grin and an eye patch on George Washington. I hadn't told anybody that I couldn't read and that looking at the words and math problems made me feel dumb. For a while, though, I was the talk of school. I may have been a dummy in class but I was a hero on the field. I was a good football player, which made girls flirt with me and guys look to me as a leader. I was invited to parties, over to kids' houses, swimming, but since I couldn't go or explain why I couldn't go, I lied that I had things to do, places to go, and generally gave them the impression that my life was full of activities. I must have looked like a fool; my poverty and aloneness in life was apparent. People don't like liars, and after a while they quit inviting me. But what was I going to do, invite them to the D-Home to meet the guards and watch TV with the rest of my homeboys behind bars in a cell? I'm sure they would've enjoyed getting patted down, and escorted to a cell, filled with a bunch of guys who saw them as the enemy. I was ashamed to admit that I was a ward of the state, a piece of property with official papers attached. At any time, I could be swept up by the state, put in handcuffs, and given over to a stranger. I was at the mercy of state officials—state-clothed, housed, and fed, a number on a case file in an office. I was going to wake up here, go to sleep here, eat and live here.

Life at the D-Home was as predictable as it had been at the orphanage. New kids came and went. We woke up at the same time every day and went to bed at the same time every night. Every weekend visitors came and visited their loved ones for an hour. And just as I had done at the Boys' Home, every night, before falling asleep, I'd imagine my mother's voice whispering good night to me. I'd think of my father and brother; I'd see in my mind the carefree kids at school, older than at the Boys' Home but laughing and playing the same, and gradually I'd fall asleep, pretending that tomorrow would be the day when everything was going to turn out well in my life.

Coach Tracy pulled me out of class one day and took me over to the gym. In his office, he sat behind his desk and said he was concerned because I was failing every class. At that time, I'd close up anytime an adult asked me questions; I didn't trust them. And though Coach Tracy was different, I stared out the window, thinking of my brother and resenting the coach's intrusion. He should have just been a coach and not worried about me or my grades. So what if I was failing? I was out of place here. The students were not from my world and I was not part of theirs.

I knew Coach Tracy was trying to be a good friend, so I said I'd try harder. He smiled. "Just give it a shot, that's all I'm asking." But after that he sought me out when I was going from class to class, asking, "How's it going? Keep at them books, Jimmy, it'll pay off." Sometimes, expecting a response, he'd pause, but I never said anything. He'd prod. "Everything okay? Something bothering you?" I played him off, saying I was doing fine, but it was a lie; I wasn't studying at night.

I hated books, I hated reading, I hated everything about school except football. So far we were undefeated. I was a fullback, trampling opponents with relish; on defense I was headhunter, roaming behind the linemen and following the ball carrier, whom I demolished. I was also the extra-point kicker. I kicked the ball so far one time that the refs had to stop the game to go and find it, over the fence in the weeds. We were on our way to becoming city champs.

After one important game, Coach Tracy surprised me by announcing I was staying at his house for the weekend. He was taking me to his home to meet his family.

I didn't know it at the time, but it was a trial run for future adoption. I met his wife and two sons, ages five and eight. They lived in a moderate-sized red-brick house down a street bordered with elm trees in a middle-class neighborhood. He took me in and showed me the bedroom where I'd sleep that night. I felt detached and confused and anxious. Was this a ploy to get me away from my father and brother? Was I being taken away again, this time by myself? Ever since I was seven I'd been boarding in a state rental, and now at fourteen I was being offered my own bedroom. I forced a smile of appreciation but I was self-conscious about being regarded with such attentive courtesy. Over supper, the kids innocently questioned me, while his pretty wife stacked pork chops and string beans and mashed potatoes on my plate. Coach Tracy was telling me that if I could get a handle on the books and keep a good grade average, it'd be no problem getting a college scholarship for football. I didn't want to go to college. I ate stiffly, feeling constrained by their deference, so unfamiliar. These were the kind of people I had a grudge against; if they knew that, they wouldn't be so nice to me. These were the people I'd assumed didn't care about us street kids. They were a part of the white world that had helped to destroy my family, made my father suffer, made my grandpa and grandma work in their fields dawn to dusk. If I lived with them, wouldn't I be betraying everything I had been taught to believe in? I'd be going against my father and brother. I was sitting in the living room with the enemy, and yet in my heart I liked them; they were not harming me in any way. The fact that they were so generous made me feel worse for my bad thoughts. In my world, they represented everything bad, and yet they were not prejudiced, mean, greedy, or money-hungry. I decided that not all white people were the same, but it still didn't make my stay any more comfortable.

I'd begun to feel early on that the state and society at large considered me a stain on their illusion of a perfect America. In the American dream there weren't supposed to be children going hungry or sleeping under bridges. In me, the state—and society by extension—had yet another mouth to feed, another body to clothe. I felt like a nuisance; I suspected that if basic human decency didn't warrant it, society would gladly dismiss me. Yet there were people like Coach Tracy and his family who went against the grain. And while I didn't want to hurt them and was willing to go along for a while, there was no way I could let myself be adopted into a white family. It just couldn't happen. I'd be like my mother then, turning my back on my people—my grandparents, my father, my brother and sister—and living a lie about who I really was. I was not going anywhere. My grandpa had always prided himself in his loyalty to his customs and traditions and people. I'd rather live on the streets and keep my loyalty, my memories and stories, than take on the gringo's way of living, which tried to make me forget where I came from, and sometimes even put down my culture and ridiculed my grandparents as lazy foreigners.

Friday night I'd had bad dreams of my brother dying, and Saturday morning, after breakfast, I decided to walk to the park up the street. I took the younger kid with me. When I stopped to light a cigarette, cradling him in one arm, a floating ash burned his cheek and he screamed. I don't know why his scream affected me so deeply. Perhaps it echoed the sentiments of my mother and the nuns, who insinuated that I was the cause of all the pain and hurt in my family's life. Perhaps, it was the same chilling scream that was buried in me and never came out, the hot cry I stifled throughout my mother's departure, my father's violence, my brother's absence, my terror of being alone in the world. I was not able to put my feelings or thoughts in words, but feeling guilty as hell, I sat on the street curb and kept telling the kid I was sorry, I didn't mean to burn his cheek, it was an accident. He wanted to go home so I carried him back, thinking the whole time I belonged in the D-Home.

Coach Tracy and his wife begged me to tell them what was wrong. My silence aggravated their confusion, and they appealed all the more for an explanation, imploring me to say something. Even if I could've expressed myself, I was confused about what I was supposed to say or not say, and my response to any question was always "I don't know."

That's exactly what I told Coach Tracy and his wife: I didn't know why, I just wanted to go back. On Sunday afternoon, Coach Tracy drove me down. We said very little. His eyes were red, his face drawn from exhaustion. I was tremendously sad when I said good-bye and shut the car door and walked to the entrance of the D-Home. I thought I had spoiled everything for him and I wanted to apologize, but I didn't know how to explain myself. I wasn't strong enough to admit that I felt worthless and was nothing but a troublemaker. I quit school the next day.

◆

I lived at the detention center for a few months more until one cold December morning when Mieyo came by on a brand-new motorcycle. I was so excited to see him that I begged Nestor, the D-Home director, to let me go with him for the day. I told him that Christmas and my fifteenth birthday, January 5, were around the corner, and that spending a day with Mieyo would be all the Christmas and birthday present I would ever want. Nestor sensed my elation and kindly agreed to let me go for the day, warning me to be back by supper. Mieyo had brought extra gloves, a coat, and a beanie cap. I put them on, and we roared out of the D-Home parking lot. I knew I was not coming back.

It didn't take me long to graduate to the kind of jails where the bars were meant to keep me in. Fortunately, I was never there for very long. I was still a juvenile, and the charges never got more serious than disturbing the peace, vagrancy, or petty theft, none of which they were very good at proving. I'd be held for a while, have a few conversations with child welfare authorities or a probation officer, and then be released into the custody of my father, who was supposed to be taking care of me but whom I never saw.

My father had lost his job with the DMV and now got his drinking money selling shoes. He spent his nights at cantinas and hardly ever came back to the shack in Albuquerque that Mieyo and I were calling home. I couldn't believe he was still searching for my mother. She still haunted him. He even questioned us to see if we knew where she was. When he did show up he'd be drunk, and if Mieyo and I were around we'd keep our distance, because we might get beaten up.

We stayed in a gardener's shack, more or less like the one I'd grown up in, converted into sleeping quarters for the three of us. Mieyo and I would eat at friends' houses, and we roamed around town with a group of like-minded kids with equally unsavory pasts. Mieyo was fifteen and trying to go to school and sometimes worked as a hotel bellboy; I was fourteen and worked occasionally, but school wasn't for me. Mostly we cruised, looking for something to do, any kind of action. We'd steal a bicycle or a tire and resell it, or earn enough—digging ditches for a plumbing contractor, cleaning yards, washing windows, or painting—to put something in our stomachs and then party. When my brother had picked me up at the D-Home, I was surprised that he had already started drinking. I followed suit. Soon there were other things: LSD, pot, harder stuff. We'd get high, cruise around, maybe get in a fight, stoke up again, and then crash wherever we could—abandoned shacks, someone's car, or on a bench or under a tree in the town square. Occasionally, I would wake up in jail.

I don't know when the process of criminalization began for any one of the kids I hung out with or woke up with in a prison cell. For me, it was when my mother first dropped my brother and sister and me off in Estancia; it was reinforced when Mieyo and I were driven through the gates of Saint Anthony's, and it started to take on a more antisocial reality at the detention center. It was at the detention center that I first learned how to intimidate others with my stare, how to lie to the authorities with a smile, how to join a group and think of myself as me against the others. It was at the detention center that I first came in contact with boys who were already well on their way to becoming criminals; whose friendship taught me I was more like them than like the boys outside the cells, living in a society that would never accept me, in a world made of parents, nice clothes, and loving care. You could see the narrowing of life's possibilities in the cold, challenging eyes of the homeboys in the detention center; you could see the numbing of their hearts in their swaggering postures. All of them had been wounded, hurt, abused, ignored; already, aggression was in their talk, in the way they let off steam over their disappointments, in the way they expressed themselves. It was all they allowed themselves to express, for each of them knew they could be hurt again if they tried anything different. So instead they refined what they did know to its own kind of perfection.

I watched and listened and learned in the detention center. I understood that if I was to get by on the streets I would have to do it by fighting. If only through my experience on the football field, I knew I had enough frustrated anger in me to funnel into destructive behavior. But it wasn't until Mieyo told me that he'd been raped during our separation that my world suddenly shifted from passive observer to violent engagement. I was not going to let the world trample my brother and me down like dogs in the street. My faith in the goodness of people began to tremble around the edges until it shattered like glass subjected to a high-pitched sound. My hope that society would one day invite us in was gone. The world was against us. Rather than let the world beat us down, I had to fight back, and I did, on the day Mieyo finally came to get me.

He fetched me on his new motorcycle, and we went over to where he was living. He told me that when I was taken to the detention center, the nuns had located our father and released Mieyo into his care. Father was living in a small shack with barely enough room for two people. He drank all the time. There was never any food, and Mieyo was sometimes beaten. So he left and was living on the streets until one day two older white men picked him up and treated him to a big meal, bought him some clothes, and invited him to their house when he didn't have a place to stay. He thought they were simply being kind, but they raped him and used legal jargon to threaten him. He would go to prison for breaking and entering, they said. They would accuse him of robbing them. Besides, who would believe a young Chicano kid anyway—certainly not over the word of two successful white men with good jobs, a nice house, and social standing.

I had known boys who had been raped before, both in the orphanage and in the detention center. But this was my brother. I found his shame excruciating to bear. I wanted to protect him—I was willing to do anything to protect him—and I began to lash out at every opportunity. We had a kind of gang going; no colors, no rules or rituals, just a bunch of us boys who had already been cast off and who didn't have much else to do but cruise around together and get in trouble. We fought other gangs, white kids mostly, and more and more I would step out and be the point man in any fight situation.

I was good at it, just like my father had said I would be on those nights when he drank and we watched the Gillette fights, or at Grandma's when I was small. Crouching down and protecting my face and ribs, I'd lash out with jabs and kicks on street corners and in alleys; the difference was that now my fighting was fueled by my rage at the world. I wouldn't stop until I was panting with exhaustion as I stared at my opponent bleeding on the pavement. I fought for my brother because I knew that inside him he was hurting in a way that only someone who gets raped can hurt.

I wanted to take his hurt away by hurting others, but it never seemed to work. When I finished a fight and we were alone again, he would explode. To vent his anger, he berated and demeaned me, and then he beat me, and I let him. I knew it wasn't right, but in all the confusion of my life I felt this one thing was helping him live. And somewhere along the line I started fighting just for the sake of fighting, because I was good at it and it felt good to beat other people up.

Fighting, drinking, and getting high, driving around, this was my life for three or four years. We'd rent a cheap apartment in a bad section of town, get drunk, burn down the apartment, and take off, a bunch of wild kids in cars prowling affluent white neighborhoods, looking to steal something or break a car window just for something to do. We'd hang out at a burger joint looking to fight other gangs or we'd cruise around to score some drugs, get off, sleep it off until late in the afternoon, and then start all over again.

I'd ride out to Estancia sometimes to visit Grandma, but it didn't feel right. La Casita made me think of my mother and father and the few good memories we had. Her being with me at the park, us lying in bed and talking, but mostly of her at the window, worried and waiting for my father. I never did hear from her after she dropped us off, and I wondered bitterly whether she thought of us and, if so, in what way. With remorse? Gladness? Or, living a carefree life in California, had she completely forgotten we were ever born? Grandma was shrinking with age. She was blind but still caring for Refugio, who came in drunk each night. Martina married at fifteen, a guy from another village, and lived in a trailer in Albuquerque. Jesusita, Julian, and Carlos came on weekends to visit, but Santiago still lived in Estancia, caring for Grandma and working at Grandpa's old job as janitor at the high school. When Grandma asked about my father and brother, I lied and said they were okay. I didn't tell her that occasionally, late at night, I'd see my father stumbling down the sidewalk on his way to the next cantina. I'd be in the backseat of someone's car, and I'd swing my head to the window to catch the expression on his face as we cruised by. It was always the same, but even through my stoned haze I'd feel the same welling of contempt with a weird measure of satisfaction that I had already surpassed him. I was going farther than he'd ever dared.

◆

My brother and I were alone in the world. I was fifteen and he sixteen, and we were accountable to no one. All I had to do was not get caught doing petty crimes, and I could continue to wander with no direction, going along on a day-to-day basis with any suggestion or impulse a friend might come up with. It wasn't so bad. Each day was a new adventure. But there were hard times, too—waking up on the ground with nothing but a stubbed-out cigarette, a half-finished beer warming in the morning sun, and a full, absolutely empty day before me. I felt as lost and useless as I ever had before or have since.

Mieyo got tired of our poverty because he liked money: having nice clothes and new Converse sneakers, eating out, buying things. He was always looking for one job or another, and still trying to go to school, but he had to quit to put food in his stomach. For a long time he had a job at the Desert Sands Hotel on Central as a bellboy. I'd go by and he'd give me tip change to buy burgers or we'd eat together. He got to see another side of life while working there, meeting people who traveled and stayed in hotels. Their exciting lives made him dream of achieving the same. He talked a lot about being a millionaire and buying a house and car.

With Mieyo always working, occasionally the formlessness of my own existence would become so boring and tiresome I'd try to get it together for a while and take a job. I was a laborer at Walker Plumbing, jackhammering concrete all day or crawling under scorpion- and spider-infested trailers or digging trenches. I'd work pumping gas or walk onto a construction site and do some manual labor. Once I had a job out at the airport, unloading and loading the food service on the planes on the night shift. It was one of the best jobs I ever had. I remember getting off one quiet windless morning in the middle of winter and stopping my bike at the fence next to a runway covered with fresh snow, the red and blue runway lights glimmering like Christmas bulbs in the distance. I stood there for the longest time, my fingers cold as I gripped the metal fence, my breath hovering about me like a small cloud, wondering why my life couldn't have been different.

Throughout those years I always had an appreciation for beautiful, quiet scenes. I just never told anybody. I'd always had a secret longing to have a place in the desert, all alone with the wind and the coyotes, or in the mountains by a stream, the forest beyond my door full of wildlife: birds, deer, elk, mountain lions, wolves. That was the happiest scene I could imagine. When I really needed to feel safe, I'd go out to the mountains and hang out with nature. The ponderosa pines and running streams appealed to me, but I always had to come back to the city, where I never lasted long on jobs. I resented the way I was treated, and when someone would call me a dumb spic or insult me another way, I'd storm off or get in a fight. I didn't understand how my brother could be content carrying suitcases and meals and washing floors for the convenience of people who didn't even look at him. Sometimes I'd try to convince him to quit, and when he wouldn't, when he'd just go back to emptying ashtrays or delivering laundry, I'd run out and hook up with the old crew. I'd get in a fight, steal something, get busted, and end up in jail again.

◆

During my last year in Albuquerque, when I was seventeen, I ended up getting picked up and charged with murder. Some guy got himself killed at a gas station, and I was walking along the street with my T-shirt wrapped around my arm, trying to staunch the blood pouring from a gash I'd gotten from punching a windshield in anger. The police took me to the hospital, had a doctor sew my arm up with eighty-two stitches, and then hauled me down to the station, booked me, and showed me into a cell. I didn't say a word from the time I was picked up to being locked up, but I had an alibi. I didn't protest because I knew that sooner or later I would get out. The police always accused me and my friends of crimes we didn't commit. With no money for a lawyer, and no family to challenge the injustice, we were easy targets for the police to hang something on. It gave them the illusion they were fighting crime and winning. Besides, three meals a day and a warm cot with a roof over my head was a vacation. It was often better in jail than on the streets; I didn't have to worry for a while about surviving.

This time, however, I was moody and dark-tempered because I'd just had my heart broken by a woman I believed I loved, and I didn't want to talk to anyone. It made me pissed and sad that I was in the same place my father had been in when I came to visit him. Except I was even worse, because while he was always thrown in the drunk tank, I was in a cell for felons accused of a capital offense.

After being released, I had a brief period where things went okay. I was off the streets and working for a vending machine company. I'd even been able to rent myself a room in a boardinghouse, with a small fridge and its own bathroom. My own car was parked outside. My life was good enough that I'd even started to allow myself the thought that things could get even better, that I was on my way to the kind of existence I imagined others had. I'd forged a birth certificate to make me over eighteen and old enough to be bonded. When I wasn't in Santa Fe I'd be on the road, traveling all over northern New Mexico, servicing vending machines in the small one-cantina towns that clung to the dry hills or perched on the banks of the brown rivers that flowed through the high desert. Those long stretches between stops gave me my first opportunities to truly relax. I was good with people. Every time I went into a bar or a café to refill the cigarettes or the Coke machine, they'd offer me a free meal or soda and ask where I'd been keeping myself. It was like I was just one of the regular guys. I looked forward to dropping by and bullshitting with waitresses and customers. The scenery relaxed me—broad fields with Queen Anne's lace, hefty sunflowers, and wind-blown grasses, poplars, and cottonwoods, shimmering creeks snaking through canyons—it offered me a placid repose from the hectic pace of urban life. I'd let the mountains and prairie beauty empty my mind of all its anxious worry and look forward to seeing my girlfriend, Theresa, waiting for me back in Albuquerque.

I'd met Theresa in the aftermath of a fight when my brother had called me down to Albuquerque. Three guys had been threatening him, and by the time I showed up two more had joined them, all white guys, and one of them had a knife. I had a big old wrench handy and went after them in my fashion and only stopped when police sirens sounded in the distance. Afterward, Theresa was waiting by my car, a brown-skinned, brown-eyed, black-haired Chicana who quietly asked me for a ride. I took her home and we began to see each other. She went to Highland High School and was impressed with my toughness and independence, and I by her beauty, kisses, and high-spirited nature. She was a normal high school girl, with parents and an older brother and sister. She was my first girlfriend.

Nothing could have been sweeter at first. We went to drive-ins, burger joints, parties, bars, campsites, and we necked late into the night in her parents' basement. But I had a difficult time getting along with her friends. They were middle-class Hispanics, whose parents made good money and bought them what they wanted, and they couldn't speak Spanish and had never been in a cell. They'd known each other since childhood, and I felt left out of their collective experience. They'd laugh about what had happened to someone in the past and I would stare at them, wanting to be included, wishing I knew what they were referring to. The only way I seemed to impress them was by my fighting. It was what had attracted Theresa in the first place, and she, and then her friends, began to encourage me to step out with just about anyone they didn't like the look of. I didn't mind it at first; my fighting skills made me somewhat of a hero in their eyes and I liked being feared and respected. But later it made me feel like the reason they ever invited me anywhere with them was to see if I could keep my unbeaten record intact. I was always fighting guys who had bullied them or made them afraid. I'd fight like a pit bull, my violence fueled by the fact that I had nothing to lose. I provided entertainment only; when it came to social gatherings, they ignored me unless there was a fight. Most of the guys I was fighting were big Anglos, and I guess in some way I was taking up where my grandfather left off. He used to fight in barns and sheds against farm-circuit prizefighters to make extra money for his family. I wasn't getting anything out of it except back slaps and free beer.

This went on for some time until I realized I was feeling used, and I began to resent the people Theresa hung out with. They were a bunch of cowards, spineless spoiled brats who had had everything given to them. To gain Theresa's affection, I was willing to oblige them, even though it undermined my self-respect. But when the dust settled and Theresa and I were left alone, we didn't grow any closer. I didn't know how to nurture a friendship, let alone love. We really didn't have much in common except violence and drinking. She wasn't interested in talking about crime, and I wasn't interested in talking about my family or my past. Our conversations were usually superficial and glib, and I was shy around her. My silence annoyed her, but it frustrated me even more because for the first time I could sense the possibility of a real closeness, however elusive.

Our meetings became sour, stiff, and unbearably tentative. I grew jealous of her friends who seemed to speak with her so easily, and I was suspicious of anyone she even looked at. A month after I turned seventeen I had bought a used trailer, hoping to persuade her to move in with me. It was a snowy February afternoon. I was asleep when she walked in. "I hear you been acting stupid again!" she said. I knew she was referring to her friends, whom I had recently threatened to beat up. I was tired of how they reveled in my fighting prowess and afterward sniggered openly at my desperation to make Theresa love me. I'd found out that she was sleeping around. She looked at me with hate in her eyes. She accused me of being a romantic fool, someone who made sex into something special. It was plain and simple fucking, not love. She didn't want an intimate relationship. She just wanted to have fun, to fuck and be done with it, with no attachment or commitment.

I put on my shirt and laced my boots up, hoping she'd want to go out for hot cocoa and a burger, but when I stood in front of her, she slapped me. Again and again, until she yelled, "Slap me back! Why don't you hit me?" She slapped me until her hand was red and puffy. In the silence between us, her eyes simmered with festering resentment. She wanted me to accept her desire to make love to other guys; she wanted to quit hiding it; she even wanted to break off our relationship. And my naïveté rankled and disgusted her. She found my meekness repulsive, my torment indecent, my loyalty vulgar and obscene. In her eyes, everything about me was repugnant. I lived in a stupid imaginary world where I worshiped her as the most beautiful woman ever. To her, it was the pitiful fantasy of a child. She wanted to be free of me. My faithfulness to her was keeping her from enjoying life. She had to hide and lie, hating herself for what she was doing. Our love meant nothing more to her than licking the bottom of every moment's pleasure. She wanted to punish me for my fidelity; she wanted me to be more like her. She gripped my arms and screamed, "Hit me back!"

But I was at the trailer door already. I fled. As I started off in a jog, the chill air and snow felt good. Dogs barked. People stared out their windows. Guys working in driveways on cars looked up. I was running to the foothills of the Sandias. The mountains would make me forget what happened. Sitting up there I could have some peace of mind and try to figure the situation out. I glanced behind me. She was following, screaming, "Get back here! I hate you! I hate you!" I was surprised to find myself among the piñons and juniper trees already. I was scared and confused, but free of her for the moment. I could see her still in pursuit and behind her the trailer park. It was snowing harder. I hid behind a piñon tree and watched her in sorrow. As she neared the foothills, she fell and yelled out, "Help, I can't walk! I broke my ankle! My foot's stuck, help me!"

For a second I thought it was a trap but then decided she needed me; she was in pain. I skidded down, jumped over rocks, and was at her side instantly. My first thought was right. She lashed out, grabbed my foot, and snarled, full of malice, "You bastard!" She bit my calf, and I kicked to release her grasp, then sprang back, terrified. My adrenaline shot up and I dashed up the hill into the dense thickets. I could barely hear her yelling. I didn't understand why she was doing this, why she hated me.

Not until she had walked away and I saw her car leave, toward dusk, did I venture back to the trailer park. In case she might return, I got behind a Dumpster, hugged my knees to my chest to keep warm, and waited until dark to enter my trailer. The light and shadows played games in the snow, and I saw her wandering again in the fields, a woman wearing a white calfskin hide, dressed in feathers and moccasins, beads and shells, doing a ritual dance. The snow fell seamlessly around her and the air grew darker until she was gone.

I knew Theresa loved me but she was as afraid as I was of intimacy. I leaned against the cinder-block wall, understanding nothing. I reached down sadly and tied my bootlace, wondering if I should go see her and act like this never had happened. I waited until the next day. When I called from the road she seemed uninterested in me. Dreading another abandonment, I clung to her all the tighter, telling myself that I would be able to hold on to her if only I wanted to enough. I was in love—no, not in love, but possessed with her. I prayed to the stars every night that God would make things good between us again.

I drove down to Albuquerque unannounced to visit her. When I arrived I could feel that she was uncomfortable with my being there. She was busy, she said, and recoiled from my touch. I begged her to come out for a Coke or a ride so we could talk things through. She relented and got in but immediately seemed bored and offended by my intensity. Before I had even turned the corner, she wanted me to take her back. Feeling powerless to convey to her how much I loved her, convinced that if she only knew this she would fall back into my arms, I finally got so desperate I told her I was kidnapping her. She didn't believe me at first, but when we left the city limits and kept going on the interstate, she became quieter. I told her we were going to live in another city and love each other and start new lives together. I kept driving. In between long smoldering stretches of silence, I repeated my plans for us. We were in El Paso by nightfall, when she finally agreed to give us another chance. I turned around and drove straight back to Albuquerque. Not a word passed between us the entire time. But just as we neared her neighborhood she told me she wanted me out of her life. I pulled over, and the next thing I knew there was blood everywhere. I had shattered the windshield, put my arm through it. There was a deep ugly gash to the bone in my left forearm. She ran off and I got out of the car, wrapped my T-shirt around my arm, and started walking toward St. Joseph's emergency room.

When the cops picked me up I didn't care what they did; it didn't matter anymore. I figured I had lost Theresa for good. After I was stitched up, the cops returned and told me I was being booked on suspicion of first-degree murder. I didn't respond to their questions. I agreed to everything with an indifferent nod. I was taken to Montessa Park to await trial and stayed there for about four months, until one day my number was called and a guard informed me that I was being released. Outside, Mieyo was waiting for me. He told me he had joined the army. We spent a couple of days together, partying, drinking, and smoking weed with friends. I wasn't saying much when I walked him downtown to the recruiting station, but I hugged him before he went to join the other recruits who were waiting for a bus to take them to basic training camp. He said he'd see me in a year, when he got out.

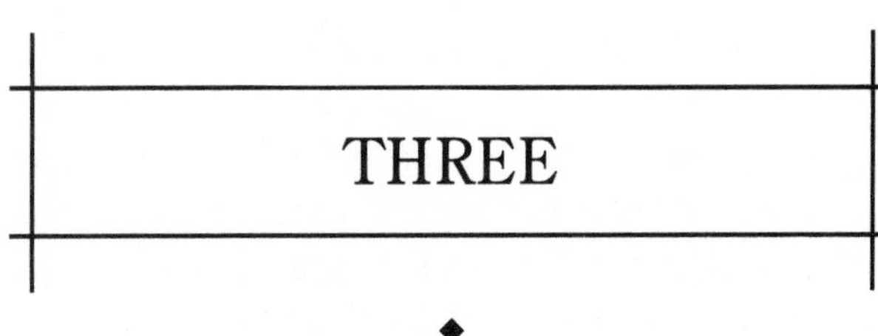

THREE

◆

After my release, I had nothing left anymore so I decided to leave Albuquerque. I headed west on I-40, with a little money in my pocket for gas and cigarettes. I was undecided about what to do or where to go but hoped traveling would help shake off the past. There was so much I couldn't explain about what was happening, but one thing was certain: No one wanted me around. I was falling apart. A long drive across the prairie would help me think. The farther I drove the more relaxed I became. My mother, father, and brother had all left me to start new lives, and maybe, with luck, I could too. All I knew was I had to keep moving, because then I didn't have to think about how messed up my life was. If I had stayed, I would almost certainly have tried again to get Theresa back and ended up in trouble. Leaving was the only way to keep from doing something stupid. I still felt frantic. I needed to put some distance between her and me, and when I finally arrived in San Diego, the humid air soothed me with its mild, salty breezes. I stood on the beach, scanning the ocean, thinking sadly that I was eighteen and worse off than the day I was born. I marveled at the force of my emotions, which had pushed me over the edge and left me without options, except to escape as far west as I could go.

It wasn't only my heartbreak over Theresa that had pushed me across the line. Beyond my obsession with her was the wreckage of my past, and most recently an encounter with my mother, who had had the bad timing to come back to town. After leaving me in Grandma's yard, she had gone to California with Richard and lived there for eleven years. She had returned to Albuquerque with two young children, moving into an affluent white-only neighborhood. My sister had talked me into paying a visit just as things with Theresa had begun to go bad. I'd gone reluctantly, but still I had some dim hope for a reconciliation, or at least for the embrace I'd longed for ever since she had abandoned us.

When the door opened and my still-attractive mother looked from me to the two children clinging to her, she introduced me to them as a friend, shattering the hope that I'd allowed to grow in my heart. Immediately, I steeled myself against showing disappointment and followed her into the bright, sunny kitchen. Richard skulked out of view, moving through adjoining rooms. She poured me a cup of coffee but didn't offer me a chair at the kitchen table. We remained standing, looking at each other across an island counter strewn with opened letters, bills, and invitations to social events. She didn't talk about herself, and she didn't need to; the evidence of the good life was all around her, from the expensive leather and wood furniture, the new refrigerator stocked with food, the sparkling pool I could see beyond the glass doors leading to the patio, to the stick-on notes on the refrigerator door instructing the maid to vacuum and wash the windows before the weekend.

She asked questions: Was I working? Had I finished school? Did I have a girl? Did I need anything? How handsome I was, how big and strong. I knew she was trying, but after that initial betrayal I wasn't going to make it easy for her. I answered her questions matter-of-factly, giving her just enough information so as not to reveal myself. I left when she ran out of questions. It was a cold, perfunctory meeting that lasted maybe ten minutes. Later, I doused the pain of her rejection in a three-day binge of whiskey and drugs. I ended up fighting some guys in a bar and getting thrown into jail. When I got out, things started crashing down on me. I hadn't seen Theresa for weeks and I drove straight to her house down in Albuquerque. She'd been worried about me and we'd ended up driving to a cheap motel on the outskirts of town. We hadn't ever been in a hurry to have sex, and I hadn't ever pressured her. Now I needed to be inside her, to be swallowed up. But it felt dirty and perverted and brought out the worst in both of us. When we finished she wept quietly into a pillow as my hunger still raged. Three weeks later, I put my arm through the windshield of my car.

◆

Above the beach, the city of San Diego rose, fronted by small shops and open-air fast-food diners, and then, like a series of giant stairs, buildings laddered up into the sky, tall glassy towers that reflected the blazing sun. Driving into the city, I hadn't paid attention to them; I'd gotten so worried about traffic and which exit to take, and was so exhilarated and anxious about the newness of it all, that I'd hardly noticed what I'd passed. I'd never seen anything like it. The towns in New Mexico were small by comparison. They nestled up against mountain foothills, shades of reddish-brown shapes hugging the earth, blending into mesquite and piñon trees. Made of adobe and flagstone, they seemed to grow up out of the earth and had a kind of quiet mystery that resonated somehow with my Spanish and Indian past. This was utterly foreign.

The seawater was cool on my feet. I'd taken off my sneakers and waded into the surf up to my ankles. I had intended to walk down to the bay but had stopped after a few paces, tantalized by the tickling sensation of the shifting sand being pulled from beneath my feet as the surf rushed back to meet the next wave. I stood looking out at the shimmering horizon as the sun lowered itself. I thought about how my life had these blank spaces, as if I were blindfolded and spun around in the dark, led on by a need to discover something to anchor me. Each time the blindfold was drawn away I found myself in new circumstances, a new place, drawn there not so much by any plan or disciplined effort as by an unconscious faith that fate would place me where I belonged, where things would go right.

By the time I started to look around, the sun was staring me straight in the eyes and I was surprised by how many people were on the beach. Had they gathered to watch the sunset, or had they been there all along, and I had simply missed them as I went straight to the water? The Chicanos looked as they did back home, dressed in clean work shirts and jeans. But they moved more easily here, and they didn't have that humble, quiet way of men fresh off the farm or ranch. I'd never seen so many hippies, the funky clothes, the girls who danced with each other, their breasts swaying like sacked kittens beneath their peasant shirts. I watched it all from a distance, imagining myself stepping into their midst, getting the walk down, the jive going. Couples strolled or nestled in the sand, kids yelped and ran, a Frisbee floated between two surfers, someone strummed a guitar, dogs chased each other, and the faint trace of pot smoke mixed with charcoal from barbecue grills. Children tunneled castles in the sand and squealed at the surf, while their mothers spread out blankets and picnic baskets. Perhaps, if I could slip into this new world, my past might flow away as the wet sand flowed back into the water.

I was hungry, so I slipped my shoes back on and walked up the boardwalk to get a burger. I could sleep in the car and tomorrow start asking around for work. It wasn't much of a plan, so I was lucky that within a few hours I met the guy who would become my friend and partner for the next couple of years.

A few cars away from my T-Bird, two cops were sipping coffee as they leaned against a railing overlooking the beach. It wasn't like they were jotting down my license plate, but I had stolen the T-Bird from a parking lot in Santa Fe and I didn't need any trouble. I had a duffel bag with a change of clothes in the trunk, a carton of cigarettes and two six-packs of Bud, and a few other things, but fuck it. If I was going to have any chance of getting off on the right foot, I'd have to leave the car where it was and play it cool. And that meant playing it straight, at least for a while. I didn't want to go back to the old games that might get me into a fight with cops or land me in jail or put me on the run, looking over my shoulder. Just ahead were a set of stairs that led down to the beach, and I headed down them, thinking, This is your best shot, dude, make it count, and don't blow it. I never broke stride and I never went back to the car.

I'd just taken off my shoes and settled down in the sand when this lanky dude came up. He had on red high-top sneakers, bomber glasses, a faded T-shirt, torn jeans, and a white hanky around his head to keep his long brown hair from falling in his face. He was puffing a joint as he sat down, took off one of his sneakers, and emptied sand from it. He wasn't wearing socks. He was about my age, eighteen, and after dragging on the joint, holding his breath back, he said, "There's killer waves at dawn. Water comes up all crazy. I sleep under the stars sometimes, listening to them. Want a blast?" I toked and passed it back. He gestured to a bonfire and the hippies gathered around it. "They probably wouldn't mind us paying a neighborly visit. We're in flower-power country. Bet they got munchies, and maybe I won't have to sleep alone tonight. C'mon, let's truck, chicks like to have someone to keep 'em warm on summer evenings like this."

The fire, the waves, and the moon made me wish Theresa were with me. We drank wine, smoked weed, and ate hot dogs, and the whole time I quietly listened to my friend's history as he tried to pick up on this chick. Marcos was an Italian from Michigan, and he'd been in town just a little over a month. His pride and joy was his new black Duster. I stared at the flames, poking a stick in the fire, shifting embers to keep the fire going. The chick and Marcos went to his car, but she returned by herself, brushing her hair, straightening out her blouse, and Marcos followed, looking sheepish, flushed on weed and wine. He tossed me a blanket. Enjoying himself immensely, he said, "Lose some, win some, but never give up!" He was trying for another chick as I lay back and fell asleep.

The next morning Marcos treated me to breakfast at a local hangout and helped me look through the want ads for plumbing work. I'd done enough back in Albuquerque and Santa Fe that I could get through most situations. By noon I'd gotten myself an interview and Marcos had dropped me off at a small green-and-orange bungalow office in Ocean Beach. One of their regular guys had hurt his shoulder yanking his pipe wrench to loosen a rusty fitting and was laid up at home with his arm in a sling. They threw me the keys to my own rig, a rusty panel van with PACIFIC PLUMBING stenciled on the side, and sent me out on my first job. It wasn't much more difficult than a clogged drain, and after I'd finished it I was sent out on another. I did four other similar jobs that day, shit that anyone with a set of tools could have figured out if they took the time, but it must have impressed the boss because he asked me to show up the next day at eight. Marcos and I got a place, a circular one-room bachelor pad; Marcos slept on one side and I on the other. Our sleeping quarters were each by bead curtains hanging from floss tied to a roof pole. The living space in between was soon the partying area, littered with dirty clothes, beer cans, ashtrays, wine bottles, and other junk. We sat, drank beer, smoked weed, listened to music, and talked.

After work at night, in what would become a routine, I'd pick up a six-pack and find Marcos on the beach. We'd polish off the beer as the sun went down, brush the sand off our butts, and get something to eat at a beachside diner. Afterward there were the bars and the green felt pool tables. Under the lights that hung over the pool tables, Chicanos bantered freely with the longhairs they were taking to the cleaners. Marcos was good. The winters were long in Michigan, and there hadn't been much else to do. He shot with a smooth strong stroke, and soon enough we were going against other guys in five-dollar games and winning most of the time. During the day he'd polish his car, and when I met him back at the beach we'd go out and cruise. It was the cleanest, meanest machine on the beach. Slumped low in the seat, elbows crooked out the window, wearing shades, moving our heads to the beat of Marvin Gaye or a Grateful Dead song, we'd look for a party at the parks. Maybe we'd go to Chicano Park, where muralists on scaffolds worked beneath the freeway underpass, painting Chicano history on the concrete beams. There'd always be some people there; if not, we'd find a grove of palm trees close to the beach and kick back, music up loud, car doors open, and maybe join a group of Frisbee players on the beach.

Marcos was living off money he'd earned back home as a mechanic. He kept it stashed at the bottom of his ratty old toilet kit. After brushing my teeth and before heading out the door, I'd count the dwindling pile of twenty-dollar bills. It wouldn't last much longer, but he wasn't in any hurry to get a job. Partying was his thing, and his day revolved around picking up chicks. His problem was that his easygoing nature made chicks like him as a brother. His mellow manner piqued a girl's interest and he was endearing to them but he had no passion to his rap. Chicks would read poetry to him, share their hurt feelings about what another guy did to them, and Marcos, like a sullen therapist listening to a patient's contrition, would make a play to get into her jeans and be told she wasn't ready yet. He hated that, because after we rented our thatched-roof bungalow, a lot of chicks were coming over to have counseling sessions with him. It annoyed him even more because I seemed to have an outlaw edge and severe mood swings that attracted them. He'd have girls over, and when one of them came over to talk, I'd keep my head down, my thoughts to myself, and quietly sit. I'd let Marcos do all the work, a faint smile on my lips, not saying much, but sure enough, eyes would swivel in my direction, and then a chick would start asking if I had a girlfriend. I'd tell her I didn't, but in truth every girl reminded me of Theresa's black hair and brown eyes, and I couldn't help wanting my hands to feel her hips, my palms to caress the inside of her thighs.

I wasn't ready for a relationship or commitment, and maybe my indifference was part of the attraction. Sometimes I'd be kissing a girl on the beach or on the futon in my room and suddenly stop because it didn't feel right. I felt I was being untrue to Theresa. It'd been only a few months since I said good-bye to her. After getting out of jail, I went to see her and it turned out bad, but I couldn't get her out of my mind. Memories of us together ruined romantic moments now. Aching with longing, I'd walk alone on the breezy beach. The rainy days made me miss her so much. My mind would play tricks on me, and I'd plan to return, thinking she would take me back. But I knew deep down she didn't want me. I was still alive and healthy; I could bounce back. I just needed time.

Being Chicano in California was cool. Everybody was dancing and partying to bands like Santana and Los Lobos, singing about our Indio-Mexican culture, and I dug it despite not understanding much about my own roots. The air was charged with Chicano political activism, and I still had a smoldering edge that chicks seemed to attribute to my nonexistent counterculture activity. Whatever it was, they wanted to find out what I was all about, what wound lay beneath my pensive silence and shy smile. They were mostly white girls who were on their way to college or had already dropped out. They thought it was cool that I was working and doing okay on my own. I'd go to college if I could, I told them, and then I'd serve up some line about how life was harder if you happened to be born brown. Usually, Marcos eavesdropped on my rap, smoking a joint and reading a *Popular Mechanics* magazine, picking up on my street-activist speeches, which got the chicks rolling with me on the grass outside the front step of our beach apartment, our bodies wrapped around each other, kissing and hugging.

For the next month and a half I replaced faucets, washer rings, rusty pipes, and sink traps. I was feeling good about making money and I didn't mind working late, taking on the hard jobs, coming home covered in cement dust from breaking concrete with a jackhammer, in some office being renovated, or caked in mud from crawling around in alley trenches. I hustled extra hard on Fridays to finish around noon so I could start the weekend early. I'd shower and put on a pair of old but clean jeans and a T-shirt and go look for Marcos. Most tenants left their doors open and I'd go door to door until I'd find him, sitting on the floor, reading album covers, sipping a beer with a chick, and listening to the stereo. We'd split, buy some cold beer, smoke a doobie, and head out to a park concert announced on handouts we found under our windshield wipers.

I was living day-to-day, meeting chicks and guys who left as easily as they appeared. Trying not to think so much of the past and inspired by Marcos to enjoy life, I exerted myself in the moment, not planning for tomorrow or saving up for the future. I'd meet a chick and go her way or she'd go mine, never knowing where we might end up or what we might do. Marcos and I followed the music and chicks, dope, and booze, and when these were finished, we'd move on to find more. Still, there were times when Marcos and I would be on our way to a movie or the pool hall, and I'd see a woman through a window having dinner with her kids. I'd think of my mother, how we were complete strangers, tied only by birth, and that we'd both come out to California—she to escape from my father and us kids, and I to leave a rotten past and a girlfriend who didn't want me anymore. But the pain of my regret would be quickly blurred by Marcos's offering me a joint, turning up the music, slapping the dashboard, and yelling as he moved his head to the beat, his long hair all over, or saying something funny about not getting chicks, like, "The sun even shines on a dog's ass some days."

I worked hard at my job. Everything was going fine. I prided myself on doing well. I'd be up at the crack of dawn to arrange my tools and organize the fittings. Then it was off to Aunt Lou's Diner for coffee before hitting the shop, a cinder-block building with two back bays lined with floor-to-ceiling pipe racks. I even liked the people I worked for. Martinez was about sixty, religious, in good health. He ran the back shop and the front office, keeping it stocked with packaged plumbing supplies for walk-in customers. The owner, a wiry guy named Clark, and his statuesque wife, Brenda, spent most of their time scouting for fixer-uppers and cheap lots to buy. Clark wasn't happy about this arrangement. He didn't like being behind a desk in a white shirt and spectacles where his wife had him. He longed for the days when he rode out with his employees on plumbing jobs. Every morning when he handed me my job slips, I could see the longing in his eyes.

Then one Monday morning I had a bit of bad luck. My first call was to fix a leaky copper pipe on a garage slop sink. I traced my finger along the map route and made my way to a white stucco house with pink trim and green tin window awnings. The job would be no big deal. I pushed the buzzer, and an attractive woman with long red hair answered the door in a cotton housecoat. Loosely cinched, it fell open as her bare leg stepped carelessly against it, revealing her bra and black panties. She clutched her robe closed and told me she'd just woken up, but she seemed pretty awake as she continued to gaze at me. I got nervous and didn't know what to say so I asked her to show me the slop sink. I'd have it fixed right away, I said, and added that I had another call to go to. I worked faster than usual. I cut the sheet rock, turned off the water, cut the pipe, slipped on couplings and a length of new copper pipe, and soldered it back. Then I went inside to hand her the bill.

She studied it carelessly and offered me a cup of coffee. She crossed her legs and swung the cotton hem so it slipped, up to her thigh. She reached across the table and took my palm, saying she wanted to see the calluses. She began to rub my palm in a way that we both knew meant more. I asked her if she'd left something burning on the stove, and then I saw smoke coming from the garage door. I bolted outside. A two-by-four stud had caught fire when I was soldering the fittings with the acetylene torch. I doused the flames with buckets of water and mopped up the charred swampy mess as best I could. After I left, finished my calls, and got back in the shop, Clark's wife berated me for making romantic advances to the woman, who had called screaming into the phone that she was going to sue me. Brenda said I was a hazard to her customers and I was fired. Clark was in the bay, and I told him I'd do anything to stay on, but he nodded toward the office and said once her mind was made up, there was no changing it.

◆

After applying for half a dozen plumbing jobs, I gave up. I was better than most plumbers but I didn't have a California license. I was offered jackhammer labor and minimum wage bullshit. We'd gotten low on money, and what little we had left we decided to invest. We bought marijuana to sell to Marcos's friends in Michigan. We were going to ship the weed on the bus. It was only a pound but it would double our investment and get us by until something else came our way.

Marcos and I stood in the bus ticket line behind backpacking hippies smelling of incense and the wild. Outside, under the I-beam canopy, buses pulled in, groaning steam and squealing brakes, and weary travelers straggled into the lobby. The ticket agent, a thin old man wearing a Greyhound cap with a green plastic bill, his face mottled with age spots, wire-rim spectacles low on his hawk nose, puckered his chapped lips and whispered hoarsely, "Next." The line moved slowly because he was having a hard time understanding the Mexicans. I asked Marcos again how this was going to work. Marcos explained how his buddies in Michigan would love this weed. "I got the whole thing set up," he said. "Soon as it's shipped, I'll call and they'll Western Union the money. By tomorrow morning, we'll have enough for rent, food, pool, beer, and partying."

We'd left a party earlier and were eager to return. We'd been tape-wrapping the box like a Christmas present when our neighbor Jo-Jo came by with a six-pack. After tasting the weed he said he'd take a hundred dollars' worth. Maggie and her boyfriend Squirrel brought some pizza and more beer, smoked, and said they'd buy some weed too; Exclusive, a black dude with a huge Afro and a dog named Bullet, put in two orders. If Michigan worked out, we could even have enough money to buy enough to sell locally too. Bernice and two girls came over and sat on the floor listening to music and talking and smoking weed. I'd left the dope and papers in a bake pan and told them to have a good time, we'd be back.

At the station, kids shrieked playing tag in the lobby as their solemn Mexican parents sat stone still in molded yellow chairs clutching bundles tied with string. They had swarthy complexions and broad faces, with serapes and sandals and white cotton peasant pants. "Next? Next?" The teller peered at us. "Fill out a shipping tag with name and address."

We handed him the box to weigh it and Marcos took a pen from the coffee can on the counter and was writing when two guys cut in line behind us. A voice came from behind me. "Boy, you guys stink of weed." I turned around and one flashed a wallet badge:

Narcotic Agents. "We'd like to look in that box." He used a box cutter to open it and found the weed. I put my head down, ashamed, as they led us through the lobby handcuffed, past those people who looked like my grandparents, people who worked hard all their lives and earned their money honestly.

The next day we pled guilty to a misdemeanor and were sentenced to thirty days. Marcos had never been in jail before, but I told him not to sweat it. Sitting on a bunk and playing poker, I told him I'd been in jail a few times and then gave him the unwritten jail rules. Bum a smoke but tell the guy you'll catch him on the rebound on commissary day. Don't join guys in a circle talking unless you're invited. If a guy mad-dogs you, never back up. If shit comes down, I'll take care of it. You watch my back, I watch yours. We spent most of our time in an open common area with five stainless-steel tables where we ate, played checkers, dominoes, cards, sat smoking, and shot the breeze. Marcos was too friendly at first, so when a guy named Flyer, a tall, ex-All-American collegiate basketball star turned pimp, gave Marcos a carton of Camels, I took them back and told Flyer to quit playing Marcos for a punk.

A few days later we sat down to eat and Flyer told Bluebird, this faggot he was bunking with, to take Marcos's orange. Bluebird hit Marcos when Marcos tried to take it back, and immediately Raven and Squeaky, two guys I played poker with, and I were on them. Marcos was scared but I kind of shielded him during the fight, placing him behind me in a way that nobody would think Marcos was chicken. Raven was nobody to mess with, a Chicano from Oakland. He had showed us all what he could do when a big guy named Mac-Daddy stepped on his Stacy Adams and Raven tore him up. Marcos was scared after the fight. Things didn't get better when Raven and Squeaky were given their walking papers. It was tense, and Marcos and I stayed on guard in case the other guys tried to jump us. Marcos didn't mellow out until he started writing another inmate's sister in Los Angeles. He taped her picture on his bunk and was always responding to her perfumed letters full of romantic dreams of their living happily ever after when he got out. He was playing along with her just to fill the time.

The days dragged on monotonously as Marcos busily wrote love letters. For cards and dominoes I partnered up with a guy named Tecolote—Spanish for Owl, because he could see DEA agents in the dark and run drugs right under their noses. I had been on the jail-house phone talking to a chick and heard Tecolote next to me, speaking rapidly in a language I'd never heard. He must have called ten people, using avid gestures as if the party he'd called was in front of him. Later I asked him what language he was talking, and he said it was Pig Latin. In fact, he could repeat anything I said backwards, sounding like an auctioneer. When he wasn't on the phone or playing cards, he was figuring out stuff, showing me a legal pad with numbers on it, saying, "That's what I make in a month." It was a five-figure digit. After visits he came back and drank salt water and threw up a balloon of hash his wife had tongued him in a kiss. Smoking from a pipe made from a toilet-paper cylinder with a screen made from the tinfoil from a cigarette pack, he suggested Marcos and I might make a little money and start selling hash and weed for him. I told him it sounded like a good idea but that Marcos and I were leaving within days. We had work and housing vouchers the jail counselor had given us. After our last experience I wanted to avoid drugs. I was looking forward to life again without having to be looking over my shoulder or worrying about being thrown in jail.

On the last night, when the lights went off, Marcos tossed and turned in the bunk above me. I finally asked what the problem was. "You usually sleep like a log, dude, what's up? Squeezing that turkey of yours?"

But instead of joking back as he usually did, he said, "I want to thank you for being my friend." I felt a little embarrassed by his admission because it just wasn't done; loyalty and friendship spoke for itself in just hanging out. And because no one had ever thanked me before for being a friend, I was kind of lost for words. I told him he was the best friend I had ever had, too, my voice sounding forced, like a child saying he liked to eat vegetables to please the grown-ups. He said he was wondering about the game plan once we got out. "What's to wonder?" I responded. "We're getting out, man: freedom, chicks, and party time."

"Things gonna be the same?"

"It's never changed," I said. "We're partners until the wheels fall off that car of yours. Go to sleep, Marcos. Good night."

◆

The police had had Marcos's car impounded so we took a bus to our old apartment, but the landlord had put our belongings in storage and wouldn't return them until we paid him back rent. We bussed over to the hotel for which the jail had given us vouchers. We were feeling good about being free, staring out the window at chicks, until we arrived at our "hotel" to find a squalid dope fiend's den and seedy whorehouse with ex-cons sitting on lumpy, ragged sofas watching soaps on television in a foul-smelling, dingy lobby. We wanted to turn around and walk out but we had no place to go. We handed the vouchers to a wrinkled, hunch-backed man at the desk, who was puffing on a cigar and playing poker with a floozy in a red miniskirt, pink fish-net stockings, and black stiletto heels. He tapped a coffee-stained black book, "Sign it," he said, coughing. "Room six, first floor. Ruby, your turn." The woman batted her false eyelashes at Marcos, her makeup crumbling in chunks at the smile lines. Beneath her black wig, gray strands stuck out.

We walked up the creaky steps into a narrow hallway rancid with the stench of decay and bleach fumes so strong I had trouble breathing. The rooms had no doors, hot electrical wires stuck out from wall outlets, gashes gouged the wooden floor, water dripped from cracked toilets and sinks. In one room a woman was passed out on the floor, her dress above her waist. In the next, two guys and a chick were cooking up heroin in a spoon. My stomach soured. I counted the rooms from the front of the hall and went into the fifth. A haggard-looking couple with shrunken cheeks and puffed-out eyes, scabbed faces, and blood-caked hair looked at us, and the guy said, "Sorry, man, sorry," and they scurried out to the hallway and into another vacant room. Marcos read my thoughts when he whispered, "This is where they send them to rehabilitate?"

To get us the hell out of the dump as quickly as we could, I called Tecolote and set up a deal. It wasn't like we were going to be big dealers or anything, it was a temporary but convenient jump start, to help us get on our feet. The judge had sentenced us to a couple of months of community service, but this ended up by helping us sell more. We reported to a Ms. Gonzalez, who met us outside a cinder-block green-tarpapered pitched-roof house, converted into a social service office. She made us wait outside on a dilapidated porch with warped boards and peeling paint. A huge ponderosa pine flanked the smooth-grooved steps leading to the door, its milky oval window cracked and repaired with duct tape. Ms. Gonzalez, a cordial heavy-shouldered Chicana with graying hair, led us into a room where we shot pool on a beat-up table until the crew boss, Luke, came in. He was a big guy, barging in from the back, roughly kicking the screen door open. A retired cop, he coached a basketball team comprised of ex-gang members at the Boys' Club. The rest of the guys filed in and after a while Luke announced that the truck had arrived and we all went out the back door to begin our deliveries of food staples to welfare food banks. At every stop, while we unloaded boxes of macaroni and block cheese, all these black and Chicano dudes would line up in the back of the racks and shelves and we'd sell quarter and half ounces.

Using the welfare delivery system as our front was a great cover. We were not going to make the same mistake and get drunk and high or use the buses when we could be cabbed all over San Diego and Ocean Beach, compliments of the city, doing our business. Our clients were generally depressed and down on their luck and needed something to lift their spirits. Site to site, on the truck bed, waving to women, whistling, yelling, and making happy eyesore spectacles of ourselves, we'd reach one food bank and while the guys unloaded commodity cereal, powdered milk, and other stuff, Marcos and I'd be in the back of the warehouse doing our thing. And what better way to package our product than in generic macaroni boxes? We'd drive down the road a bit, unload, sell our weed, and drive on and unload at another food-bank site. We went all over San Diego, joking and laughing, rolling in dough, our pockets brimming with stamps; we pointed out different houses we were going to rent, shops we were going to buy clothes in, chicks we were going to take out. We reveled in the ocean air and warm sunshine; life couldn't have been better. We got the car out of the pound, paid our back rent, got our stuff back, and rented a nice pad facing the ocean with a walkway down to the beach.

◆

After our community service work was done, Marcos and I resumed living the life we'd had before jail. We'd wash and wax his car and then hang out at Pub and Pockets, a sports bar with shapely waitresses carrying trays of food and beer pitchers to college kids watching TVs suspended from the ceiling showing different games. I was racking another pool game when these two lovely Chicanas took a table next to ours. Marcos shot me a glance. The more beautiful of the two reminded me of Theresa with her caramel complexion; in a yellow skirt and off-rose silk blouse, black mane of hair, red lips, she glowed with a sensual sweetness. She chalked her stick and bent over to break, the stick caressing her breast with each stroke. She didn't get a ball in and abruptly turned to me and said, "Almost." I blushed and looked down because she kept looking. Marcos missed, teasing me, "Jimmy, it's your shot; make it count, dude; don't let a beautiful woman distract you; come on, concentrate, I'm giving you a little mercy, dude." He purposely set the cue ball on the side closest to them. I stepped around the table, trying to think of what to say to her, taking a long time eyeing the balls for an angle. Then from behind me, she asked, "Are you going to shoot?" Caught by surprise, I hurried my shot and missed the cue ball, smacking my stick against the stained-glass umbrella lamp hanging over the table. Embarrassed, I returned to my chair to sip my rum and Coke, wanting to say something but lost for words.

We ended up playing teams, and later followed them to their hangout—Surf's Up, an open-air watering hole jamming with a beach band and a rowdy crowd. Attached to bamboo in the palm ceiling, Chinese paper lanterns came on at dusk, illuminating red roses painted on the shades, swaying slightly in the breeze. Marcos and Clara split in her car and left Lonnie and me drinking margaritas. After we drained the last one, she kissed me, long and passionately. She was the first woman since Theresa who made me believe that I could love again, and from that first kiss we were inseparable.

The next morning I took her home to change clothes. She lived with her parents in an older upper-class neighborhood in a beige two-story clapboard-and-brick house. Lofty palm trees lined the shrub-bordered street, and the lawns and hedges were geometrically perfect. Her father was in the two-car garage, tinkering with his Cessna plane. I waited in the car, and after a while Lonnie came out of the house wearing jeans and a red shirt. She had a carefree air about her that made her seem like a little girl skipping squares at hopscotch. She went to the garage to kiss her father good-bye. He turned on her angrily, ordering her to stay and commanding her to get rid of me. She had words with him, but they only made him more demanding. When she came to the car, I leaned over to the passenger side and suggested, "Maybe you should stay. I can come back later." But she got in and said, "Don't let it bother you, he's always mad." She was on the verge of tears. She looked at me, eyes wet. "I'm okay. I just want to be with you." I downshifted, turned a corner, and sped under trees whose shade and sunlight glimmered off the windshield. We had not planned for her to leave home only after one night with me, it just happened that way. It felt like a new beginning, though I was afraid I might not be the man she thought I was.

On the freeway, going to the beach, I said, "I heard your father back there. You don't have a home anymore. I'm sorry. I didn't mean to mess things up." She scooted over and squeezed my hand. "I love you." I looked at her and asked, "Are you sure you want this?" She answered by giving me a long kiss until I pulled away and veered to avoid hitting a guard rail. I wanted to say much more to her, but I didn't have the words.

◆

The three of us hung out, and I became as comfortable with Lonnie as I was with Marcos. To get our relationship more grounded, and being tired of looking over my shoulder for narcs, I told Marcos we should stop selling weed. I reminded him that we were just doing lightweight dealing to get on our feet; it wasn't like we wanted to become millionaires in drugs and make it our life.

"I'm with you all the way, long as we don't end up back at that grungy hotel." With Marcos, it was never a question of whether it was right or wrong—friendship was more important to him. He swiped his hair from his face, looked at me, and added, "So where do we go and how do we get by?"

I told him I'd gone to an employment agency, where I had leafed through a magazine about Arizona in the waiting room. I pulled the pictures I'd torn out from my pocket and showed them to him. "Don't look too bad, do they?" He studied the magazine pictures and asked, "Did you get a job?" I said that the counselor asked me in the interview if I knew what the word tangible meant. I imagined a jar of Tang. "It's a drink," I told the counselor. "Athletes drink it on commercials." Marcos broke out laughing. "Tangible ain't got nothing to do with Tang." And then I told him, "Yeah, I know that now. I figured it out when, after my answer, the jerk walks me to the door with a strange look on his face as if I'd just farted in church or something." Marcos said, "We go to Arizona, then."

My life hinged on the precarious belief that sooner or later I was bound to fall into step with life around me if I continued to move and try out new things, new places, meet new people. If I opened myself to enough new experiences, I was bound to hit on the right one sooner or later.

The next day, three hundred miles later, Marcos, Lonnie, and I were driving into a town that wasn't what we'd expected from the magazine pictures. Yuma, Arizona, was no oasis in the desert; we didn't see the Colorado River glimmering between green fields or any friendly faces under a Chamber of Commerce sign welcoming newcomers. We drove in at dawn, startling crows from stick fences lining the dusty roads damp with night dew. We jostled on the outskirts over rutted roads, gradually winding into residential areas. It was a small-enough town that we could cover it in an hour. The morning was cool and minty as cedar berries, and lunch-pail workers drowsily trucked their way to work. We found the tracks dividing whites and Mexicans and drove through the Mexican barrio, where jeans hung on clotheslines and chickens nested under wrecked cars. Outhouses lay on the edge of small cornfields and a goat stood licking the drip puddles from hand-pump water spigots in a weedy yard. Here and there gardens of squash and chile grew beside shacks built from tin and timber scraps. We saw a young boy taking a bucket by the front door to haul water; at another house, melons and green beans were piled by a ravaged screen door; from nearby came the faint strains of Mexican music. Hoes and rakes and shovels clustered together by the east wall near clay pits to mix mud and repair the adobe cracks. I'd grown used to big-city noise, and here a silence lay over everything like an invisible spirit invoking memories of the past that made me realize how much my life had changed in a few years. It reminded me of Estancia, and maybe because of the promise it held for a new life, I talked about my brother and sister for the first time, and told my two friends about how my parents abandoned us. Closer to me than my own family had ever been, Marcos and Lonnie brought out the best in me and were the most accepting people I'd ever been with. They'd come to see me as someone they could rely on, who was strong, with a clear idea of what we should do. But I didn't trust myself, nor did I tell them that I was searching for something to make me feel more a part of the world, and while they helped me in that search, I couldn't share with anyone the pain that still drove my exploration to find a place to stand comfortably in my skin.

◆

That afternoon we rented an old clapboard house in the Mexican section, where most of the families worked in fields surrounding their houses. Mr. William Purvis, a doddering, bow-legged, weathered old cowboy, met us at the house and gave us the do's and don'ts, scanning us with his one good eye while his lifeless glass eye stared off askew. We gave him a hundred-dollar damage deposit and a hundred dollars for the first month's rent, then handed him the rental sign which had been nailed to the tattered screen door. We used a hammer to take off the plywood nailed over the door. I was excited about moving in but it was strange and I felt like an actor with a domestic role to play. I rolled up my sleeves and started in with the box of cleaning and repair supplies we'd picked up at a hardware store. Lonnie swept, dusted, and scrubbed. I hung the door I found in the back bedroom, nailed loose porch planks, and oiled kitchen drawer runners. Marcos, smoking a fat doobie and blasting his boom box, put on his mechanic's overalls and repaired window screens, tarred and papered roof holes, and replaced rotted wood on the side of the house with wood scraps he found out back in the decaying chicken coops.

I had a new life and good friends. In the days that followed, there were moments of genuine intense emotion. After getting the house in order, with a door to walk through, I carried Lonnie over the threshold as if she were my bride. I was brimming over, not only with a sense of accomplishment but with a warm feeling that I had my first real home. One night, lying on the floor on blankets, Lonnie asked why I couldn't say the word *love.* I whispered to her, "It's like a secret wish, supposed to keep it secret. Like a birthday wish: Never let anyone know what you wished for and it'll come true."

She was intuitive. "You ever have a birthday cake or birthday party?" I didn't say anything back, but I lay in the dark remembering how my brother Mieyo stole a candle from the altar at the orphanage, and for my birthday we hid under his bunk with the candle lit and he sang a happy birthday song to me. He gave me a handful of hard candy he'd stolen from the living quarters of Father Gallagher, the priest.

I wished Mieyo were with me, that we could be together like this, the way we always said we would as kids. Every other place I'd had, in Albuquerque or Santa Fe, was to party in, hide from the world, or just crash. This was different. I didn't feel the emptiness or despair that I normally felt in those other places. I turned over and hugged Lonnie. From the living room, Marcos gave a choked cough from the bong he was smoking before snuggling into his sleeping bag. In the dark, Lonnie whispered, as if she knew what I'd been thinking, "Welcome home, sweetheart, I love you. Tomorrow I'll clean the yard and plant some roses for you." It was usually difficult for me to feel good about anything I did, but I did feel certain about Lonnie. Hoping it would last, I fell asleep, a part of me still yearning to call Theresa to tell her I was doing well.

◆

A couple of weeks later we got our phone hooked up and left Xeroxed flyers with our number at the Laundromat, the gas station, and the hardware store. While we were leaving them in mailboxes on the white side of town with their extravagant lawns and shrubs, a police cruiser rolled up. The officer said there'd been a rash of burglaries and folks in the area were suspicious. "If you're looking for work," he advised, "Mexicans and hippies gather at dawn on Main Street." But later that afternoon, canvassing the motel strip, we landed our first job at the Cactus Rose Motel, fixing rooms trashed by army guys partying from the nearby base. The proprietor, a bony guy from India, kept us as regular groundskeepers. Three bucks an hour for each of us paid for groceries. Better still, he referred us to other innkeepers, and within weeks we were changing swamp-cooler pads, painting motel rooms, and landscaping. Marcos and I traded work for a junked truck rusting in the weeds behind one of the motels. We got it running and painted our company name and phone number on the doors—HANDYMAN EXPRESS— with a guy with a hammer in one hand and a tool box in the other dashing off to a call. Lonnie brought hot lunches to the job site; after working in the hundred-degree heat, we'd return at sunset exhausted and sit before the air conditioner, shower, eat a meal, and kick back in the living room drinking beer until the late news, after which we hit the sack. The straight life wasn't as hard as it was boring, but it gave a regularity to my life.

Everything was going great until one morning we were trimming out a house—tacking floorboards, screwing in cabinet doors, doorknobs, and light fixtures—when this guy appeared in the doorway. He was from the state. He said we needed a contractor's license and, until we applied for one in Phoenix, at the State Labor Board, we had to "cease operations."

I had no idea what the idiot was talking about, as I told Lonnie later, sitting on the back doorstep of our house. Marcos and I had our shirts off; we were as dark as the Mexicans living around us in shacks separated by fields of weeds and cactus. Marcos was on a crate, drinking his beer, saying, "We were getting all the work, so the competition sicced the law on us. In the meantime, we should probably pick up that tile in San Luis for the landlord. Kill some time."

Marcos went for another beer. I told him to grab beers for us and then turned to Lonnie, saying, "You look sad." She had told me earlier in the week how she missed her parents and the piano and dance lessons she'd taken twice a week for years. On weekends, she and her father flew his plane. She had said it wasn't their fault she wasn't happy, they'd tried. I wanted to say something but I got up and hugged her as Marcos came with our beers.

"Yeah, lovebirds, I got a suggestion. What say we have a party after we come back from San Luis?" Lonnie and I both agreed, and Marcos went into one of his fishing stories.

Half listening, I scanned the fields shimmering with heat from the sun-baked soil. After a truck or car went by on the dirt road, dust clouds hung on the air. Mexican music floated faintly across the quiet parched fields, triggering memories of Estancia: Grandpa in his hard-backed chair by the back door, rolling a cigarette and smoking meditatively, reading his Bible and looking up to think about the words; me at his work boots playing with his bootlaces, inventing games in the dirt with sticks, pebbles, and insects. Marcos was still telling his story. "The fish couldn't even fit in the bathtub. I weighed it at the county store—a state record. I'd snuck in behind Lambley's house and caught it in his pond! And Lambley hated me after that; he'd been trying to catch that fish since he was a kid, and here I go, snagging it with nothing more than a black rubber worm. Nothing to it."

The whole time Marcos was telling his story, I watched Mexicans butchering a pig in the distance. They didn't pay much attention to a half-starved mongrel sniffing the air spiced with skillet scents of pig's feet, fried intestines, tortillas, beans, and rice. And they didn't have time to stop it before it snatched a pig's foot and dashed off as they cursed and threw rocks at it. I was happy it got away. Above us, a hawk scanned the prickly desert weeds, checking out the dog. Marcos gulped his beer and ended his story. "Bet them bass are biting now."

"Why'd you leave?" Lonnie asked.

"My daddy used to tell me stories about the world, from books, and I guess I took them to heart and wanted to see for myself. Up there was God's country, but God didn't stop me and my dad from fighting—he wanted me to go to school, join the service, get married, settle down. We didn't get along much at the end." His eyes had a soft remembering, and to break the pain he asked, "Hey, Jimmy? What you'all do back home?"

"Not much," I said. "I can tell you one thing, Marcos, you should talk to your dad, make up with him."

Marcos had hurt in his voice. "Why? He started it."

I said, "The last time I saw my dad, he was drunk and beating me. I kept telling him to stop, but he wouldn't. So I hit him. That was the last time I saw him. I regret that; I wish I could tell him I'm sorry. When I left I wasn't going *to* someplace, I was running away from all the shit in my life."

We were quiet.

"Here's to the best friends I ever had." Marcos toasted, then scratched at the dirt, tossing a little of it, and said, "I do miss hunting with him, though. I could smell a buck a mile away, better than that mongrel dog. I could survive off the land too. I know about plants, which to eat and stuff like that."

Some of the Mexican kids were chasing the dog and I realized they had my family's faces, my own among them, shooing chickens and throwing pebbles at sparrows on telephone lines; tired grandparents, resting in chairs on porches, talked about the chile plants and corn in their small garden plots. I got up and walked in the field. I broke a flowery weed and came back and gave it to Lonnie. She was brushing red nail polish on her toenails.

She took my gift and said, "I fell in love with you, Jimmy, that's why I left home. And I have no regrets."

◆

In San Luis, Mexico, ten minutes south of the border, they sold bathroom tile cheap, but we didn't know where. The border checkpoint was a small cubicle with a guard who didn't bother to come out, sleepily waving a finger for us to proceed.

We drove around. It was a decrepit, chalky town, dust and silence its main features. Dirt yards surrounded bricked-up dismantled car hulls. Chickens clawed the crusty dirt, and children scraped the hard ground to play games. Now and then noises rattled in the silence, loose tin slapped, and stray pack dogs emitted pained yelps. The town seemed weary of itself, every trace of life drained as it clung to the scantiest survival. Burros and roosters dozed in the shade of abandoned adobes beside cinder-block walls and stick houses buried in stickers and weeds. I wondered what supported its existence. I was thirsty and told Marcos to find a place to have a beer. He asked if I remembered the guy's name that we had met in the county jail. Tecolote, I told him, and he asked, "Wasn't this the town he was talking about, about this big dealer here?"

"Yeah," I said."I think the guy's name was Galvan."

We parked behind a few battered cars in front of a weathered adobe building, the lettering on the facade faded but readable, EL TIGRE cantina. We went inside, eyeing the rough-looking Mexicans brooding over their beers at other tables, and took a seat at one of the rickety round tables set up haphazardly around the room under a slow-turning ceiling fan. On the earthen walls hung peeling paintings depicting bullfighters, famous cowboys, and revolutionaries. I ordered two beers and wondered where we could find floor tiles.

Marcos pointed to the bartender, gulping and putting his bottle down. "I'll tell you, this place reminds me of those old Western movies I used to watch as a kid." He looked around. "Wish I knew Spanish. How d'you say beer?"

"*Cerveza.*"

Marcos got up. "I'll get two more." He came back with beers in hand and asked, "What does *pelao* mean?"

"Country bumpkin, or foolish kid."

Marcos stared at the bartender, who grinned at him. "Country bumpkin, huh?" Marcos said, and went over to the bartender.

By the bartender's expression, whatever Marcos told him, he didn't like it. He glared at Marcos all the way back to our table. When Marcos told me he had said *Metalo,* which was slang for "Up yours," I warned him to be careful about what he said to people. "They take it personal here."

"I just wanted to show him a thing or two," Marcos countered. "See that look on his face when I mentioned Galvan's name?"

I drained my beer, a little nervous, and said, "Let's find that tile and get home." The bartender was slowly pacing behind the counter as if padlocked to a chain attached to an iron collar around his thick neck. When we rose to leave he nodded us over to the counter and poured us each a free shot of tequila and a beer. I didn't want to stay, but Marcos had already downed his shot.

"Mexico ain't such a bad place." He smacked his lips, pleased.

The bartender pointed to my shot, indicating with his finger for me to drink. I sensed something was off. The bartender returned to washing glasses and drying them on his apron. As we were sipping our beers, a man dressed in cheap nightclub rayon entered and sat at the counter next to us.

"You looking for Galvan?" he asked. I wondered how he knew.

"Yeah." Marcos added, before I could stop him, "Recommended by a friend."

The stranger motioned us to follow him to the end of the bar, where he knuckle-rapped the countertop and shot three fingers up. The bartender slid three tequila shots down the counter, his disregard indicating no payment necessary. We slugged them down in a swallow. Feeling the tequila, we got in our car and followed the guy in his to a motel at the edge of town. He opened a door to a room, said, "I'll be back," and left.

I was worried and tried to tell Marcos we should leave. "People get killed like this. We could be robbed, left for dead. You ever think they might be setting us up? Did the bartender see you pull that wad of money out for the tile?" I was uneasy about the whole thing, but Marcos was nonchalant, savoring the dope-buyer role.

"Chill, Jimmy. You remember that boat we seen docked in Marina del Sol in San Diego, its name was ONE TIME? Remember? You said, Yeah, that would be nice, a one-time score that would put us over the top. This is Tecolote's main connect! This is the man!"

Before I could tell him that was before I met Lonnie and things changed, I heard a car outside. I stared at the door anxiously. It opened, and the same slick guy came in the room and closed the door. I gave Marcos a tense look that conveyed I didn't like what was going down. "We wait," the stranger said. I wanted to get the hell out of there. I was feeling trapped. Just as I was going to say, Forget the meeting, forget we ever asked, I heard another car drive in and three doors slam shut.

Three men came in. One asked our escort who was the lead man, and he pointed to me, mostly because I spoke Spanish. "You, come with us." We'd already gone too far. The last thing I wanted to do with these gangsters was play head games. If I backed out now, they'd think we were narcs and kill us.

Outside, one of them opened the passenger door in front and I slid in. We drove in a cloud of dust away from town into the desert, out far enough that the town disappeared. The driver parked under a dead mesquite tree and killed the engine. I stared at the dead bugs on the windshield. No sight of another human being, nothing except the haunting *whoo* of the breeze and the two menacing henchmen in the backseat. The driver ordered me to step out. One of the men patted me down for weapons, and then I got back in.

"What do you want with Galvan?" the driver asked, his brown eyes icy. He was short and plump with rounded shoulders, hair combed into a ponytail. He wore a tight-fitting black silk shirt and designer jeans. His face was gouged with smallpox pits.

The seriousness of my situation hit me. This was the real deal. These guys were heavy hitters, and if my answers were not right they'd put a bullet in the back of my head.

"A friend of a friend, you said. Who's the friend?" He repeated my words with grim calm, hissing the sibilants.

"In the county jail, a guy—we were in jail together—he said Galvan could get some good weed."

The driver smiled. "How much?"

"A hundred pounds—but we don't have the money now."

"I shit a hundred pounds!" he laughed."How about a ton?"

"A ton?"

"Otherwise it is not worth my time."

I didn't know what to say. I looked out the windshield, chilled with dread. "I can sell it," I heard myself say, "but you have to front it to us, give us a week or two."

"This friend in jail with you . . . his name?"

I was still stunned by my answer.

"His name?" he asked again.

"His name? Tecolote." Was Tecolote his friend or his enemy?

The driver sighed. "Ahh?"

I exhaled, wanting to get through this ordeal. "They slammed him down for distribution." The presence of the two men in the backseat was unnerving. A sinking feeling came over me, making my mouth sticky and dry. "He told me Galvan could give me quantity and price, quality weed. And that Galvan was a man of his word."

"He told you that? The sonofabitch owes me money. But it's true, not only price and quality but doorstep service. Yuma? No problem. I will front it to you, but how much time?"

"A week or two?"

"We'll give you a trial run—a sample, okay, fifty pounds tomorrow. Diego will see where you live. You pay in a week."

I nodded and gave a weak smile, relieved.

"Seven days . . . or you're buzzard shit." He hunched forward, reached under the seat, and took out a chrome-plated nine millimeter. He threw it on the seat between us, felt under the seat again, and brought out a thick object wrapped in newspaper. He handed it to me and I carefully unwrapped the porno tabloid pages. It was a marijuana stalk with resinous, crystalline ocher buds. It represented money, easy money.

FOUR

There was a point in that car out on the desert when I quit thinking—my mental circuits closed down, and I was compelled to do whatever the circumstances required. It was as if there were something beyond my will driving me on. I was hoping the chance to deal dope again would never come but wishing it would, dreading and wanting it simultaneously. My bluff had been called. No matter how I wanted to back out, I had to go through with it. Drugs were the way, providing the only opportunity at hand to make money quickly. I knew I didn't have the patience to work for years at landscaping; it was too repetitive and, most importantly, did not meet my dream of living an exciting life. I feared getting stuck with doing landscaping the rest of my life. I'd have to work years to save enough for a house. That life was only a temporary solution to making enough money to get by. I wanted more than going to work at dawn, busting my ass all day, and getting home so tired I fell right to sleep. So I was going to make the best of dealing drugs: get in and get out as fast as possible. Part of me rejected the whole idea of dealing as a stupid mistake; another part was already calculating how to take advantage of it. I didn't want to jeopardize what Lonnie and I had going, a normal life and a secure eight-to-five job, but, with the IRS shutting us down, this deal gave me an opportunity to turn some fast cash. We'd have the money to get a license and jump-start our business again on firmer financial footing. We could even expand it: buy new trucks and hire other workers to do the menial labor while Lonnie and I traveled.

Yet Galvan was no ordinary street dealer. Fueled by tequilas and beer chasers, buzzed on the adrenaline of the deal, I'd gotten myself into a serious situation. Despite the obvious hazards of working with a man who killed people when things didn't go his way, the electric jolt of the deal counteracted the dulling anesthetic effects of normal life. The sun shone brighter, the day felt more adventurous, and I sensed a multitude of exciting possibilities. Dealing was hard to get out of the blood, and I stepped right back into it as if I'd never left.

◆

When we'd had our repair business, we'd gotten so busy that we had hired Carey as a part-time helper. He was an army serviceman living off-base in a trailer with another military roommate. Carey turned out to be perfect for delivering weed—a Kentucky country boy, blond hair, large blue eyes, with a farm-boy innocence and disarming simpleness. After tasting a sample of the weed, he said he could definitely sell quite a bit on-base. He'd need a couple of days to put the word out and collect the money. To our surprise, Carey sold all fifty pounds.

In the cantina the next week I gave Galvan the money, and after a few tequila shots we went to his house. It was a whitewashed hacienda with endless rooms enclosing a large courtyard. Parched palm trees and awnings kept the heat down but it still was oppressive; hot breezes whipped the sombrero brims of the groundskeepers. Brawny bodyguards with bull torsos and tattooed arms brooded with guns strapped around their huge guts. Antique ranch spurs and mule saddles were nailed to the exterior walls. Inside, wagon-wheel candle chandeliers hung from rusting chains. The red-brick floors had corded throw rugs at all doorways; see-through lace curtains covered the arched windows. The rooms were decorated with pre-Columbian gold figurines, Mayan and Aztec artifacts that Galvan boasted were sold to him by Mexican grave robbers. Several beautiful Mexican women floated around the place like dark swans against the white adobe. We lounged poolside, drinking tequilas, as he told me I had nothing to worry about as far as the locals went—border guards, judges, police, and lawyers were eating out of his hand. But, he warned, "Keep your eyes open for DEA. Yuma's a wholesale port of entry and DEA are like cockroaches here."

Two days later, five hundred pounds of weed arrived at our doorstep.

Lonnie thought we were moving too fast and began to worry. She said I was gritting my teeth at night. When we ate out once a week she said I'd look at every face, suspecting every glance. I was indeed now more careful than I had been in San Diego, looking in my rearview every few minutes, discussing the biz with Marcos only when no others were around, putting my index finger to my lips when Marcos started talking in a café.

"You're too paranoid," he said. "Gotta enjoy it while it's here."

"Marcos," I said, "it can only work if we're careful. We can't just be throwing our shit around, buying a new car, eating out all the time and flaunting it."

Lonnie was alarmed by the amount of money we counted each night on the bed, stacking and tying it in five-thousand-dollar piles and stuffing it in pillowcases. She explained that dealing was touching every aspect of our lives. Every knock on the door, every phone call, took on a whole different meaning. I reassured her it was only temporary and promised to quit after we had saved enough to move back to New Mexico.

But privately, I knew I was in over my head. I had to keep riding Marcos because he wanted to go on a shopping spree. He wanted to buy a boat and paint TWO TIMES on it. I asked him, "Wouldn't it be a bit weird to have a new boat parked in the middle of the desert?" All he could think of was going back to La Zona to screw the Mexican babes at the brothels in San Luis. I told him after we had some money stashed and got out of dealing we could do all the partying we wanted. In the meantime, we had to keep our business under wraps and act normal. Even though Marcos was still getting high, I couldn't because it made me too paranoid. Carey would show up at night and we'd load his trunk with half the load, and the following night he'd show up with the money and load up the other half. It was 1972, the weed business was just starting to boom, and we were at the right place at the right time.

Carey was selling between five and six hundred pounds a month, and Galvan was forcing more and more on us, and we couldn't keep up with the quantities. Sometimes at night, separating the fives, tens, twenties, and hundreds on the bed, I'd tell Lonnie how poor we were when I was a child. When I lived with my mom in La Casita we had an outhouse, cold running water, and one bed. The most common phrase that I could remember from childhood was *"No hay con que."* It meant there was not enough of whatever was needed to go around. The fights, the worry, and even my parents' breaking up resulted in no small part from poverty. We never went to a movie and seldom bought new clothes unless it was work gloves, boots, or thermal underwear.

I let my imagination run away, telling Lonnie how I wanted to buy Grandma a new stove and phone and get her the best medical help money could buy because she was blind and arthritic. I'd buy my brother a new truck and my sister a new car once we got home. I'd like to put my dad in the hospital to get him to stop drinking and then buy him his own house and car. Lonnie suggested we take a vacation to relieve the stress from being pent up like we'd been since we started dealing. Marcos was more than up for it. It was the first planned vacation I ever had. We gave the house keys to Carey and left him in charge of everything.

◆

We drove to San Diego and dropped Lonnie off at her parents' house; we'd pick her up later in the evening. For old times, Marcos and I were going to shoot pool at our old hangout, but while cruising there we spotted Cadillac Cuz, the dealer/pimp at the old Sleazeball Hotel. We pulled into the alley behind his Caddy and, after slapping fives and bullshitting, he smoked a sample and said Bingo! In his Superfly talk, sliding his pink sunglasses down his nose and cocking his red hat to one side, he asked, "What's the P.R. on an L.B.?" We quoted our prices and locked him in for a load a week.

When we picked Lonnie up, she was jubilant because her parents had accepted her decision to live with me and were no longer mad. I told her we were extending the vacation. Might as well try to make up with *my* father too. We were going up to San Francisco to find my dad, who had gone there in search of my mother. My sister had given me his address.

Also in San Francisco was a guy we'd met in jail. We headed north on 101 to see Big Tommy, a biker from Redwood City. Driving along the breathtaking coast road, we laughed and sang and played music and smoked. We stopped in at old missions and lighthouses and took lots of pictures. Lonnie and I walked on the beach boardwalks of a tourist hamlet to eat and stretch our legs, and we kissed and made promises never to leave each other. It was romantic and passionate and gave our hearts a sorely needed lift, a push back into the real world away from dealing and Galvan and paranoia. Feeling caught up in the moment, I told her I used to be in love with an old girlfriend, Theresa. And that while I sometimes still thought of her, the pain from those days was slowly fading. Lonnie hugged me, whispering, "I'm always going to be yours and love you forever."

We got into Frisco eight hours later and found Big Tommy in his garage with other bikers, customizing Harley motors and frames. He had a full-blown three-bay shop with a black-lacquered tool chest the size of a bedroom on wheels. He took us into his office, and we laid out the bud we'd hidden in the car's door panel. He grabbed one stalk by the stem and hurled it against the window, saying, "Here you go, we're going to do a line or two of this, what I call Raising the Dead meth, and after we're done talking, if that bud don't slip and fall, I'll take five hundred a month." It didn't, and the deal was sealed.

The next morning, after breakfast, we went to find my father. After a while we found the Tenderloin district. I grew very quiet, seeing the tramps passed out in the gutters, winos rummaging through Dumpsters, guys slinging heroin and cocaine on street corners, buildings boarded up and secured with barb-wire fences. I didn't say anything. Marcos was tracking the streets by alphabetical order, until we found the address and pulled over in front of a crumbling brownstone. "This is it, Jimmy. Eighteen-thirty-eight Duran Street."

"He doesn't even know my mother's back in New Mexico," I said, staring out the window at the gray skies. I thought of the times riding with him in the car as a child, fearing we might be killed. Him crying about Mother, begging to know where she was. I kept wanting to get out and walk up the stairs and see him. But I knew my fantasy of a father was only that, a fantasy. It went something like me entering his room to find a well-dressed and sober man, embracing him, and going out to eat and talk. Taking him with me, waking up in a nice hotel room and having breakfast with him and buying him an airline ticket and flying him out to New Mexico, where I'd meet him and we'd get a place. But if I went up those stairs, he'd be on the bed half naked, puking his guts out, screaming that he needed a drink. What was I going to tell him when he asked about Mother? That she was married with two kids and another life and never wanted to see him again? I shouldn't have come. "Drive on," I told Marcos. "Drive—drive, get the fuck out of here!" Lonnie grabbed my hands because I was picking my bloody cuticles. I pushed her hands back. I squeezed myself with my arms crossed, trying to rock the pain out of me.

Marcos screeched the tires, fishtailing through the red-light district, past the nightmare of drunks and addicts and hookers. I didn't want to see my father like this. "Where to?" Marcos asked. "Home," I said. "Open this motherfucker up, let's see what she's got." I hoped the speed would take away the bad feelings, take away my grief. Marcos asked me something, but I couldn't talk. Lonnie was sniffling and I couldn't comfort her. I sat there cold and distant as we drove out of San Francisco, up and down the hilly streets. The thunder rolled ominously and the rain turned everything gray. I pictured my father lurching and stumbling in the rain, moaning for my mother. He sincerely believed an encounter would miraculously mend years of destruction and that they would live happily ever after. I rolled my window down and threw away the piece of paper with his address on it.

◆

The weed, eight hundred to a thousand pounds a month, was bricked and wrapped in plastic and yellow butcher paper, then stuffed in gunnysacks and delivered by Carey. The DEA relocated from Florida were easy to avoid because they stood out like blond, rosy-cheeked, suntanned stop signs. But neither the burgeoning weed business nor the profits lessened the depression I suffered after coming back from our vacation. I started getting high and drinking at bars with Marcos. Instead of going right in and out when delivering money to Galvan, I now took his invitation to stay longer and party with him, doing cocaine and messing around with La Zona girls. Feeling guilty about that, I took Lonnie on shopping sprees, buying her expensive dresses and jewelry.

I began to grow more nervous; the volume was taking over my life. Marcos and I spent a lot of time with Galvan partying at his ranch, joining him for dinners with lawyers, judges, cops from Yuma, and big shots from Chicago. Lonnie didn't trust Galvan; neither did I. Suspicious of his overly gracious manner, I went back to staying straight. I worried about being watched or slipping up. Marcos and I took care of the paperwork and returned to landscaping, light pruning, and molding hedges. Carey was still handling the base and making his runs to California. Lonnie kept the books on how much money we owed and how much we were making. We took our cut and hid it in the broom closet. Often, we'd sit out in the backyard and talk as in the old days, watching the sunset on the horizon. Other times we'd watch basketball or football on the color TV and drink beer and relax. But dealing was always in the back of my mind. The weed was in high demand, and orders kept coming in.

Things were getting crazier, faster, reeling out of control. There was no structure to my life. Day and night, situations came up, and after six months it was getting to my nerves. New customers, heavier loads, phone calls at all hours of the night, waiting and worrying if so-and-so could be trusted; fronting weed and waiting for the money; waiting for word from loads en route to destinations, and a hundred other details. To relax, Lonnie and I went to a lake outside of Yuma one Sunday. Carey had scored some PCP on the base. He said it was okay to take. Lonnie and I mixed some of the white powder in our sodas, and within the hour we were drowning in the worst nightmare of our lives. It lasted two days, and when we came out of it, we decided then and there to quit the business. Lonnie and I got into praying after that, something we had never done, but the demons and ghosts that attacked our minds while tripping made us both certain we were lucky to be alive. We were only twenty. We didn't want to spend the rest of our lives vegetating in a loony bin.

We'd saved up enough of a nest egg to go home, and I asked Lonnie to marry me and she agreed. It was a big move, but if I was going to do it, now was the time. She wanted to return with me to Albuquerque, buy a house of our own, and have a family.

At La Zona I told Galvan and he shrugged with little dismay. He had expected the news and said he was not going to dissuade me. "I am always here," he said, and raised his glass to the good times. I spent a couple of hours with him drinking and doing a few lines. He kidded a lot, saying I had to do what I had to do, but that in his opinion I had dealing in my blood and I had a certain way about me that attracted money and customers. Swaying his index finger at me, he said, "You'll be back." I was certain he was wrong, and when Marcos returned from Ocean Beach where he'd taken a girl to party, I told him too. He was laid back about it, and even seemed anxious to hit the road for home too. That evening during supper Marcos suggested we go to La Zona one last time to end our partnership with a party and commemorate our parting with a good old bottle of tequila. So that night we went to party for the last time. After half a bottle of tequila, Marcos went to one of the rooms with a woman and I sat in the booth nursing my drink and remembering the months in Yuma and the business deals we'd done. Reminiscing, enjoying the mariachis and sexy women, I waited for Marcos until a vendor boy with a box of cigarettes came up to me and slapped a pack of Marlboros down on the table next to my glass.

"*No quiero cigarros,*" I told him, handing them back.

"*Me dijo que traiera cigarros.*" Someone told him to bring me cigarettes. I couldn't figure out who. I told him to leave and forced the pack back on him.

Marcos finished with the woman in the back room. When he came up, I told him, "Let's jam, my man. No ands, ifs, or buts—we're outa here." I suddenly felt like a mouse about to get trapped. I don't know why, but alarms were going off in me. Marcos, flushed and beaming from sexual exertion, put his arm around my shoulder and we walked out. It was good to see him so happy, but as soon as we were outside two Federales escorting the cigarette boy approached us with rifles racked.

"*Esos son, esos dos.*" The vendor pointed at us.

"*¡Paganse cabrones!*" the Federale ordered us. Pay the vendor.

"What are you talking about? For what?" I asked.

"*Los cigarros, los cigarros,*" the vendor kept bleating like a wind-up toy. "*¡Me robaron!*" He insisted we robbed him.

"We didn't steal any cigarettes," I stated, directing my comments to the Federales holding their rifles on us.

A paddy wagon pulled up, and one of the Federales motioned to Marcos to get in.

"You can't be serious?" Marcos asked incredulously.

"*¡Pa entro!*" the Federale ordered.

The van driver swung the back panel door open and Marcos got in. The Federale gestured for me to depart but I couldn't leave Marcos to fend for himself. I leaned low and entered the wagon with Marcos. "You're not going alone," I said to him. They slammed the doors, and it was immediately pitch black. The wagon jostled over the ruts and made us grip the steel bench. A small grated window frame separated the front seat from the prisoners. I knocked on it; a Federale slid it back. His cap band shimmered and his polished black brim shaded an arrogant leer on his lips.

I tried to bribe him. *"Dejanos aqui y te doy cien dolas."*

"A ver, pasalo."

He went for it. I twisted a hundred-dollar bill into a straw and pushed it through the mesh screen. The Federale took it, laughed, and slid the shutter closed.

"Yeah, man, leave us here, we gave you the money!"

The Federale slid the slot open again. *"¿Qué quieres?"*

"Drop us off! You got the money!"

He lifted a leather thong and slapped it against his palm. *"¡Qiete!"*

"You shut up, muthafucker!" I cried back.

The slot slammed and the paddy wagon lunged forward, jostling us for twenty minutes until it lurched to a stop. Keys scratched at the lock and the door swung open. An impeccably dressed guard reached in, and grabbed Marcos by the back of the shirt, and threw him out, sprawling him on the ground. Another Federale butted me in the back with his rifle.

We were led into a dank concrete facility. Hostile noises from prisoners in the cavernous labyrinth echoed as from a deep chamber. We were stripped and searched, and all our money was pocketed by the Commandante. He smoked a cigar and sported a huge Pancho Villa mustache. Without asking what our charges were or speaking a word, we submitted. Had we uttered a word we would have been beaten. We were led down a corridor leading to cells. I paused to tie my shoelace. Bent over as I was, it hurt even worse when the guard kicked me in the chest and ordered me to move. We went into a courtyard blockhouse with communal cells on two sides facing each other and a compound in the middle. The guard opened a gate to a cell and pushed us inside.

Most of the men were Indian peasant opium runners, squatting shoulder to shoulder around the cell. I squeezed out a space to stand by the latrine, a hole in the floor, and Marcos crammed in between snoring Mexicans. The overwhelming stench of hangover breath was nauseating, compounded by layers of drunk vomit ingrained and putrefying in cement pores. Above us a guard patrolled, walking around the catwalk, cradling a rifle and peering down into the cells.

The cell could accommodate at most twenty prisoners, but it held about sixty. Marcos and I exchanged looks of despair. For weeks I slept standing up, ate corn meal for breakfast, tacos for lunch, and soup and tortillas for supper. We washed once a day at the spigot and took our turn at the horrible-smelling latrine, which was just a hole in the concrete.

We were released about three months later, Marcos to go home and I to the cantina for a meeting with Galvan.

Galvan was expecting me.

"You are angry about the Commandante? I cannot put my reputation on the line for one who does not work for me."

"That's fine, I'm finished. I don't want anything to do with selling weed."

He said nothing. He just stared.

◆

The time in prison had only strengthened my resolve to quit the business entirely and return home as quickly as I could. While in the cell, my only reprieve from constant tedium had been thoughts of going to Albuquerque with Lonnie. Soon as I walked through the door, never feeling happier to see her, I told her we were leaving as soon as our stuff was packed. I had to settle her down because she was frantic. She kept hugging me and repeating, "Don't ever do that, call me, tell me what's going on, I would have taken you money!" I told her there was no way of communicating with her and I apologized and also to look on the bright side of things, we still had our money that we had saved up. She hugged and kissed me, suddenly scared that something might happen to ruin all our plans. While we packed she kept cursing Galvan. I kissed her on the mouth and set out to get some packing boxes.

Marcos and I had a last meal at the café on Main Street. He'd given me his address and phone number and was doing all he could to keep our farewell from being solemn or emotional. He promised to be best man at our wedding. I told him he was the best friend I had ever had and I would call him as soon as we got our house. We recounted the crazy times: our first meeting on the beach in San Diego, two years ago, the party girls, the jail, and La Zona. He'd hidden weed in the false bottom of his trunk and he had his cut of the money to buy himself that dream cabin in the mountains and live the life he always wanted—hunting, fishing, and hiking in the woods in upstate Michigan. I had to keep myself together because I didn't want to let him go. I managed a smile and walked him out and watched him drive off, burning rubber down the street, as if to say, We did it, brother, we did it! I never saw him after that, but I'm pretty sure he stayed in the Michigan backcountry to hunt and fish.

When I got back to the pad, Rick, Carey's roommate, had come over to help us load the truck. Carey hadn't really talked about him much except to say they were close friends. He wore polished combat boots, jeans, and a muscle shirt. After getting the heavy stuff packed, he said Carey had invited us over for a glass of wine. I still had a lot of things to do but we drove to Rick and Carey's trailer the next day, in the evening. I figured I owed Carey a visit because he'd always been on call, ready to drive at a moment's notice to San Diego or do pickups.

I was eager to leave, hardly able to contain my excitement of going home with Lonnie and money. But leaving made me anxious about a whole new set of problems. Things didn't feel right.

There was an unsettling stirring in the air that I picked up when going out for boxes. Maybe it was seeing the sheriff at the post office when I went in to buy packing tape, or the siren I'd heard last night, or the unmarked DEA cars gathered in the motel parking lot. It was probably just my jittery nerves. There was also the unresolved anxiety of seeing Theresa again. And what about my mother? Would it work out when I moved my father in with us? I was also planning to see Grandma and Santiago and help them out. I convinced myself that there was nothing weird or menacing about the guy in the suit who had slowed his car to point at me. He wasn't pointing at me but at another person on the sidewalk. The jeep that followed me a few blocks before turning off was not tailing me, it was just going on its own business. There was no one monitoring me in the grocery aisle when I was buying groceries for the road. I had to let go of my paranoia. After everything was packed and ready for our departure, a few glasses of wine were just what I needed to relax.

Lonnie and I sat in Carey's kitchen, sipping wine and talking. Someone knocked, and Carey's roommate, Rick, came out of the back bedroom. Through a curtain that partitioned off the living room, I could hear Rick and a man whispering. I also heard movement in the bushes outside.

Something was wrong.

"What's up?" I asked

"Selling to a customer," Carey said. "It's okay."

I went into the living room. Rick was weighing out an ounce of heroin for the guy.

"Do it when we're not here," I said.

"Everything's cool; this is Wade." Rick smiled.

"Bullshit. The guy's a narc!"

"Carey, tell your buddy to chill his wheels," Rick said.

"What's up?" Carey asked.

"Get me a pistol," I said. "This guy's not leaving here."

"What?" Carey said.

"He's a narc. I know it."

"That's crazy, I've known him for years," Rick lied.

"You're a fucking narc!" I hissed at the guy and grabbed him by his shirt and shoved him against the wall. My whole life was slipping out of my grasp. In a moment's time, everything spun out of control. My plans, future, dreams collided with the immediate reality, a smoldering wreck.

"I told you I know him!" Rick lied again.

"He's a narc, " I repeated.

"I have the money in my car. I'm outa here," the narc said.

They walked out.

I stood in the frame of the open door and watched them go toward a car under a streetlight. Carey was behind me, with a pistol. Lonnie sat at the table, her eyes wide with fright.

I saw the narc open the truck and the tip of a rifle barrel rising. The narc's voice shattered the silence.

"This is a bust! Federal agents!"

Screaming, Rick hit the ground, begging, "Don't shoot, don't shoot!"

The sky and the grounds lit up like midday, with spotlights from the air and the ground. From cars, bushes, trees, and the air, they opened fire. Jeeps, helicopters, and agents' cars whirled around the trailer.

I turned and yelled, "Get down, Lonnie!" She crouched in a corner on the floor.

I was in the doorway and I leaped out onto the ground, zigzagging and rolling as bullets bit the dust and gouged the trailer's tin siding. Carey returned fire. My ears burned with a stinging pain, and blood reddened my right side from head to waist. A disembodied arm still clutching a pistol flew by. It belonged to an agent who had crept behind me with the intent of executing me; he was aiming behind me to shoot me in the head when Carey blasted him, tearing his arm off.

It was all-out war. Except there was only one of us returning fire, and scores of FBI sharpshooters raining bullets on us.

I couldn't hear anything, I only saw the bullets ripping the dirt around my feet. I raced into an orchard at the side of the trailer. Agents pursued me. Adrenaline exploding in me, I tore my white T-shirt away, kicked my cowboy boots off, and bolted through the orchard.

Bullets zinged in branches and spattered the trunks of trees.

Gunfire paused and frenzied voices cried out. They had them. I shot a glance over my shoulder to measure the distance between me and the pursuing agents.

I reached the end of the orchard and climbed over a cinder-block fence topped with barb wire. The thorns pierced my palms and raked my stomach. I was bleeding as if mauled by a tiger.

On the other side, I was equally as startled as the old woman who was standing there, clutching her nightgown and staring up at the hovering helicopter, its strobe lights sweeping the area.

"It's okay," I said, and ran through her yard and into a field with a warehouse. On one side of the warehouse was a pile of old lumber. I crawled into it and piled planks over me. I would wait here for an opportunity to cross the road.

A police car pulled within a foot me. A policeman got out, his black boots inches from my face, the engine exhaust and heat stifling me.

"I don't see a thing here. Make sure them cars stay close together. He ain't gonna cross the road," he said into the mike, and drove off.

Unaware that I dozed off, I was woken later by headlights. I had thrown the boards off in my sleep.

"What the hell happened to you?" a man said, standing by his headlights. I couldn't see his face.

I stood.

He was a watchman, making the rounds.

"I got beat up at a party," I said lamely.

"Need a ride?"

I directed him to my house. The cops must've known him, because on the way we passed freely through a roadblock.

"Turn here," I said. "Stop."

"In the middle of the—?"

But I was gone, darting in and out of the palm tree grove. I guessed the driver had given the cops a sign.

Instead of going into my house, I jumped the wall of the vacant house next door. No sooner had my feet landed on the backyard grass than a swarm of police and agents converged on my house with weapons drawn and bullhorns roaring orders to surrender.

I watched the whole scene: bullets shredding the house, battering ram shattering the door. They searched what was left of the house and left.

The back door of the vacant house was open. I went in to rest a bit on the couch. I fell asleep, then was awakened by a voice talking to another neighbor. A man's hand was on the doorknob, the door an inch open, and I crept off the couch and snuck out the back before the man came in.

I crawled on my belly to the road and stood up and walked as if everything was normal. The two on the porch stared but said nothing.

About thirty yards up I paused at the ditch to look back and saw them talking again. I sprinted down the ditch to Billy's house. Billy was a long-haired hippy who sampled our weed shipments and sold small quantities to friends in the area. He showed me the headlines and read me an article about how I was a drug kingpin, now with a felony warrant. A reward was being offered to anyone with information leading to my capture. Of the many lies it contained, it claimed that I had tried to murder an FBI agent. One of them had been shot and seriously wounded and was in the hospital. I was considered armed and dangerous. Lonnie, Carey, and Rick had been caught. Billy told me the area was swarming with agents. I called my sister and told her I couldn't explain the details, but my life was in great danger. She had to come get me right away. Billy stashed me until she arrived a day later. We made it through the roadblocks and all the way to Albuquerque with me hiding under the backseat of her Bronco. In the darkness, with the driveshaft spinning next to my ear, the tires sizzling on asphalt, I was in shock. My ears had a ringing buzz that wouldn't go away. Everything had blown up. One moment my girl and I were having wine with a friend, and the next I was a fugitive with an attempted murder rap. I tried to place things in order, but my mind was a kaleidoscope of lights and gun blasts and terror, and my heart raced wildly. My peaceful dream had exploded in a convulsion of death and destruction. I was supposed to be driving this road with Lonnie to get married and settle down and prove to everyone how I had made it and how wrong they were about me.

◆

The day after I got to Albuquerque, I called a lawyer, who checked on what the cops had. I was shattered by the news that the FBI had issued an all points bulletin for my arrest. I felt trapped. I thought briefly of fleeing to Mexico or Canada, but I didn't even have money for coffee, so I decided to turn myself in. First, though, I hot-wired a '63 Impala from the downtown municipal parking lot and drove northeast out of Albuqueque to the Sandia Mountains. I was petrified with fear and needed some time to drive and think. Being in the mountains gave me the illusion that everything was going to turn out all right.

By the time I reached Sandia Peak it was night. The sky was cold and brilliant and the air pungent with pines and chilled granite. I needed to be out here. This was as close as I'd ever come to believing in God. I'd prayed for salvation before but I wasn't praying for salvation this time. I couldn't bring myself to kneel on the ground and talk to God, so I sat on a boulder and looked up and awkwardly pleaded with him to set things straight. Looking down at the valley of lights, I gazed at the general area where my mother's house lay. Her maid would be washing supper dishes now. My mom would be preparing her kids for bed, reading stories to them, kissing them good night.

In the other direction, I looked to where my brother and father and I had lived in a small gardener's shack behind Mrs. Larazola's red-brick Victorian. I thought, If only I had one more chance to make it right again. Just one more chance to take it all back and make it the way it was. I could cope with my father's alcoholism, my mother's abandonment, my brother's violence toward me, my sister's indifference.

Farther south was Estancia, a handful of glimmering beads in a sea of black. I knew Grandma was kneeling at her cot and praying for me. Prayers might help others but not me. I wasn't strong enough to deal with life on these terms. With remorse, I recalled the warning Lonnie's father gave her: Don't go with him, you'll end up in trouble. He was right; she was in jail with Carey and Rick. I should have known better than to take her with me. I was on the verge of being gunned down in the streets like a dog. Now everybody could point and say, I knew it. I told you. He's no good. He's nothing but a criminal. It hurt to admit they were right. Still, I wanted to explain to someone that it was all a mistake. All I ever wanted was to have what others had. I didn't want sympathy or pity. I just wanted a fair go at the things they had. But to get those opportunities, I had to go outside the law. Now I just wanted peace.

I asked God that if he was going to let me die, let it come quickly and without suffering. I'd had enough. I didn't know what I'd done to deserve my life, but I'd done the best I could with what I had. I raised my head to the moon and wondered if my grandfather was watching me from heaven. Looking up at the stars, I wished he could tell me what to do. I missed him, missed his Indio roots and the Indio culture that offered kindness and understanding. I wished I knew how to survive in the woods like Marcos. I wanted to take off across the snow and lose myself in the forest, moving over boulders and through trees, my path illuminated by the moonlight. The sad fact was that there was nothing to keep me in society—no family, no friends, nothing at all. I was utterly alone.

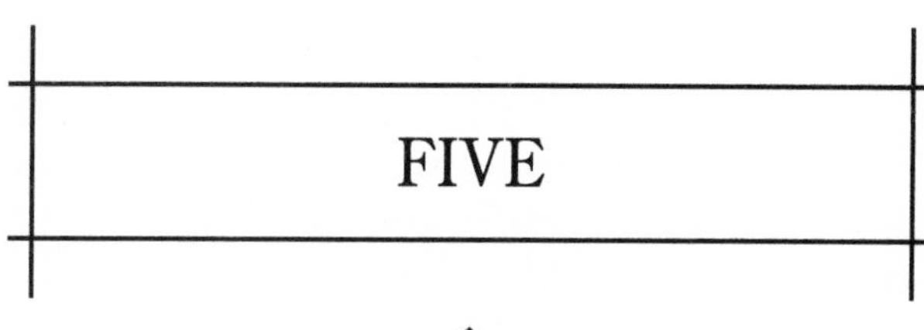

FIVE

◆

I had been extradited from New Mexico and was in the Yuma County Jail. I had seen the court counselor from Galvan's parties, a two-bit hustler who sold Galvan information from trial transcripts. He let me use the jail phone to call my sister in Albuquerque. A criminal defense attorney specializing in drug cases had agreed to represent me if I could pay the fifty-dollar fare to fly him in, and I was calling to borrow the money from Martina. It was strange to hear her kids quarreling in the background, accompanied by Saturday morning TV cartoons, slamming pans, and Martina's voice saying the pancakes were almost ready. Behind me, in the jail, other life sounds echoed—curses, banging, pissed-off convicts hollering, and guards barking orders into their crackling walkie-talkies. Our worlds were galaxies apart. Between her screams at little Chris to get ready for soccer practice and to order Chad and Cindy to get dressed, I asked if she could lend me fifty bucks. It seemed like such an insignificant request at her end of the phone, but from mine it was life or death. She threw the phone down and slapped one of the kids, who started crying. "Don't you start that! Wipe those tears and pick up those clothes!" It was a scene I knew well. Every holiday I would drop by for dinner and then take them to the park or to play pinball at a burger joint. My visits were rare, but enough to keep my relationship as their uncle intact.

I expected her to lend me the money. When she said no, I wanted to beg her to reconsider but was too proud. I realized that my mother had already succeeded in turning Martina against me.

I felt bitter because I'd always done things for her. When she and Chris had married, they'd rented a cockroach trailer at Dead Man's Corner, in Southside barrio. Mieyo and I would push Chris's junker on the cold mornings to get it started and helped them out as much as we could until Chris got into the Carpenters' Union. Eventually, with Chris's GI Bill, they'd bought their first house close to my mother's. When Chris had been promoted to journeyman carpenter, it doubled his salary and they'd purchased a small apartment complex and bought two new cars. That's why I couldn't believe it when she said no. I knew that cops scared her and thought maybe she was afraid that she was helping me escape, or that lending me money was illegal. But it was more than that. It had been four months since I had last seen her, and she was much more guarded and wary of me now. She'd been hanging around our mother, and Mother's rejection of me was rubbing off on her. Since Martina's insular white middle-class life had no room for problems like me, being loyal to that white world meant turning her back on me and believing my mother and the Feds, who accused me of being a dangerous criminal. She went into labored apologies about how bills had to be paid on time, and how they were barely making ends meet. I cut her short by saying I had to go; it was okay. I was staring at the phone wondering who to call next when the counselor came up behind me and took me into his office.

"How'd it go?" He wore a gold watch, tassel loafers, gold neck chain, new clothes. Galvan was paying him well.

"I'll be out in no time," I forced myself to say.

"That's good. Lonnie told me to give you this." He opened a drawer, took out a letter, and tossed it toward me on his desk.

"Can you read it to me?" I stared out the barred window as he read how Lonnie was sorry for the way things turned out. No matter what it took, Carey had promised to get her out. He'd written the judge on her behalf, blaming himself and agreeing to do her time. They'd found my wallet in her purse, with my driver's license in it, and that was how they knew who I was. She launched into how sorry she was and how she still cared about me, but during the time

I'd been in jail in Mexico, she and Carey had fallen in love. It wasn't on purpose; Carey made her feel safe and loved, especially when she doubted that she'd ever see me again. He'd called her every day, put money in her account, and consoled her in the visiting room. They had started by holding hands, then embracing, and finally kissing. Things happen, she wrote. Please don't be mad at me.

There was a discomforting pause. After a while the counselor said smugly, "You want a little blast to pick you up?" He laid a line of cocaine on his desk and snorted half of it. He offered me the straw and I shook my head no. He did the rest.

To conceal my shame and embarrassment, I faked a smile. "She's just another chick." I crushed the letter up and threw it in the trash can.

For a second, I angrily blamed Rick aloud. "Fucking snitch!"

The counselor already knew all about it, because he added, "Galvan's put the word out that he ratted. They'll take him out in the joint."

But it wasn't only Rick. My sister had turned me down. Lonnie and Carey became lovers behind my back. They had all been there when they wanted something but had turned their backs on me now. I never thought Lonnie would do that. I was too proud to admit that any of it hurt; too proud to think even for a second it could faze me. I'd bury their deceptions and lies where I buried all the rest, in a dark place in my heart where I would never have to think about them.

Since I had no money to retain competent counsel, I was stuck with the court-appointed lackey. A week earlier he'd come by: a blue-eyed, blond-haired man, wearing a gray suit. He'd handed me a Mormon's Bible from his briefcase and I told him to keep it. Then he summed up my situation bluntly. "Plead guilty to the charges and they'll go easy. Don't, and you haven't a prayer in hell. This is what they want."

He'd handed me a list of charges written in longhand on yellow legal pad paper. I stared at the page as if I knew what I was reading.

"You picked the wrong time to get busted," he said. "It's reelection time, and you're the judge's ride to a second term."

"What do you mean?"

"With all the play you got in the papers, you're going to be made an example, put behind bars, so voters'll feel safer from criminals like you. The court'll be lenient if you waive your right to trial and plead guilty, but if you persist in your innocence, the DA'll tack on more time."

I didn't understand what he was saying. I was ignorant of court procedure and intimidated by legal jargon. The truth was, I was more panicked by having rights than losing them. Dreading what he threatened they might do to me, I felt there was no way out. And I was wearied by the mounting apprehension of not knowing what was going to happen, so I shrugged. "Do whatever you think best."

◆

I'd gone over the recent past, trying to understand how it all happened. After I'd turned myself in in Albuquerque, my fantasies of starting over anew were a distant memory and the reality of prison life had become second nature to me. It hadn't been the smoothest of reintroductions. I had shown up at the Albuquerque police station, believing that the misunderstanding would be cleared up. I was willing to describe the events in Yuma, the shootout, ready to explain that I hadn't done anything, I was just in the place when the deal went down. But everything backfired. After the officer checked the wanted files, he stepped out from behind his desk without giving me a chance to explain anything, drew his pistol from his holster, and ordered me to turn around and place my palms flat on the wall.

Minutes later, several detectives dressed in identical blue suits, black shoes, and sunglasses dashed out of the elevator and begin to kick and pistol-whip me. They handcuffed and dragged me in an elevator up to an office to be interrogated, then pummeled me more until I couldn't feel the blows or see out of my eyes. My jaw was on fire as I forced myself to swallow blood, gagging on bits of flesh and teeth chips. Later, I was taken out through a basement exit and shoved into an unmarked car and driven away. I was beaten back and forth between two detectives in the backseat until we reached the outskirts of Albuquerque. The detective to my right clambered over into the front seat, turned around, and flung the door open so I could see the road blurring beneath and feel the wind on my face. The detective to my left had braced his back against his door and had started kicking me to force me out where a police cruiser behind us could run over me on the road. Still handcuffed, I had hunched up, propping my foot against the doorframe and floor, turned my head toward the guy kicking me, and barreled into him with all my force. Through the welter of blows, all my efforts were on keeping my head against the detective's belly, pushing as hard as I could against him to keep from being thrown out of the car.

Things didn't let up for the next few weeks. They were extra hard on me because they thought I had set up the FBI agent, and even though the agent wounded in the shootout hadn't died, he was still in serious condition in the hospital. Guards would visit my cell at night and threaten to take me out and shoot me. They'd terrify me with sudden earsplitting batterings on my steel cell door in the middle of the night, and day-shift goons would curse me every time they passed my cell. I lost track of time and days. I would look out the port window of my cell and see prisoners marching to and from chow. I could hardly stand, my legs bruised blue from being hit with batons and my heels whacked by leather straps. Yet when I stood or tried to walk, I welcomed my body's pain; it grounded me during a time when nothing else seemed real. Life had little value now. I was irrational; one moment I panicked, the next I didn't care if I lived or died. One moment my previous life was real, the next it didn't seem like I had lived it. With frayed nerves and body aching with welts and wounds, I did everything I could to keep myself together, mostly by thinking of the preceding two years, which seemed like a dream. I couldn't hold a thought for more than a second. On my bunk, my eyes closed, Lonnie and I would be riding happily in the car one moment, and the next her memory would scatter into unrecognizable images that I'd only imagined.

My mind was riddled with misgivings and suspicions. I was second-guessing everything. The last year with Marcos and Lonnie seemed so far away and vague. I tried again and again to conjure up a portrait of her: Lonnie cooking supper or us sitting behind the house, her soft voice when she whispered me awake at dawn, the plans we'd written out of how we'd decorate our house, the list of names we'd chosen for our first baby. All those images swirled in a void with no reference to my life, memories splashed like black paint on a white canvas with no meaning or structure. From time to time, my dreaming was interrupted by chilling screams from jail cells, solid steel doors slamming, keys jangling, guards yelling. I hadn't talked to anyone in a long time. I was locked away in my sullen silence, afraid of what was happening to me, my memories of life before jail being slowly sucked out of existence. Perhaps my mind was playing tricks on me because of the severe stress and shock from the shootout. The beatings had traumatized me, and any coherent sense of my recent history was beyond my grasp, leaving me a mental invalid on my bunk, picking at scabs on my face, trying to sift through my elusive experience, guessing at what was real and what was not.

I'd managed, however, to get through not only their beatings but also their two previous attempts at extradition to Arizona. It was the law that you had to extradite someone within ninety days. On the two other appearances, the judge had taken issue with the Arizona marshals for failing to produce evidence to justify my extradition. He told them not to waste his time with hearsay and sent them away. Arizona had to provide legitimate proof to extradite me, and their time had almost expired. I knew that if they couldn't do it soon the judge would have to let me go. I reasoned they couldn't have any proof because I hadn't sold any heroin to the narc that night. I was expecting to be set free when, on the eighty-ninth day of confinement in the Albuquerque county jail, I'd limped into the courtroom for my last extradition hearing. Though I was handcuffed and hobbled, my spirits were high as I sat in the hard-backed chair in the jury box in my orange jumpsuit and shower thongs.

I was ashamed to meet my sister's gaze in the public seating section beyond the railing. She'd had enough pain in her life without my piling on more, but I'd forced myself to search for her. When our eyes met, her gaze went to her hands, wringing a paper tissue in her lap. She was dressed like the sister I once knew, in a white sweater and head veil, a blue blouse and long black skirt. We forced ourselves to smile, hoping with all our hearts that this would be the last hour of my confinement.

The bailiff escorted me to the bench. I waited anxiously to hear the words that I was free. Once I was out, I'd never again get into any trouble. When my case number was called, two Arizona marshals approached the bench. They handed a sworn statement to the judge, signed by Governor Babbitt of Arizona. Rick, testifying under oath, had sworn that I had sold him drugs, that I was a big heroin dealer, and that I'd masterminded the deal the night of the shootout. When I heard the words "Extradition granted," I couldn't believe my ears. I fought down the despair that was overwhelming me. I disconnected myself from the courtroom, the people, my sister, and the marshals and focused my eyes on the wall plaque behind the judge, which read, TRUST IN GOD. The courtroom had turned quiet. I felt people's eyes on me; the hot fluorescent lights penetrated beneath my jumpsuit, clawed under my skin, burning intense as an interrogation light. Disengaging myself from the judge's words and spectators' eyes, I stared like a blind man at the plaque. *This wasn't happening, this couldn't happen.* My eyes watered at the corners and I turned my head sideways and wiped them against my sleeve. I resumed staring at the wall plaque, as if I were deaf and the words didn't mean anything. I didn't want anyone to see me cry. All they were entitled to was a glassy stare—a deep unwavering stare of anger and defiance.

When the marshals turned me around, my sister was weeping, her teary face smeared with makeup. Long black rivulets of eyeliner ran down her cheeks. Her black tears gave her a frightful expression. She was superstitious and religious in the extreme, and I knew that when I left the courtroom, she'd go to Saint Mary's down the street and light candles for me and pray before the La Virgen de Guadalupe, pleading with her to reverse this bad fortune and protect my soul. She'd visit the palm reader and the psychic, and they'd tell her what she wanted to hear. Later, she'd tell my mother what happened, and my mother would convince her that I needed to go to prison.

It didn't seem to matter that Rick was the guilty one—he had ratted on us, done the drug deal, taken the stand against us, and committed perjury by saying that we were all big-time shot-callers. The marshals had trumped up a paper saying I had sold heroin to Rick, and Rick had signed it. He was a state witness; according to the snitch, I'd been dealing heroin to him for years. The truth was I'd only met him a few times when I had gone to pick up Carey, and I had never given him so much as a seed of marijuana.

◆

The morning after my hearing I was driven from Albuquerque to the Yuma County Jail. For a week or so, I wasn't allowed out of my cell. I'd been in plenty of cells, but the Yuma County Jail cell beat them all with its horrid smell. The rusting bunk was anchored to a shit-smeared wall, and the putrid commode was barely attached to the wall with rotten bolts. Every time someone in another cell flushed their toilet, particles of sewage bubbled up from my commode and puddled on the floor. Most of the day, I stood at the bars rapping with the porters. Holding the steel tray outside the bars with one hand, I ate with the other, balancing each spoonful of lumpy oatmeal through the bars. I deciphered the graffiti on walls and checked the six-by-nine cell for a way to escape. Luckily, a day-shift guard had recognized me from La Zona and made me a trusty. I hung out at the kitchen and visiting room, even going outside to empty the trash, where the guard and I would lean against the wall in the shade, smoking cigarettes. I'd see a truck rumbling by with its bed bulging with clipped branches and mown grass, and I'd think of Marcos. While the guard rambled on about titty bars he'd visited with his buddies, I'd hear an NFL game coming from a cell, which reminded me of how Marcos and I would sit in the living room, rooting for our Oakland Raiders.

My situation contrasted painfully to life just a few months ago and I continued to struggle to make sense of the dreamlike quality of my memories. I'd wake up at 6 A.M., my head filled with memories of Lonnie and me walking hand in hand across the fields, following dirt paths made by kids on bikes. I'd point out what were good omens: two hummingbirds flitting in the sagebrush; a coyote and her young pups in the distance; red anthills and an upturned centipede in our path. After a tasteless breakfast, I'd scrub a tier by a window that opened to the streets, and passing cars and pedestrian voices drew my mind from the suds and mop pail to foamy wind spray on the beach, Lonnie waving away seagulls from the reefs in San Diego, blowing dust and the stormy horizon threatening a downpour as we snuggled close, face-to-face, and she'd ask if I loved her.

As I looked back from behind bars on the life I tried to make with Lonnie, it seemed my efforts had been nothing more than useless illusions. At night in my cot, when the lights went off, I'd stare at the ceiling and realize that everything I had said to Lonnie was partially to suppress memories of Theresa. At the time, our lives had seemed to be leading Lonnie and me toward true love and marriage. But now my heart was pulsing out memories of Theresa. I'd drift back to recollections of Lonnie and realize, in the quiet night, that it wasn't Lonnie I had dreamed of but Theresa. Along with the dreams came the pain of those times, and the disconsolate longing. I was back in the world I belonged in. I had altered the superficial details of my life, but nothing had really changed—I was still the same confused, hurt, angry man underneath. The same foul stink and cell bars surrounded me that I'd left behind when I moved to San Diego.

Had I been allowed to leave the jail, I would have gone to see Theresa, not Lonnie. Every morning, standing at my cell bars, waiting to be let out to porter, the bright dawn and sparse clouds through the cell windows made me want to talk with Theresa.

◆

On November 16, I changed my original plea from innocent to a plea bargain of guilty of possession of heroin with intent to distribute. When I first balked at pleading guilty, my PD hadn't even pretended an interest in my innocence. "Plead guilty," he had said, "and stop wasting everyone's time." Nor was he bothered by the fact that I couldn't read the papers I had signed. I was a negligible nuisance to him. He was in a hurry for me to agree so he could leave right away. By the chummy way he laughed and talked with the prosecutor, it was obvious they were good buddies and the least of their concerns was a twenty-one-year-old illiterate Chicano kid. When the judge entered, I recognized him as the guy who owned the Texaco gas station where I used to fill up the truck once a week. He usually had on oily overalls and greasy cap instead of a black robe, with a socket wrench instead of a gavel. He gave no indication, however, that he'd ever seen me. After I pled guilty, he set a sentencing date and I was led back to jail.

To keep my mind from worrying what my sentence might be, I kept busy scouring the drunk tanks, slapping lice from rancid mattresses with a broom, scrubbing spit and blood off grime-caked walls, and carrying blankets stiff with urine and vomit to the laundry room. In the afternoon I'd mop tiers, cart meals to cons on lockdown, hand out toiletries, and run notes, or "kites," from one con to another.

I'd been flirting with this blond-haired girl, Tara, a clerk at the booking desk who worked the graveyard shift. She'd mentioned that she was going to college, and I thought she was pretty cool until one night when I was dusting the filing cabinets. Two detectives had come in, roughly shoving a drunk Chicano to the booking desk. I didn't like being around them so I started to leave, but Tara asked me to put away the wax bottles and roll the cord up on the big buffing machine. Meanwhile, they'd stripped the drunk down, but he'd resisted their efforts to take off the talisman pouch around his neck. I knew it was considered magic to protect his soul and ward off evil. He howled in terror but they laughed, as they ripped it off. Tara joined in their fun, chuckling over the drunk's superstitions. After locking the drunk up, the detectives went into the bathroom to wash their hands. When Tara turned to get the Chicano's file from the record cabinets, I reached through the bars, swiped one of her college textbooks, and hid it under my jail overalls. After putting the mop and buffer away, I told the duty guard that I was done for the evening, and he escorted me to my cell.

Sitting on my cot, I smoked a cigarette, opened the big hardcover book, and leafed through it. Parts of the text were highlighted with yellow, and on page margins she'd scribbled notes in red ink. I set my cigarette down on the concrete floor and murmured the words, sounding out the letters deliberately to see if I could understand them. I had trouble. It seemed each letter was fighting me. Reading was frustrating because each letter slowed me down. While sounding them out, I had to remember what they meant when combined. It was a lot harder than I expected. As I struggled, time, jail noise, cells, and walls all vanished. I was engrossed in the simple story of a man and his pond. How he spent his days there. How he loved to watch the birds. How he sat on its bank and meditated. How he compared the water's sensuous currents to making love with a woman.

Each letter had its own voice, and as I put the sounds together to make words, they told a story. The more I read the more I thought about the pond in Estancia. I put my finger under each word, sounding them out all the way to the bottom of the page. It was confusing, but I'd gathered it was about a man named Wordsworth and Cool-ridge. Word cool, cool word. Wool. Coolo. I smiled because *coolo* in slang meant "stingy chump." Farther down, breaking off from the rest of the long-lined text, about the middle of the page, were shorter lines called a poem. I spent a long time figuring it out, until I was interrupted by my neighbor, Enrique. He asked me to brew some coffee, and I took out the red Folger's coffee can I'd found in one of the vacated cells and filled it with water. I tore some pages out of the book and lit them to heat the water. I crouched on my haunches and watched the words burn on the page, the balled-up paper unwrinkling into dark ash.

I saw the thirty-dollar hardcover price. No matter how much I liked the story, I would never spend money on a book. Guys like me hung out and bullshitted all day. We told stories but they didn't mean much; they were just to pass the time behind a drugstore or on a street corner. I'd never owned a book and had no desire to own one. But still, I did enjoy this one, if for no other reason than it alleviated the boredom of waiting. I hadn't forgotten, though, that I took it to hurt her for laughing at the man who could've been my father. To my way of thinking, books had always been used to hurt and inflict pain. Books separated me from people like her and those two detectives, who used lawbooks to perpetrate wanton violence against poor people, and from greedy lawyers, who used lawbooks to twist the truth. There were only two ways to learn things: on the street, fighting to prove you were right, or sharing a fifth of whiskey or a six-pack and hanging out with homies and listening to their stories.

When I went to bed, I stared at the ceiling in the dark, thinking of that guy walking around the pond, connecting him to my mom, sister, and brother. I kept spelling the word: p-o-n-d, keeping it as mine. I mouthed it over and over. I dozed off, blending Cool and Word into my memories of Mother at the pond, in the sun, the breeze blowing over her, and all of us lying in the grass and napping as dragonflies skimmed the surface and fishes popped the silver surface, rippling rings.

◆

The next morning I was back in court, admiring the stenographer's legs as she stocked her machine with paper. Handcuffs had become as normal to me as a wristwatch is to a free man. The DA glared at me with hard gray eyes. I watched him grab my folder from a stack on his table and give it to the bailiff, who in turn handed it to the judge. The bailiff called my name and pronounced my crimes. As I stood before the judge, adrenaline raced wildly through my body. Gripped with fear, I wanted to say that I was willing to go to a drug program, a halfway house, do community work, anything but prison. I didn't say a word—yet I couldn't help but hope that somehow a merciful Samaritan would burst through the doors and set things straight. But these officials were not in the business of pardoning poor people. Their faces only reflected impatience, with no inclination for listening to convicts' explanations or litanies of regret. The process had a momentum all its own. For it to work, there could be no sentiment or discretion. To them, I was a criminal without soul, heart, or feelings.

Standing before the judge, I remembered an event that happened when I was fourteen. I'd been staying with my Aunt Charlotte, one of my mother's sisters, and one morning my Uncle Tranquelino, her husband, asked me to go with him to the pigpen. I grabbed a pail of grain and shook it as a pig innocently came to the feeder. It was a beautiful morning, resinous with manure and livestock smells, birds in the blue sky, a comfortable awakening chill in the air that excited me. When the pig muzzled his pink snout into the pail and crunched up the grain, my uncle shot it between the eyes. It shuddered, awkwardly spread its legs to hold itself up, and flopped to the ground. My ears ringing, my nerves shredded, I dropped the pail as its brothers and sisters trundled around to slurp the blood up. "We'll butcher it today," my uncle had said.

"Do you have anything to say before I pass sentence?" the judge asked.

I remained silent. I felt ashamed because I was the first one in my family to go to prison. I'd sold drugs only to get back to Albuquerque, to be with someone I loved, to be respected, to be part of a community. I didn't wanted to be like Galvan or these lawyers, earning money by screwing people.

"Very well." The judge sighed and sentenced me to a mandatory no-parole five to ten years, with five years flat, day for day, in a maximum-security state prison. They were giving me six months, the three I had put in at Albuquerque awaiting extradition and the three at the Yuma jail. I was twenty-one and I figured I'd be out when I was twenty-six. It was no surprise that the judge had given me the harshest sentence allowed by law. The nuns had always said I was a bad boy, and here was the judge making the same condemnation. I was sure I was convicted mostly because of who I was, expunged from a society that didn't want people like me in it. I sat back in my wooden chair as they signed the paperwork and stared down at the arm rests, studying the various layers of paint, the chips and cracks. How many hands had gripped them? I wondered. What lives were attached to those hands, what dreams were shattered, what sorrows were they trying to squeeze out of their souls?

◆

At daybreak on January 2, we got on the road to Florence State Prison. I was brought out to the booking desk and chained up with another prisoner, Wedo, a tall wiry nineteen-year-old Chicano with green eyes, tattoos, and a crew cut. He had a disarming grin that conveyed mockery, defiance, or genuine cordiality, depending on his mood. He engaged anyone in his vicinity in small talk, making fun of the guards, jiving at cons in cells. Muscled like a gymnast, he looked at me and smiled ear to ear.

"Be nice to rabbit-hunt today. Ever see a mountain lion? I seen one. Since I was a boy I've camped around these hills."

The marshals chained us and stuffed Wedo's ring, watch, and pocket change into a manila envelope. Wedo harassed them the whole time.

They escorted us to the car, handling Wedo rougher than me, grunting that they were going to kick his ass if he didn't shut up. We waited by the car as one marshal went inside to get some papers while the other sat in the car eating a sandwich. Even this early, it was starting to get hot. I gazed at the facade of Yuma County Courthouse, a squat sandstone building that housed the jail cells, courtrooms, and the office for paying traffic tickets. Visitors clustered around the doors, waiting to attend a family member's trial. Two women had infants in their arms, screaming as their mothers shifted them around to the other arm. A younger kid with black hair and large brown eyes clung to his mother's hand. He could have been me, when I was visiting my father in jail.

The familiarity of the summer streets I had once driven had a desolate, barren sadness. Pigeons on concrete ledges of municipal buildings cooed and cuddled wing to wing, staring down at us; blue-collar Chicanos with black lunch pails and white construction hard hats, waiting for the bus to take them to job sites, eyed the marshal's car with a cold aloofness; store windows facing the bright sunny street glimmered, tempting the customers who were already waiting, parked in their cars, for the doors to open. That I was actually going to prison made the sights and scenes all the more unreal. Life would go on without me.

Soon, we were accelerating away from a café, where the marshals had picked up a box of doughnuts and filled their coffee thermos, up the ramp, and onto the freeway, heading east toward Florence State Prison. Lonnie, Carey, and Rick had already been sentenced; she to time in the Florence State Women's Prison and they to sentences in the men's. Wedo started badgering the marshals again. Heat shimmered above the asphalt as we headed out of Yuma in the same direction I'd once intended to leave with Lonnie.

On the road, the marshals turned the radio to a hick station playing a cowboy tune about riding the range. Through the grill, I could see a double-barrel shotgun, set upright and strapped between them. I fantasized putting it against their double chins, making them undress, watching them walk naked, two albino buffaloes across the prairie, as I drove straight to the border, dumped the car in El Paso in the Kmart parking lot, and walked across the

International Bridge to Juarez. There were a million places to hide in Mexico. I imagined myself living in a highland village in El Canyon del Cobre—Copper Canyon— near Chihuahua, which my grandfather had told me was beautiful and wild. I imagined apparitions of my grandmother under a salt cedar, strapping the infant cradle to her back as she prepared to walk to the village with medicinal herbs she had collected in the prairie. I'd lie down and press my ear to the ground to hear Mother Earth breathing.

Looking out the window, at the open space all around me, I saw myself as a boy on the prairie, my legs pumping fast and sweat beading my forehead. More than anything else, I loved open space. I had always run to the fields. Escaping from the D-Home, I'd crawl over security fences, belly and arms cut by barb wire; the pain was worth it to be walking happily along a winding dirt road in the South Valley. I'd run when my parents fought; when my purple-faced brother raged jealously after me; when Theresa slapped me and I dashed from the trailer across frozen fields to the Sandia Mountain foothills in a heavy snowfall. I always felt more comfortable alone. I'd cup my palms under the cold windmill-tank pipe and splash my face with cold water and keep moving; while everyone else was in the company of friends and family, I enjoyed nature in the open fields.

I drew kindness from the silence of the prairie at noon and the streams trickling between rocks and through canyons where I roamed; from the birds that crowded fence lines, the horses I stopped to pet along the road, the dogs that trailed me. In the same way that nature broke down leaves and stones, it broke down the hardness in my heart.

On the way to Florence, among the cactus, tumbleweeds rolled like buffaloes and dust devils spun up whirling into cones. Our car sped around a sharp curve and startled prairie doves feasting on a dead rattlesnake in the middle of the road. I thought how even my last years with Marcos and Lonnie now seemed like a long run to get away from my past life. Running had always cleared my mind, had always been my escape from the violence in my life: over the next wall, across ditches, under branches, fleeing like a fugitive, hiding in trash cans, alleys, neighborhood nooks, and abandoned houses. The reality was that for a very long time I would not have open space to run to anymore.

◆

We pulled in at a weathered truck stop to use the bathroom and fill up the gas tank. Wedo and I had to sit in the car while the two marshals went in and ate, made calls, had coffee. The attendant, a wiry farm boy, avoided my eyes as he wiped the bugs off the windshield, checked the oil, and aired up the tires. Finally one of the marshals let us out, sore and stiff, and we walked past the cynical glares of customers staring at us in our shackles hobbling into the bathroom. Wedo didn't care; he smiled at them and mouthed the words *fuck you.* But I felt ashamed. I assumed an attitude of disregard and they pretended not to notice me, their passive ranchers' and glum truckers' faces turned down to their coffee and plates of sausage, scrambled eggs, and toast.

On the road again, with the two marshals up front munching another box of doughnuts and sipping coffee from paper cups, we sped past parched junipers, piñon trees, sage, and scrub brush. I stared at a decrepit holding pen in the trees and, beyond that, barely visible, nestled in and blending with the brown surrounding hills, a rough-hewn lumber shack with a man standing at its side in worn workman's clothes, a shovel in his right hand. The man looked like my Uncle Santiago, broad and thick-muscled, with a red clay complexion. The sun had passed its apex and moved west with us, throwing the landscape into shadows and light. I peered at the man, craning my neck around, until the trees and hills erased him. He'd be the last farmer I'd see for a long time.

I leaned back in my seat and closed my eyes, trying to ignore Wedo ordering the marshals to give him some doughnuts. He wouldn't let up; high-strung and cocky, he was getting under their skin. He didn't flinch when they pulled over and threatened to beat him if he didn't shut up. He just glared at them and leered.

"Oh, yeah, let's see what you got. Ain't nothing but a bunch of meatball muthafuckers." When they didn't respond, he turned to me and declared that he'd lived in the prairie outside of Tucson all his life, and these fat-ass marshals would die out there without their doughnuts and badges. He turned back to them and challenged them to give him five minutes to run, and if they caught him they could kill him.

The driver smirked at his buddy. "Where you're headed, you'll get fucked soon enough."

◆

The steady hum of the engine, the sizzle of tires, and the whir of the air conditioner made me think of times when I rode in the new red-and-white Ford with my father. He was probably out there drinking in a cheap motel with a prostitute, whiskey drippings at his mouth as he chain-smoked Pall Malls. When I rode with him, his Old Spice cologne would fill the car. My eyes would water from the cigarette smoke as I'd gaze at the moon, wishing we could catch up to it. It always seemed so close, only to settle just beyond my reach, in a pasture over the next hill.

The spell of reverie was broken as we passed a dairy plant with hundreds of cows muzzling hay in troughs facing the highway, because suddenly a black dog darted from the manure lots into the road, and the driver veered sharply to the right. "I oughta shoot that sumbitch!" the driver huffed. Red-faced and unnerved, he let go two shots from his pistol and missed. Wedo laughed at them and told the marshals to turn that hick shit off the radio. He kept interrupting my thoughts, boasting about all the things he could do. He sounded the way my father did when he bragged what he was going to do: buy a new house, land, get us new clothes, be home every night, stop drinking, take us to the zoo, eat out. How he could have been a senator or congressman; he was always on his way; every bartender between Albuquerque and Santa Fe knew him; the politicians liked him.

This kind of empty braggadocio ran rampant among criminals, and I was looking at five long years of listening to it.

◆

The wind rushed through the marshal's open window. The sun shone harshly over the prairie. In the distance, beyond low rolling hills to the south, was the town of Florence. I smelled the green resinous scent as trucks passed us, bulging with brown gunnysacks of fresh-picked green chiles. An old woman was washing clothes in an old roller-wringer washer in the yard. Work jeans and shirts hung on the clothesline. Her husband was out back burning weeds. Farther down the road, Wedo pointed out the Florence State Prison. My throat constricted. Rows of convicts were burning ditch weeds and others were cutting weeds on the roadside. Menacing granite and razor-wire coils unspooled the length of the looming wall enclosing the prison. Manned gun towers jutted up, with guards in sunglasses cradling rifles and pacing catwalks, clocking the cons, monitoring their every step.

Off to one side of the prison a bunch of cons were playing baseball. I watched them as we slowed and turned down a long tree-lined lane with a checkpoint midway. The baseball game reminded me of a story I was told by a healer-man, a friend of my grandpa's. My mother was playing baseball in the scrub-brush field beside the ranch house in Willard with her four sisters late one afternoon. After catching a long fly ball she'd doubled over in pain. Too pregnant to ride one of her brothers' horses, she'd dashed off to the healer's house two miles away, her four sisters laughing one moment and throwing the ball and the next worriedly looking at each other across the breeze-blown dust and sunlight. Holding her enlarged abdomen, my mother ran like any country girl, across the arroyos and over chamiso, and then felt a rattler's sting at her ankle. At the healer's house, on a blanket under the stars and moon and prairie night sky, I was born. It was a special birth. Since the venom had mixed in my blood, I'd have skills to see in the dark, and I'd change many times in life just as the snake sluffs its skin.

We pulled up, went through a series of checkpoints, and parked in front of a massive iron gate. The guards wore beige uniforms, caps, and black boots and carried lead-filled batons. Some were leaving and others arriving for shift change, joking and giving each other last-minute job details. I tried to look without being noticed, wearing an attitude that it was no big deal, just another day, that I had done this before, but my survival instincts were red hot. A few cons walking with brooms and rakes glanced over as if I had insulted them, coldly and frankly appraising Wedo and me and then looking away as if they knew everything they needed to know about us.

My stomach churned. We got out and were escorted to the gate. The marshals turned to leave after signing us over; then one glared at Wedo and smacked him across the mouth. "You're going to get fucked here, punk!" Wedo lunged at him, forgetting he was wrapped in waist and wrist chains and hobbled at the ankles; he fell to the ground, cursing. The marshals mocked him, laughing, and left. A guard yelled up to another guard on the catwalk above the main gate, and he lowered a tin bucket from a rope on a pulley. The guard took a key out of the bucket, turned the lock, deposited the key back in the bucket, and the guard hoisted it up again. Another guard came with a roster and jotted our names down. With a wave he signaled one of the tower guards up on the main gate, and it slowly and begrudgingly creaked and squealed to the left, opening on my new world. Maybe I could get some schooling and learn to read and write. Maybe I could learn heating and refrigeration to go with my plumbing trade. It was time to change.

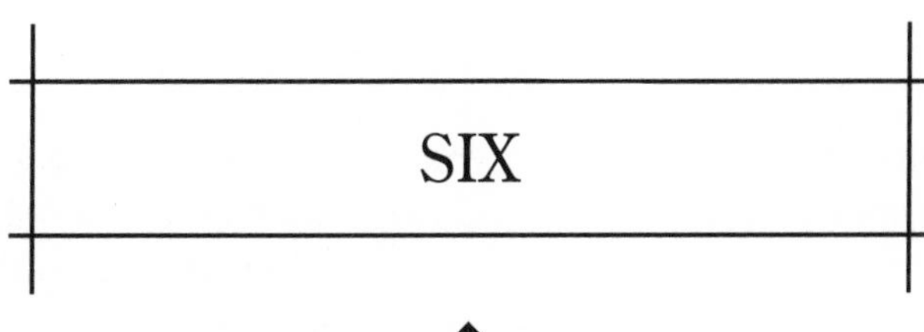

SIX

I had made up my mind to blend in, attract no attention, do my time, and get out alive. It's true, as convicts know, that you seldom make real friends in prison, just acquaintances, allied by mutual need. All of us had lived in projects, reservations, and barrios, as addicts, hustlers, or nothing at all, existing in aimless desperation. And though we didn't want to admit it, many of us were begrudgingly relieved to have three meals a day, a bed, and a roof over our heads. The key was to survive prison, not let it kill your spirit, crush your heart, or have you wheeled out with your toe tagged.

DC—Diagnostic Center—the block I was temporarily in, housed all new arrivals. Florence is in the desert, so like almost everyone else I wore boxer shorts, dressing in prison blues and brogans only for family visits, counselor interviews, chow time, or infirmary. Even if you had been here ten times, you started here, the newest high-tech cell block in the yard, four tiers high, thirty cells a tier, facing one another across a broad landing. There were three cell blocks in the main yard, all with various security levels, and every block had one or two tiers reserved for special cases: Nut Run for the mentally disturbed; lockdown cells for suspected gang members; the Dungeon for dangerous psychos; isolation cells with degrees of deprivation; and then maximum-security and protective-custody cells. For various reasons, I would eventually visit all of them.

When I first came in, every eye in the block checked me out. I felt vulnerable, with nothing to hide behind, veil my confusion, or conceal my fear. When cons looked at me I would turn away, not wanting to provoke a confrontation by returning an icy glare back. But I felt their eyes on my back, gauging my walk and gestures, searching for anything that might expose a weakness, looking to detect the most insignificant sign that would give me away. Nothing went unnoticed by them. It was useless to try and fake my way through this world where the weak were devoured.

Four times a day, before meals and bedtime, guards roamed for count time under the fluorescent tier lights, threatening cons with disciplinary write-ups if they didn't get in their cells. Since our only freedom was going to the chow hall, we generally tried to scam extra freedom when we could. From the moment a con entered the block, passing through arches with built-in electronic metal detectors that scanned for weapons, he stayed out of his cell as much as possible. It was worth having the guard yelling at you by waiting until the last second before he reached for his pen. Eventually, the tiers cleared and the thick-necked beer-bellied bulls went cell to cell, checking numbers off on a clipboard.

I'd lean my face between my cell bars to study their beige uniforms and black boots, brass skeleton keys jangling at three-inch black belts, rank stripes on sleeves, gold braid and black-billed visor cap, lead-filled club slapping their thighs. The cons across the landing—Chicanos, Mexicans, blacks, whites, and a small group of Indios who hung with the Chicanos—looked at us and we looked back. Chicanos hand-signed to homeboys across the landing, a coded language that went on for hours. Others whistled elaborate bird chirps or hawk cries that ricocheted off the cavernous slate granite walls. After count time, in the bulletproof Plexiglas cubicle at the entrance, in the glare of sunlight that glimmered off the polished linoleum, a fat guard sat on a swivel chair punching panel buttons and crackling intercom orders through the mike by number—Tier 3, out for showers! . . . 14772, kitchen duty! . . . 16730, counselor! . . . 23911, infirmary! . . . 30225, chow detail! The earsplitting roar sounded all day as the control cage guard opened the main block gates to let in new cons being escorted to cells up the black angle-iron stairwells on both sides of the block.

The fat guard in the main guard station also buzzed the cells to let out cons who'd completed their diagnostic process in DC and were joining general population.

Every day, I anxiously waited for my number to be called for a counselor interview. Most of the guys on two-for-one sentences earned good time—for every day you served without getting in trouble, you got another day knocked off your sentence—but only if you were eligible, which I wasn't. Because I was convicted and sentenced under a new law for drug dealers, I had to do what they called flat time, day for day. Still, once on the yard, I'd make twelve cents an hour working and I could buy street cigarettes, toiletries, and candy at the canteen; learn a trade, or get my GED; even go to college if I could get smart enough. In general population, you were allowed to have a TV and radio and to go to the exercise field, movies, and library. To break up the boring hours, I'd gotten into doing push-ups and sit-ups, standing at the bars watching cons, then exercising some more. The only thing that broke up the monotony was rapping to Macaron, the con in the next cell.

My harmonica had been confiscated in Albuquerque, but it had made its way here and I was jamming a Leadbelly blues one day when Macaron asked to borrow it. I expected him to blow a few notes but he handed it back to me through the bars in three pieces, the main body and two side plates, charred inside where he had cooked heroin. I didn't know how to respond. I knew enough from my past street life that if you let a guy get over on you, the rest of the wolves will follow. I paced up and down, thinking. Should I tell him he had to buy me a new one? This would lead to a fight, and I didn't want trouble. There was a thin line between fear and respect. He might be testing me, and I knew if I didn't say anything he might think I was a punk. When I heard him stirring around next door, rousing out of his heroin doze, I was trying to decide what to do when he tapped my bars and his hand shot around the bars with two packs of Camels. That showed respect. I put my harmonica back together and ultimately found that the heat had actually seasoned the reeds and allowed them to bend more easily when I blew into it. I was later glad that I didn't jump to any rash conclusions, because he invited me to sit at his table in the dining room. This was a big deal—it meant I was being accepted.

At night, when the block darkened—except for the control cage glowing at the entrance in the foyer—graveyard guards patrolled tiers every hour, shining a flashlight into each cell on their rounds, keys rattling against their hips. I often had trouble sleeping. The heat, the starched sheets, and the coarse blanket made it worse. I lay in the dark listening to a few voices talk across the landing; to the dripping shower stall down the tier; to the opening and closing gates echoing in the block; to cons groaning and sighing in their troubled sleep. I'd sit down by the bars, staring into the dark landing, and whisper to ask if Macaron was awake. If he was, we'd talk sitting on the floor with our backs against the bars. Macaron (nicknamed so because he loved macaroni) grew up in Phoenix. He dropped out in eighth grade, got into drugs, and spent most of his youth in institutions. It was the same story we all had, but now in his late forties with a graying crew cut, all he had to show for it were tattoos and scars covering his stout brown muscled frame. He had gotten into drugs to escape the pain of a fucked-up life, and as he got more addicted, he committed more burglaries. He'd been in and out of prison six times, for fourteen years all told. He was what they called a *veterano,* a con who knew the ropes and had earned a rep. The others respected him; porters kept coming by to drop off smokes, coffee, comics, and heroin and give him information about what was going on.

"That guy you came in with, over in B-Twelve," he said, one afternoon before supper. "They're gonna make a play on him."

Wedo had been his usual self, yelling for hours, crossing back and forth on the tier when he was out for a shower, bumming cigarettes, borrowing coffee, begging credit from drug dealers. But other than that, my untrained eye hadn't noticed anything out of the ordinary. A few days later, though, during shower time in the evening, Macaron called me to the bars. "The two bangers at the end of the tier, check them out. They're La eMe, Mexican mafia."

I whistled to get his attention, but only the bangers turned to look at me.

"Do that again," Macaron warned, "and it'll get you killed."

"I can't warn him?" I asked, feeling some allegiance because we had arrived together.

"Do your time, not his. He stands the line or punks out."

They strutted, towels in hand, in boxer shorts and thongs, down the tier. Wedo was lying down, feet to the bars toward the tier. They stopped in front of his cell. One of them slipped a toothbrush from his towel and ran the bristles up the pads of Wedo's bare feet. Then they walked away, stuffing the toothbrush back in the rolled towel. Blood gushed from Wedo's feet. He got up, wedged his face between the bars, and yelled, "I'll show you how it's done, punks!" Grinning, he said, "Ain't nothing but a meatball," and he sat down, tore his sheet in strips, and wrapped his feet.

"They had a razor blade in the brush," Macaron said.

"Why?"

"Trying to get him to pay protection. It happens to 'fish'—first-timers."

Macaron explained it further the next morning. At 5 A.M. the cell-block speakers blasted, "Chow time! Chow time! Hubba-hubba! Come 'n' git it!" We dressed out in jeans and T-shirt, rolled down the stairwell onto the landing and out under the stars and moon. The main yard was awash in klieg lights. We stood in a line of twos, facing the front gate, waiting in the semi-dark as a chain gang was marched out of the mess hall and across the main yard, filing out through a series of Cyclone-fence gates that led to trucks waiting to carry them to the fields. They passed the infirmary and library to the left. As each one stepped through the last gate exiting the main yard, he spread his arms and feet apart; guards scanned them with a hand metal detector and moved them on. They were sunburned from working under a blazing sun and looked exhausted in faded jeans and T-shirts and scuffed prison brogans. Even though there were hundreds of them, their withdrawn hardness made the yard eerily vacant and quiet. Guards stationed up and down the line talked into radio receivers attached to their belts, coordinating movements of prisoners coming and going from the chow hall. I kept my eyes on the horizon of coiled razor wire, above which the red light of dawn spread out across the sky. One of the line guards yelled, and we marched past a thirty-foot-high concrete cylinder cone in the middle of the yard. It was the Wheelhouse, or administrative center, where our "jackets," or court transcripts, were kept. A con coming out of it nodded at Macaron, who was next to me. The bangers ran it, so before you hit DC, they knew everything about you. The guards on its catwalk cradled loaded rifles and followed us with their stares. One of them had a small transistor radio that I could barely hear; it was playing Led Zeppelin's "Stairway to Heaven." Two captains that everybody knew, Mad Dog Madril and Five Hundred, strode back and forth across the yard, yelling at cons and guards alike. Beyond the Wheelhouse, already this early in the morning, the main gates were creaking open as marshals brought in new fish, just as sunrise reached over the granite walls, glimmered on the razor wire, and spread over the main yard.

We marched in through the north side of the chow hall, a low-roofed cinder-block building with gray painted-steel doors and reinforced chicken-wire windows. Whites sat with whites, blacks with blacks, and Chicanos with Chicanos. It held about a hundred cons at a time; as one group finished eating, deposited their trays at the wash window next to the slop cans, and went out at the south end, a new set of cons came in through the north. We were allowed fifteen minutes to eat, and if we took longer we got a write-up. Guards flanked doors on opposite ends of the dining room, others were stationed by the serving line and juice machines, and more guards roamed around the tables. Behind Macaron, I took a tray and spoon, went through the serving line, and stuck my tray under a plastic partition, and the kitchen workers slopped down powdered scrambled eggs, toast, and sausage patties. I filled my plastic cup at the milk machine and followed Macaron to a table. Two other *veteranos* joined us, and I listened as they talked about friends in Phoenix who got busted and were on their way back; about visiting on Sundays and drugs being smuggled in; about getting classified to minimum security, where they had more freedom.

Wedo approached, breaking in on the conversation. "What's up? Fucking brogans are too big! What's with all this baggy shit? These clothes don't fit! I want some real threads!" Macaron shot me a jaded glance. Wedo clenched inches of loose waistline and snugged his belt over it tightly to keep his pants up. "Motherfuckers." He smiled, looking over the heads in the chow hall. "A carton of smokes a week or get fucked?" He pointed at his chest and raised his eyebrows. "Me? You talking to me?" His eyes were glazed and he was limping a little, but seeming otherwise okay, he left.

Instead of following his tier out, he unexpectedly went left, heading straight for the table where the two bangers were sitting. He pulled something from his waistline and plunged it into the back of one of them, shouting, "Pay protection, motherfuckers!" Guards blew whistles as the two bangers leaped up on Wedo. He kept stabbing them wildly with a metal shank, sharpened to an ice-pick point. Led by Mad Dog Madril and Five Hundred, goons rushed into the mess hall, clubbing Wedo and dragging him away. All the way out, Mad Dog Madril kept whipping Wedo's head and body with a flat leather paddle. Another guard, Big Foot, who was about three hundred and fifty pounds, kicked at the bangers until they were clutching their ribs and heads on the floor.

As the guards took the two stabbed cons to the infirmary, we went on eating. One of Macaron's homeboys gave me an irritable look. "Tell him never to come to our table again."

"They rode in together," Macaron offered. "He doesn't know the guy." The *veterano* nodded at Macaron and sipped his coffee.

I waited for them to finish eating, studying their tattooed hands and arms, covered in religious symbols of La Virgen de

Guadalupe or Jesus' crown of thorns, or nightmarish depictions of violence and bloodshed, or names of lovers in hearts. On one man sitting across from me, I saw the upside-down tattoo of La eMe initials, camouflaged in a labyrinth of flowers and crosses. I rested my hand under my chin to keep the nervous twitch in my cheek from being noticed. When we left, I made sure I was behind them.

◆

There were times, usually as we came out for meals, when Macaron signaled me with a nod to tell me to hold back; minutes later, a fight would break out in line or in the landing below. I was thankful to him for taking me under his wing. He advised me not to give the future or the past much thought. "It'll drive you crazy," he said. "Keep your mind on the present, forget about the streets and freedom, and things will work out." Yet when we crossed and recrossed the yard, I sometimes experienced powerful yearnings for freedom; regret at allowing life to pass me by pressed so hard against my heart that I felt it might never end. Nights were sometimes worse, especially when cons talked aloud in the dark about girlfriends, small towns they had come from, things they remembered doing. My brain would start boiling forth so many memories that I had to put toilet paper in my ears to block out the voices. Other times, however, nothing helped and I would wake up sweating and frightened, feeling I had no chance of ever having a decent life.

When the counselor interviewed me, he told me that if I behaved well and obeyed the institutional rules, I'd be permitted to go to school. I'd have to do my time behind the wall because of the aggravating circumstances of my crime (an FBI agent's getting shot), but he assured me that after sixty days in the kitchen without a disciplinary report, the Reclassification Committee would let me attend school to get my GED.

◆

Macaron had a homeboy clerking for the counselor, who arranged for us to be neighbors in Cell Block 2 and work in the kitchen together. Beneath the everyday routine of prison life, this secret system operated through the intricate network of homeboys, messengers, porters, trusties, and corrupt guards. Macaron said the system could be used to your advantage, but he also warned that a twenty-dollar bribe or a bottle cap of heroin residue was enough of a pay-off that some cons and guards would do anything, even kill or set you up. "It works both ways," he said, "and you always have to be aware of it—remember, the money's easy and drugs are an addict's god."

CB2 was an archaic tomb of concrete and iron that smelled clammy and damp. The noise waved out in mind-numbing shocks: iron bars clanged, concrete hummed, radios and TVs jumbled out English and Spanish, speakers blared numbers and crackled orders. Guards ambled down tiers all day and all night. Everyone was hollering and signing and involved in a clandestine scheme of one sort or another: trying to get drugs, avoiding a poker bill, setting up a sister with another con through letters, making bets on sports games, preparing legal paperwork in another attempt at freedom, grieving over a wife's letter that informed the con she was getting married to another guy. It was a world within a world, the difference being that you lived in a cage with a thousand other caged men. Macaron and I were put into B9 and B10, second tier. Solemn faces stared from cells smaller than in DC, their serene demeanor suppressing a violence behind calm brown eyes. Water dripped from plumbing pipes in the maintenance space behind the cells; often, two cons were cramped in cells smaller than in DC; the oxidized iron and concrete floor had a dull sheen from years of human wear; rusting hanging lamps with massive tin shades created a creepy horror-house effect, making cons' shadowy faces more ominous. The three-story cell block with exposed steel-beam rooftop creaked and the rusting tin roof made it all the more eerie—a gigantic warehouse for storing unquartered human beef. The air shook with the tread of black-booted guards hurrying in squads everywhere up and down scaffolds of black-painted staircases. I'd never heard so much noise compressed into one space. Steam hissed behind the walls; pipes rattled; gates clanged. The dark granite was smoked with the ingrained body sweat of decades of caged prisoners. But it was more than that—it was as if their despair and rage had taken on a palpable presence of its own, haunting the shadows in the hollow corners of the block.

At 4 A.M., Macaron and I and four others were racked out of our cells and escorted across the yard to the kitchen. We prepared powdered eggs and toast, brewed coffee, filled up the milk machines, made oatmeal, set out the plastic glasses and spoons. In the afternoon we went to the exercise field and usually played handball, or if we were tired we'd walk around the field talking.

Things were going well until one day after work, about three months into my sentence. I stopped in the foyer for the guards to scan me before entering the block; then I went past them into the landing and toward the wrought-iron stairwell up to my cell. I noticed this huge burly black porter watching me. For a few days in a row, he stood by the guard booth, leaning on his broom, throwing me a smile. I didn't know how to handle a man looking at me like that, and with an embarrassed silence I averted my eyes. I hoped that by ignoring him he'd go away. Instead he took my indifference to mean I was frightened and accessible, and he began to rub his crotch and grin more boldly. One evening, after mail call, I came out of the shower, and he came over to my cell offering cigarettes and coffee. I shook my head no, adding a lingering glare to back him off, but he mad-dogged me back. For the moment it was a standoff, but I knew it wasn't the end. I could see in his hard dark eyes that he felt he could break me, and the thought of him thinking of me as a woman filled me with anger. Guys thinking they could beat me up weren't new to me; I could handle that. But a guy wanting to rape me got under my skin in the worst way. I was too humiliated to talk about it until a few days later, when Macaron and I had just finished playing handball. Sweating and exhausted, we sat on the grass and Macaron asked if something was bothering me. I told him about the problem with the black fag.

"Take him down, you don't wanna get turned out," he said matter-of-factly. "You can't pretend it's not happening."

"Take him down?" I asked, wanting to shift the conversation to something else.

"Show him he's messing with the wrong guy."

"I can do it with these," I said, clenching my fists, hoping Macaron would agree.

"He's a four-time loser. You can fight with your fists, but you have to use a shank, too. He'll have one. What you knew on the streets is over—this is a crazier world. When we come out tomorrow, strap down and ride. We'll watch your back." He glanced at homeboys with slicked black hair and black shades, chilling on the bleachers in starched jeans and white T-shirts.

From the southeast corner of the field where we were sitting, the expanse of parched grass spread out with a dirt track around it; surrounding the field were three rows of security fences and razor wire; in each direction were huts on stilts with armed guards wearing aviator glasses. Cons were scattered out, separated by race: north of the handball courts was the iron pit filled with tattooed Aryan warriors muscling up; beyond that were boxers sparring and pounding the speed bags and body bags in a dirt ring; more Chicanos and blacks played baseball at the southwest corner; and at the northwest corner teams divided by race ran up and down the cement basketball courts.

Macaron said, in a tired voice, "I know you're scared, but this is the way it is. In the joint you live by the convict code, no gray areas: fight or get punked, step out or be turned out, cash in the wolf tickets or be eaten—it's real. Don't show fear, 'cause you'll give your enemy the advantage. Don't intimidate or maddog him—take him out for disrespecting you. Respect is everything. It's earned. You do what you gotta do."

"What if I kill him?" The thought of spending the rest of my life in prison scared me.

"It depends how far he takes it, and you never know until you're in it. Don't stick him around the heart; you don't have to kill him. Teach him a lesson; earn your rep as a *vato* not to mess with; attack first and show no mercy. Word'll get out that you're a stand-up dude, and you got no more problems. On the streets, you lose a fight you go home; that's it. Here, you get fucked, you get sold, punked out; cons don't respect you. Cons who went to Nam say it's worse than jungle warfare. You live with your enemies here. There ain't no going home. You live hour to hour with your enemy standing next to you, eating next to you, walking next to you. The only thing that keeps him from killing you is respect. Do what you gotta do and do it now." Macaron got up and went to the bleachers. I wanted to keep talking but there was nothing more to say.

I lay back and closed my eyes, inhaling the musty scent of hot grass, sensing my aloneness and how my life seemed to lead ineluctably to this moment. All the fights I'd won to prove I was a man didn't matter; nothing mattered except what I was going to do now. The longer I postponed the inevitable showdown, the more it looked like I was afraid and the stronger it made him. The whistle sounded. We formed a single line and filed through the checkpoint back into the main yard. Tower guards with rifles paced the perimeters on top of the walls. Waiting in front of the granite wall, on the exercise field side, I glanced to my right through two fence gates where cons in pressed Levi's and shirts, clean-shaven, confidently carried their books into the educational barracks. One day I'd be one of them, I thought. I just had to take care of my business.

That evening, after showering, on my way back to my cell, Macaron called me to the bars and handed me a washcloth, warning, "Remember, wipe your prints off and toss it after you use it." I unfolded the cloth to find a piece of sharpened plastic about six inches long. Shanks were weapons made from anything you could get your hands on: melted-down plastic molded to a blade, sharpened wood, filed steel, glass, stone, tin, whatever. I slid it under my mattress, hoping I wouldn't have to use it. I couldn't sleep. I tossed and turned, unable to put the confrontation out of my mind. What if I missed a punch and he stabbed me first? What if he moved just as I was going to stab him, and I caught him by accident in the heart? The more I imagined what I would do to him, the more confident I became. I'd grown up fighting, dealing with this kind of shit all my life. I was faster. I'd keep the shank tucked away in my sock, and if he pulled his, I'd pull mine. Street-fighting rules applied here too; the difference was that the weapons were more deadly. I had to set my mind on the job and do it without hesitation. I had to prove to everyone I was not going to be messed with. My mind reeled with anger at the fact that he was fucking with me when I hadn't done anything to him. My plans for school would have to be delayed. The thoughts kept coming—how to get an advantage, what I'd counter with if he made certain moves—and after hours of rehearsing it, I finally dozed off. But before I fell asleep, I had decided that, until it was over, nothing was important to me except beating down this thug.

I climbed out of my cot the next morning, dressed, and hid the shank inside my brogan. I took it because the shakedown crews usually inspected one or two cells while cons were out on the field or working. I was too agitated to eat breakfast, and after doing my chores, I headed back to the block to change clothes and check out for field. I needed to fight and get it over with. On the yard, after I left the block, a guard swept my body with a handheld scanner and moved me on. Macaron was at my side, his homeboys in front and back. As we marched past the Wheelhouse guards staring down on us, I thought how my jacket, neatly filed away in a cabinet, would never have the true information about me—that I wanted to do right but couldn't. When the counselor read it all he saw was that I had no education and no family, and that a federal agent had been shot during a heroin sale. He didn't know, no one knew who I was. He had told me that if I stayed out of trouble, I'd go to school and get a better job. Implicit in his encouragement was that it was up to me to decide my fate, but it wasn't really like that. Others had a lot to do with whether you did good or bad.

Cons were coming out of the small chapel next to the library, and I wished for God to take all this away. Among others, I saw Wedo at the property-room window arguing with a guard about his clothes. Other cons were lined up at the canteen. The whitewashed cinder-block infirmary looked quiet. I hoped I didn't end up there. The yard was swept clean and hard. A line formed behind the checkpoint at the west end of the main yard, and another one at the gate where you entered the barracks area and then the field. I could see the distant gun towers at each corner of the field and the top ledge of the handball-court walls. As I neared the checkpoint leading to the gate to the field, I saw him on my left in the open-air welding sheds across from the school barracks. He was supposed to be in the field, not in the welding shop. Panic raced wildly through me. I went numb with the familiar sensation of anger. My mouth was dry. A graveled road for delivery trucks ran north and south between the barracks and welding shed. My brain boiled over with red mist, making me dizzy and weak. The hot sun and heat were choking me. Then something suddenly snapped, igniting in my heart, and I took off sprinting from the line.

The air was opaque, as if I were observing things through a milky quartz, and in the dim consciousness, I heard whistles. Everything blurred around me—fences, gravel road, guards, and cons merged—the only thing I saw was the black dude bending over, wearing welding goggles and smoothing the end of a leg length of cot pipe at a grinding wheel. He was glistening sweat in the torch flame from the con welding next to him. Before he knew it, I was beside him. Startled by seeing me, he dropped the pipe he was shaving on the grinder. He crouched to pick it up but I quickly picked a piece of angle iron from the trash can between us and hit him on the head. Stunned, he staggered back and turned his face right into the whirring grinding wheel. The blade ripped his goggles in half and cut into his cheek and eye. Blood squirted across the air in thick sprays and he cried out. A part of his eye and a chunk of cut cheek flesh dangled as he tripped back, covering his face. I hit him again and he fell to his knees, his muscled arms, broad shoulders, and thick legs squirming to escape. I planted my feet firmly apart and hit him until he sprawled out on the concrete floor. A voice inside my head kept yelling the whole time I was hitting him that I was doing this for Theresa, whose father had raped her, and for my brother, who'd been raped by those two white guys.

Guards in riot gear rushed in, knocking me to the floor, beating me down with boots and clubs from every direction. It was Mad Dog Madril, smashing my face in with his boot heel, and Five Hundred, clubbing my torso. I lay still, looking at the black dude groaning in a pool of blood a few feet from me. Two big goons lifted me and led me up the gravel road. For a few minutes, I was blinded by bright sunspots flashing in my eyes. I squinted and focused on the line of prisoners waiting to go into the field. I saw Macaron, who nodded his approval. I was proud and relieved it was over.

They marched me across the yard, and outside CB4 the goons stripped me down and found the shank. They ordered me to stand in an open concrete bay and blasted me against the wall with a fire hose. I tried to protect my testicles, going sideways as the velocity of the water turned me around and around. After hosing me down, they made me bend over, to check my asshole, and forward, to check my testicles, arms, ears, and mouth. I put on my boxer shorts, and four bulls escorted me down into CB4. We went through a series of old iron gates, down a long corridor. After each gate the air in each succeeding corridor grew darker. To my right there were cells, and the faces in them had an eerie, sickly paleness from lack of sunshine and fresh air. I didn't know it was death row, or that the other cells we passed were for administrative segregation—cons accused of being in gangs and indefinitely locked down by the warden. At the back of the block we climbed three floors. The guards' boots thundered on the old fire-escape steps made of mesh-wire steel. As we went up, I noticed each floor had two isolation cells off to the side in a small landing. On the third floor, the guards opened a solid-steel door, uncuffed me, and shoved me in. The cell was pitch black. They slammed the door and I listened in the darkness until their descending footsteps faded away.

◆

My body ached from being hit by the goons. I began to focus on my breathing and to pace the five-by-nine cell. I hadn't slept much the previous night, and I was drained and exhausted but jittery and high-strung. I trailed my hand along the wall until my eyes adjusted to the pitch black. I had proven myself, I thought, and I was proud, but I also felt bad because instead of changing for the better, I was becoming more violent. It was the first time I ever beat a guy with an angle iron, and an ominous dread filled my heart as I prayed that I hadn't killed him. If I did, I was only defending myself. I did what I had to. The only reason I used the iron was because he was going to use an iron pipe on me. After hours of pacing, trying to calm my mind and nerves down, I lay on the cot and closed my eyes, concentrating on trying to get some rest. I don't know if it was days or hours, but I slept for the longest time. Days and nights blurred. The only times I remember waking up were from nightmares of the fight; each time I fell back to sleep, I prayed for the guy not to die.

Over the next series of meals, I caught up on lost sleep, and then, to keep myself functioning in the same reality as before, I stayed awake from the time breakfast trays were delivered to when supper trays were picked up. As I was completely submerged in darkness for long periods, the sharp clack and loud jangling of keys at the swill slot frightened me every time meals came. As I tried to regain my composure, the guard never failed to yell, "Take the fucking tray!" Once or twice I was too slow and he let it drop, and I picked the food off the floor and ate it. I savored each morsel of whatever it was I was eating. When I managed to anticipate his coming, kneeling down, my face in the shaft of light the four-inch slot panel let in, I asked if the black guy was okay. The guard made a stupid remark I remembered from adolescence: "That's for me to know and you to find out." Then he slammed the lid over the porthole opening. I traced my fingers around the edges, hoping it might not have latched all the way, but it always did.

There were frenzied periods of paranoia, when I thought I saw big rats on the floor and crouched on the cot, my back to the wall, until I realized it was just an illusion. My eyes weren't alone in playing tricks on me: I scratched and slapped at insects crawling over my flesh, which turned out to be tiny bits of iron shavings that had been embedded in my flesh when I was smashed to the welding-floor ground by the guards. I washed and scrubbed with cold water at blood on my arms and legs until I realized they were bruises.

But these physical delusions were trivial compared to the insanity I got lost in. Ominous, howling noises came through the walls. I was certain that black gang members were coming to kill me through the crawl spaces behind the cells where the wiring and plumbing was. Lying perfectly still in the dark for hours, I could hear them gathering outside the door. Stone chips were flaking off the wall because someone was on the other side chiseling to get in. Inch by inch I ran my fingers over walls, floor, ceiling, toilet, and bunk, searching every cranny to make sure they were not getting through. They had probably bribed a guard and were just waiting for the right time to enter the hole and stab me to death. Even as I became sure they were coming, I also kept insisting it was ridiculous. I panicked for long stretches at a time, sweating, my heart thumping loudly as I listened to the thuds and hammering closing in on me. I lost track of the days. The swill slot in the door would open and a guard would hand me a tray. That was all I knew of life beyond the darkness and my madness.

To keep from going insane, I started to do sit-ups, push-ups, and jumping jacks. I'd splash cold water over my naked body and sleep on the cool concrete floor, with no blanket, mattress, or sheet. I was constantly clawing at itches in my growing beard. Here in my own dark world, I had control only over the cold button on the sink, and I pushed it a hundred times a day, gulping until I was bloated, bathing until I was drenched. To squeeze every last drop of restless energy from me I masturbated, sometimes six times a day. I tried anything to pass the time, but the moment finally came when I was tired of waiting. I was so depressed I couldn't stand it anymore. I wanted to get out. I curled up naked on the cot and quit eating. I forgot about life, forgot about myself, and just let time pass.

Then one day the guard delivered my tray, not through the swill slot but through the door. A stream of hazy late-morning light filled my squinting, sensitive eyes. "Put some fucking shorts on!" he snapped. A little later, I stood outside on the landing, shivering and skinny. I had to hold the handrail as I followed the guard down the stairs. And as we made our way down the corridors to the front of CB4, one of the guys in an administrative-segregation cell yelled, "You should've killed that black sonofabitch!"

So he was alive. Alive, and everything was new. Even the dingy green cell bars looked good. My eyes absorbed every face and cell; my ears took in all the harsh sounds and yelling; even the intercom crackling numbers wasn't as repulsive as I remembered it. He hadn't died. The slamming steel, screaming radios, and TVs were all welcome sights and sounds to me. I was led to the Reclassification Committee, where I pled guilty to assault and was given an extra six months. My new beginning had a real sweetness to it; I was eager to start doing my time from a whole different vantage point. I had respect now.

◆

I was back in CB2 again and on kitchen detail. In the days that followed I expected something to happen, if not from black gangs then from the black fag himself. But when Macaron and I sat down at our table, he said the guy had been transferred outside the walls. With respect came double servings on the chow line, guards let me stay out on the tier to porter, and when Chicanos came back from commissary runs they dropped off cigarettes and coffee at my cell. Though I secretly had mixed feelings about being rewarded for beating a man, that's the way it had always been. I noticed when I came from the chow hall to the field, or when I was on the tier, young Chicanos stuck close by me. When I jogged around the field, they strolled in threes and fours, keeping an eye on me. I felt good to be part of them.

One morning as I grabbed up empty containers from the serving line and carried full ones from the cooking area in the back to the chow line up front, I saw Carey in line with his tray. He poured a glass of milk at the machines and sat with two Aryan skinheads. They eyed me with contempt as I came up and greeted Carey. We sat at another table. He was gaunt and cautious; his disarming farm-boy mannerisms and rustic features were hardened with concern.

"Galvan has a contract on Rick," he stated.

I was expecting to talk about Lonnie or where he was working, but I could see he was seriously worried.

"Rick's got to get out of the walls or he's dead," he went on. "The counselor in Yuma smuggled in Rick's court transcripts on a client visit. Warn Rick, tell him to roll up and get out of the walls." Carey rose and followed his Aryan brothers out. I never expected to see him join the Aryan clique, but prison makes us do strange things.

Carey had done me right. Even if he fell in love with Lonnie, he had never ripped me off, and I owed him for saving my life the night that narc stepped out to blow me away. If Carey hadn't shot him, I'd be dead. Carey got fifty years for pulling the trigger.

The following day, on the field after playing handball, I asked Macaron if his homies clerking in the Wheelhouse could find where Rick was working. The next evening a kite came to my cell, informing me that Rick was in minimum security and attending school in the barracks. I flushed the note down the toilet. I knew the education cons ate lunch at eleven and the next day I hung around, instead of leaving as I usually did at nine. I finally saw him sitting by himself. I sat down and told him Carey said he had a price on his head. "Pack up and get out of the walls or you're dead."

I put the whole thing out of my mind; I didn't want to see or talk to Rick ever again. I figured the whole thing was done with until a few days later in the cell block. I was leaning on the bars looking around when I noticed a Chicano across the landing trying to stare me down. A coincidence, I thought, and looked away, but I glanced back and he was still staring. If a subtle glance became a riveting stare, it meant bad blood. Over the next few days on the field, Aryan and black bangers furtively glanced at me. On my way from work back to the block, Shorty, a dude built wider than he was tall, trailed me. I recognized the same Chicano in the block at a table near me in the dining room. Prison atmosphere, which only a week earlier seemed familiar and comforting, now filled me with tense trepidation. From my cell to work to field and back to my cell, I felt eyes at the back of my head.

On my way back to the block after exercise one afternoon, two soldiers from La eMe accosted me at the entrance.

"Yeah, *vato,* why'd you tip that snitch?" They swaggered off with a certain cockiness, meaning their business was not done. I was in a bad cross and wanted to straighten things out. I regretted doing a favor for Carey; I should have known better. The next day at dusk I was in the chow line when another mafia guy came up.

"We want that money, it's ours," a lanky Chicano said menacingly, and walked off.

Then, on my way back to CB2, another mafioso said, "Pay the two g's that was on his head."

I knew nothing would stop the mafiosos. They began to dog me even harder, shadowing me wherever I went. I tried to shine them on, giving them my fuck-you attitude, but I knew they were not making idle threats. They ran their gang like a corporate business. I'd heard they were making big bucks selling drugs and protection. The days passed slowly and I grew more scared but I didn't show it. I'd take a drink from the fountain in the block and there'd be two behind me. They followed me to the field, on the tiers, at work. Then one morning, as I sat on crates in the back having coffee with a homeboy named Chacho at the back service door of the kitchen leading into the dining room, two Mexicans appeared. A hit squad.

"*¡Ojo, águila!*" Chacho warned. Watch out! As he said it, I saw them draw shanks and move quickly toward me. Simultaneously, I leaped up and grabbed the butcher knife the chef was chopping onions with. I was behind the table, and one of them jumped over it. Unable to stop his forward momentum, he came on me from above and I slit his stomach. He clutched his intestines as they slopped out of his gut and then fell on the chopping block, his blood all over the vegetables. The other one stopped dead in his tracks and dashed out. The chef slammed the button and the alarm went off. It was that quick—pure instinct and survival. I wiped the knife handle on my white apron and dropped it and walked out the back door.

I walked into the cell block, going right to my cell, as men straggled out for breakfast. Midway down the landing, a guy named Brujo and a *clika,* about twenty Mexicans, confronted me. I didn't know who Brujo was, or his standing with La eMe, and I didn't care.

Older than the rest, Brujo combed his black-and-gray hair back and wore sunglasses that concealed his eyes. He moved like a seasoned tiger, having survived many wars. His face had nicks and scars. He wore a thin mustache, and below his left eye were three tattooed dots. He stopped and I stopped, about twenty paces apart, facing each other.

In a voice like a rusty blade, Brujo said to me, "You might have got away this morning, but there's no place you can run. Or hide. We'll get you wherever you are." His brown eyes were seething. I asked him, "You sent the hit squad? You fucking punk, what I ever do to you?" He said, "It's about your snitch friend and the money." I said, "If you have a score to settle with me, let's settle it between us now." He leered, signaling his henchmen to hold off, because when I insulted him as a coward they started for me. They were circling me, when the young bucks who had recently appointed me their leader started coming down the second-story tiers and stairwell, yelling they were backing my play. There was a big racket as they rushed down the staircase, two steps at a time.

Brujo's boys reached for shanks under their long blue winter jackets and gray sweatshirts that reached their thighs. Their black beanie caps were snugged around their heads down to their eyebrows. Brujo gave me an evil leer, showing his control of the situation and his power over life and death. "Snitches are no good," Brujo said. "We're in prison because of them; we've lost our families, our lives, our freedom because of them. They have caused us much pain, and we live in that pain every day. You dare to insult us by protecting one of them? No, no, we will take you and them down into the pain we live in every day and make you pay for every hour of it." Seven or eight of the young bucks rushing down the stairs drew up beside me. Brujo leered again. "You think these young kids can stop us? We have hundreds of soldiers. If they wish to die with you, fine, good, the more the better." And with one motion, in their prison jackets with the big pockets, the army of disciplined apostles ready to give their lives for Brujo, for what he stood for, moved past me.

I went to Macaron's cell and told him what happened, told him how I messed everything up, how I had planned to go to school and get my GED and now everything was all fucked up again.

He was sitting on his cot by the bars. He looked at me, brown eyes large in a scarred face, and said, "I was like you— hoping for a better life, working to do right— but that time passed. I remember when it happened. I was standing in front of the gates with the chain gang; we were going out to pick potatoes. Suddenly I lost hope, and I could never get it back again. My soul broke. It died. That day, I became a criminal. That day I had no more hope. I knew when the punishment was enough, and then it kept going on and on, and from that point it made no sense. . . ."

After a pause, he continued. "It happens to all of us who stay here past a certain time. You do your time; then you do more and more, and the hurt in the heart turns to bitterness, freedom turns to vengeance, and you look forward to getting out, not to resume your life but to hurt people the way they hurt you, for punishment that made no sense, for the hurting and hurting, for the day when you couldn't take it anymore but you had to and lost your humanity, lost your reason for wanting to be a human being. The day you just fell into line, knowing this is where you'd live and die."

He stood up, then, gripping the bars an inch from my face, staring deep into my eyes. "I know you're going to the hole for a long time, and I know you're in serious trouble. Remember, it's not the size of your muscles or your mouth—here, the heart is all that matters. The mind can't accept being in a six-by-nine cell for years, but the heart understands it has to be done. The mind says, There's no way I can live in prison for years, but the heart says, Deal with it and shut the fuck up. The mind senses your growing brutality, but the heart ignores it. Forget freedom, the heart commands.

"No one will help you here; you're on your own. Fuck family, dreams, hopes, plans; when it comes down to it, you do what you got to do. If you got a parole board hearing in the afternoon and someone jumps your case, you fuck them up, and if you get more time, you get more time. If you're put in a cross, no one cares. All you got here is heart—*corazón.* Only *corazón.* And if you don't have it, every day will be a hell you've never imagined. When the mind says, I am human, the heart growls, I am an animal. When you wish to scream, the heart says, Be silent. When you feel hurt, you numb yourself. When you're lonely, you push it aside. Strip yourself of every trace of the streets, because it will hurt you here. Here, you have no feelings, no soul; only your heart will help you survive. Forget everything except survival. Don't ask why—there are no reasons. There is no future, no past, only the moment; you will do what you have to do. You didn't exist before coming here; your life before here never happened. The only thought that drives you on is to be alive at the end of the day, and to be a man, or die fighting proving you are a man. That's the code of the warrior.

"You better get in your cell; they're coming for you." He gave me a cigarette. "Here, it'll be the last one you have for a while."

I smoked the Lucky Strike slowly, standing at the bars, staring out into the landing, at the goons in riot gear coming up, led by Mad Dog Madril and Five Hundred, barking at cons to stick their heads in. They kept nearing my cell. I had blood on my clothes. Who was I becoming? I felt lost, a stranger even to myself. The cell-block intercom blared my number, crackling commands for me to step out peacefully. I ignored them. Mad Dog Madril stood in my open cell door. "You want us to come in and get you?" I stared in quiet defiance and flicked the cigarette butt at him. Mad Dog stepped aside. Five Hundred was first to enter, body-slamming me against the wall, wrenching me out by the neck, and throwing me against the floor. As I was pushed in handcuffs down the stairwell, I realized it was the end of February, a time of change, when golden leaves blew across the air, returning to the earth, and spring leaves were just starting to bud in the coming warmth. I was twenty-two.

SEVEN

Most people might assume that cons spend their time thinking about what they're going to do when their time is up, fantasizing about the women they're going to fuck and scams they're going to run, or planning how they're going to go straight and everything will be different. I did think about the future sometimes, but more and more it was the past my mind began to turn to, especially during those first days and nights in solitary.

The years leading up to prison had been a never-ending series of hustles. I was constantly conniving, focused on whatever screwed-up situation was at hand that day or planning tomorrow's score. For a street kid, it was all about the basics: food, shelter, a little pocket change. Always moving forward, head down, never looking back. But things were different now. I wasn't moving anywhere anytime soon.

Lying on my cot, staring at the concrete wall for hours on end, for the first time in years my mind's eye drifted back over my shoulder, down the bleak road that had led me here. Remembering was a novelty. The territory I began to explore seemed just as fresh as anything I could dream up but free of the exhausting, overpowering ache of longing. Most of all, it helped fill the void stretching out in front of me, which was not nearly so black and terrifying this time around. It was just empty time. My first stint in the hole had been a nightmare, but I'd survived it, and I could do it again. Thirty days was just thirty days.

What began as an idle reflex became a habit of mind and then something else entirely. As my powers of concentration grew,

I would revisit places and people from my past for longer stretches of time. Stretched out flat on my back, arms covering my eyes, I would replay the events over and over again like a sexual fantasy, adding details and names, redrawing faces, until they seemed as real to me as if they were right in front of me. Occasionally I'd be distracted by the sound of a guard's footsteps or thoughts about the Mexican mafia gunning for me in the prison yard outside. But with nothing else to do but lie there and sweat, I trained my mind to shut out everything around me and travel back in time.

Revisiting the past wasn't about seeking comfort at first, it was just something to do, like push-ups. But as I thought back on my unhappy childhood, I found myself lingering more and more on images of Estancia, the small village where my grandparents lived, all by itself in the vast prairie, in a certain lonely innocence.

I'd spent a few fleeting years of happiness in Estancia, during my boyhood, before my mother left and everything changed. The village was nestled under a grove of scattered cottonwoods, in the flatlands to the southeast of the Sangre de Cristo Mountains. I could see my grandparents' small brown stucco house, the windswept dirt yard, and the barnlike-shed where I played with Grandpa's shovel and pick, their handles cracked and blackened with sweat and use, shredded gunnysacks, mule harness, old iodine bottles, and rusty cans.

I'd never gone into my memories so vividly before. I felt more outside my cell than in it. In my mind I would see the looming silver water tower on trestle stilts to the north, and next to it the three-story red-brick schoolhouse. The park and pond were to the south, the railyard to the east, and to the west the prairie rolled to the Manzano foothills.

My grandfather died years ago, but in my mind he was alive, and my brother, sister, and I were with him, in the small village where my father grew up. From the horizon, train tracks threaded through vast stretches of endless parched rabbit brush and cactus to Estancia's dusty warehouses. A few goats, horses, and cows roamed well-worn footpaths connecting adobe and clapboard houses. At the pond, used for centuries by sheepherders as a watering hole, renowned for its sweet-tasting water, there were picnic benches and tree stumps, around which villagers gathered for rodeos and religious fiestas. In the cottonwoods, owls, blackbirds, and hawks perched, scanning the prairie at sunrise, glinting off the galvanized tin roof of my grandparents' house, its blackened chimney smoking as Grandma prepared coffee, eggs, tortilla, and green chile for Grandpa and my Uncle Refugio.

It was a modest stucco house, constructed of two-by-four milled lumber, with a tiny front porch and a white wooden railing and love swing, built by the railroad as a dual-family unit for Mexican tracklayers. On sunny afternoons, Martina and Mieyo would often sit in the love swing and talk, while I walked back and forth atop the railing, trying to balance as I listened. Two brown doors faced the dirt road, and these were never opened except on hot days, to let a breeze cool the house, or for formal visits when Grandma had guests and they sat in the parlor.

◆

My Uncle Santiago arrives, as he does every morning, in his battered green truck, smelling of hay, livestock, earth, and water. The kitchen radio plays Mexican songs. He uses the back door, as everybody does, bringing a glass canning jar filled with fresh goat's milk for Grandma. A chill draft sweeps through the house as he enters and closes the door, stamping his heavy work boots. He drinks a cup of coffee, sharing news he's heard about people they know, asks how Grandpa and Grandma feel, and leaves to feed his animals on the outskirts of town. Mieyo and Martina have already eaten and gone to school. The woodstove fills the house with resinous cedar aroma; the steam from coffee, beans, chile makes me hungry. I brace myself for the ice-cold linoleum, leap out from under the warm quilt, and dash across the hall to the bathroom to pee.

"Whoaaa!" My Uncle Refugio pretends I almost knocked him over. He's tall and strong, Grandma's third son, and every day after field work he spends his pay at the Blue Ribbon bar and then staggers home, and Grandma puts him to bed, lights a candle, and prays. I'm always surprised how fresh he looks in the morning, especially after seeing him so drunk the night before. Combed and shaved, wearing starched jeans and a denim shirt, he points the straight-edge razor at me, frowning. "This is not a corral!" Hot water steams the mirror as he rinses the shaving brush, puts it in the mug, and, after drying his face, slaps Old Spice on his cheeks. I pee and sneak back to bed but Grandma catches me.

"*Puerco, ven paca,*" she scolds, and pulls me to the sink and scours my face and ears. Freezing water drops on my neck make me fidget. "Hold still," she demands, cuffing my oversized shirt and pants. Combing my hair and straightening my clothes into a presentable appearance, she complains that I stink worse than a goat.

"Wait for Grandpa. I'm going to church." She drapes a black shawl over her shoulders and leaves. I jump on the counter sink and look out the window to watch her best friend, Juanoveva, meeting her mid-field. They go on together, both slightly stooped and frail. I believe God listens to her, and I know she's praying that my parents will come back together.

Grandpa comes in from chopping wood, slapping his shoulders to shake the cold off and rubbing his hands over the woodstove. I follow him to his room and lie on his bed, watching him as he sits in a spindle chair lacing his boots. I'm amazed by his huge knuckles, all scarred and scabbed. To make extra money, he fights bare-knuckled on weekends in the railroad sheds against Mexicans or gringos the growers bring in from other towns. I want to be like him one day. He towers over me, pretending he's boxing, and I slug him in the leg as he winces. I go to hug him and realize it's a trick; he grabs me and wipes my runny nose with his handkerchief. He tosses me back on the bed and spirals an index finger above my stomach, repeating, "*Lanza, lanza, lanza la panza! Lanza, lanza, lanza la panza!*" Tickle, tickle, tickle the stomach! He zeroes in on my stomach with his index finger until I'm hiccuping giggles, trying to deflect his hands. "Up, we have to go." He sits me on his knee, swings me up and down a few times, and gently places me on the floor.

Outside, I walk alongside Grandpa, carrying his black lunch pail in the red wagon I pull behind us. He's wearing his crumpled fedora and threadbare suit coat over bib overalls. The land sparkles with dew. Roosters crow. Cows bellow. He looks at the clear sky and land and houses all around and slaps his chest lightly to indicate how he loves the dawn. I do the same. When I'm with him like this, life is beautiful. Nothing in the world can harm me. Halfway to school, he kisses me, and his rough gray stubble makes me scratch my cheek. I hand him his black lunch pail. He tells me to help Grandma and be good, that we'll meet later, and heads off to school, where he's the janitor.

Back at the house, I know Grandma will soon arrive to start tortillas and clean house and wash clothes. Entering the back door, you come into the kitchen and eating room, divided by an arched opening. The west side of the house has Refugio's bedroom facing north toward the road, then, in the middle of a small room, is a large cot for us kids, and at the foot of the cot, close by the bathroom, is a wringer washing machine. The east side of the house, through a door in the eating area, is Grandma and Grandpa's bedroom, and then the parlor, facing the road. The parlor is off limits to kids and seldom used except for special social calls by the priest or rare visitors. I'm not supposed to go into my grandparents' bedroom by myself, but I turn the brown enamel doorknob and skeleton key and enter anyway. The air is cold and stale. A fine dust covers the brittle linoleum creaking under my step. A dusty brass chamber pot glimmers at the foot of the brass four-poster and directly above it two daguerreotypes in oval frames depict a much younger Grandma and Grandpa poised on a buckboard, in somber attire, features weathered and rigorous. I try to imagine what their young lives were like but their eyes look as if they're really staring at me. Something rattles against the window and I believe it's spirit talk, warning me to leave. But instead of getting scared and tiptoeing out, I slowly open the other door, which leads into the parlor. Mexican blankets drape the couch and rocking chair. Faded pictures of Christ and Santo Nino de Atocha hang on the wall. Displayed imposingly on a cherry-wood table is the red Bible in which important papers are kept. I open it and find a photograph of Grandmother's parents standing before a red rock house. Indians and Mexicans stand before it, holding their horses. Grandma is a young girl in some kind of ceremony because she's wearing feathers and a doeskin skirt. There's another photograph of Grandpa's parents; rough-looking Mexicans with dark copper skin. Grandpa is standing next to his father, a solemn-faced man wearing a black sombrero with a thick mustache. About a dozen white mules are tethered to ground stakes with lead ropes. The men and women are dressed in clean jeans and cowboy shirts, probably on their way to a fiesta or mass.

Before Grandma comes and makes me help her work, I run out of the house, crossing the fields to the old red-brick school to visit Grandpa. I'm always complaining that I'm too sick to attend school, and my grandparents indulge me. Besides, I can only speak Spanish, and Grandma is against speaking English and prefers that I stay home as long as I can. Grandma lets me go there after school to be with Grandpa. He lets me sprinkle cottonseed oil on the dust mop, and I help him push it down the long hall. We start playing. My voice echoes in the hall with squeals of excitement as I dodge and squirm and duck under his arms and run. He spins around, growling, "Here I come, I'm going to get you!" He corners me and I'm balled up laughing with delight on the floor. I go into a classroom and draw on the chalkboard, spin the globe on the teacher's desk, and leaf through pretty picture books. Later, when I get tired of helping, I fall asleep on the floor in the gym, comforted by hearing Grandpa shaking the dust mop and running the wax buffer. When he wakes me it's dark outside, and he carries me back home under the stars and moon on his shoulders.

◆

Those days were almost happy enough for me to forget my parents, and in the hole I returned to Estancia time and time again in my mind, living as if I were there, feeling the sun on my skin, watching hawks glide above the village in the sharp blue sky, just as I had as a child. The vivid reality of my reveries made these imaginary excursions so forceful it scared me. It became much more than idly remembering this or that. I'd play a memory like a song, over and over, adding this or subtracting that, changing something in a scene or re-creating a certain episode and enhancing it with additional details. Fearful I might be losing my sanity, sometimes when I came back to the present, I'd call out my name in the cell just to hear it or bang the steel door until my hands hurt. But, whatever was happening, I felt a wholesome fulfillment that delighted me, even in this dark pit. Memories structured my day and filled my cell. It was as if all the sorrow, fear, and regret I'd carried in my bones suddenly was swept away and my heart lifted itself into a realm of innocence before all sadness and tragedy happened. In my imagination I was safe and joyous again. The darkness of my cell glowed with the bright dawn light of Estancia. The walls of my cell slowly disintegrated into trees and a pond and village people coming out of their houses. The ritual of re-creating my young life repeated itself every day after meals, almost without effort. The instant I closed my eyes, I'd picture myself back in Estancia, hear my six-year-old voice talking with my friend Mocoso as we walked along a dusty road, slipping into the brush to reach the creek and follow its cool, meandering current through groves of cottonwoods and boulders.

◆

We play outside, roaming the village, exploring the alleys, the pond, the buildings on Main Street and the railroad warehouses. We start at the pond in the park on the south side of town. I lean over the flagstone border and claw up handfuls of weed, dripping mud as minnows scatter. I hop on the flagstone border, taunting *la bruja,* the legendary witch who lives in the water. Mocoso warns me to stop; she might grab us and drown us like she did this kid Fernando a few years ago. We play on the swings and the teeter-totter, roll in the grass, and pitch pebbles, making them squirt up across the water. Perfectly still on our stomachs over the water's edge, with its reflections of tree and sky, we watch fish spurt to catch an insect skimming the surface. I cup handfuls of the sweet cold water from the natural springs that feed the pond. A truck rumbles by, carrying Mexican field workers, a large silver drinking bucket tied to its tailgate. Steam drifts from its radiator as it bounces and bangs down the dirt road toward the tracks. Behind us, in the yard of one of the houses, cows and goats spar, bucking vigorously, as hens squawk and roosters crow; from a window, Spanish mass comes from a radio. *"El Espiritu de Dios se mueve, el Espiritu de Dios se mueve dentro mi corazón."* The spirit of God moves within me, the spirit of God moves within my heart.

We talk to Mr. Gonzalez's mule, whom we've named *sordo,* deaf one, because he never listens; he just stares and doesn't want to come to us. On the way to wherever we're going, we climb over piles of firewood stacked in yards by front doors. At one, we watch Rudolfo cutting wood, and as he swings his ax we try to catch the resinous chips scattering in the air until he tells us to stop; we might get hurt. He frees the blade and swings again, cracking a log in half, and tosses the chunk on the pile. As we walk, Mocoso and I make our muscles dance. We compete to see who can flex and jiggle biceps better. Mocoso does better birdcalls and he tries to teach me but I can't do them. I lift my shirt and bloat my belly to a huge balloon, my cheeks puffed as I hold my breath. He laughs, and ropes of snot dangle from his nostrils. We walk backwards until we stop in front of the old crumbling mansion with white scrolled porch pillars, corbel edges, and trimmed filigree eaves cracked with age. It's a haunted house, where a rich gringo once lived. Mocoso says he was mean to the village people, and the wind made a tree break and fall on him. Ghosts live in the house, and during winter the cows huddle in the empty rooms for shelter against the blowing snow and freezing wind. We continue, following a goat path from the water tower, going west. The path's weeds and grass go from dark to light, thick to sparse stubble, then open to a run of hard clay bordered by short tough yellow grass. We talk about things we really don't understand, about rich white men who stole land and bandits who roamed the plains, and as we talk we add new details to the stories to make them even more scary and exciting. We turn south, into tall cattail reeds, and follow a shady, meandering stone path and clamber over field machinery and defunct livestock pens. The path snakes under rusting cattle cars, dismantled windmills, and diesel engines and around old boxcars whose rusting insides are filled with straw, vagrants' rags and wine bottles, and crusty beads of sheep manure, cow dung, and bird droppings.

We turn east. The path burrows under the *Torreon Times,* a bimonthly ranching-paper office, no longer used and boarded up, where old men now meet to sun themselves every morning. Its glass is dulled blue by tobacco and wood-smoke resin from a time when the old ones met inside by the potbelly stove and read the paper and talked. Dead flies and insects in webs hang from old iron lamps standing on the windowsill. We go north, as the path undulates up and under root-cracked foundations, driving straight toward shaggy cottonwoods. It pierces through abandoned warehouses, once used to store sacks of pinto beans, the best-tasting beans in the world. The old railroad tracks that come up to the loading dock doors are buried in sand. The path goes under great beams caved in from above, and in the rafters sparrows leap and chirp in gaping holes in the ceiling. The beams crisscross on the ground, creating a playground for us to play around in for a while. Sometimes a startled chicken squawks out from under a crevice or a snake slithers into a pile of old tools and flour sacks.

We reach the town water tower again and sit down against one of the great steel trestle legs. I look up at the narrow ladder that leads to the top. I don't realize how high it really is until Mocoso picks up a dirt clod and tries to hit the *E* of Estancia. We throw dirt clods for a long time, aiming at the large black letters painted across the silver tank. The dirt clods stick puffs of dirt where they hit. We decide on an easier target, the church butane cylinder. The gravel stones hitting it make a tinny clang and pigeons scatter from the roof bell. Mocoso wants to go bug my Cousin Stella and her boyfriend, necking in the end zone on the football field, but I tell him she'll beat us up.

After promising to meet Mocoso tomorrow at the pond, I take off for Grandma's. It's near dusk, a time when people withdraw into their homes and a somber lull falls over the pueblo and I have no words to describe how I love what I see and feel: the wispy trails of smoke from chimneys, the small stone grottos of La Virgen de Guadalupe and San Martín de Porres by doors, the aura of religious resolve that pervades the pueblo, the feeling that people have always lived here with the assistance of saints who watch over them and bless each day. Above me, the red harvest moon rises in the western sky, and large owls hoot in trees. As I run, I remember midnight rides with my father from Estancia to Santa Fe; me telling him, Go faster, catch the moon, it's just over the next hill. He swigs from his whiskey flask, and tells me the moon looks like it's close but it's really far away in the sky. But I believe it's close, and dashing to Grandma's, I make the same wish I'd made a hundred times when I was with him. Looking up at the sky, I promise myself that tomorrow, Mocoso and I will check the foothills to find the moon's home.

◆

My sleep and waking rhythms were all mixed up, whirling as I was through the gray zone between the cell and the village. I kept time of day and night with meals and shift changes. Whether I was awake or in an altered state or sleeping, Estancia was never far away. In my imagination, the more I visited Estancia, the more there was to see and do. I wanted to know more about it, to get into every person's heart and know what happened to each of them: what changed them, why things turned out as they did. I wanted to understand both the joyous and the tragic sides of their lives. Day and night, half conscious, I was consumed by the other world, always in an altered state, even when I was awake. I couldn't help but feel wonderful, and I couldn't stop myself as I went back into my memories again because of the peace it brought to my body, soul, and mind. I felt an affirmation of who I was; the person I'd almost buried forever became stronger in me. Returning to the cell from my memories, I'd find myself regenerated, despite the lack of sleep.

I went on like this for weeks, reliving the fable of my life, rediscovering from my isolation cell the boy I was and the life I'd lived. Beyond the dark and the two-inch-thick steel door, during days and nights, I'd hear keys rattling, guard boots stomping up and down stairwells, muffled screams from other isolation cells, water pipes quaking. I'd sit and listen to the sounds until they blended into the house in Estancia.

◆

From the kitchen I listen, in bed, to Grandpa shoving piñon into the woodstove to stoke it for the evening. Grandma is toasting tortillas on the stovetop so they'll be ready for the morning, with Santiago in the kitchen whispering over his coffee his anger at Refugio's drunkenness. I nestle closer to the body heat of my brother and sister next to me in bed and fall asleep. During the night, a familiar scent of cologne wakes me. I get up quietly and stand beside the hall door, peering in the kitchen. My father sits at the table, holding yet another pair of new shoes for Grandma. She has many other shoes he's brought her in the closet, none of which she could ever wear because her toes are gnarled so badly she would have to cut the shoe tips off. I know he brings shoes to her as an excuse to get information about where my mom is. He pushes the box across the kitchen table.

"Paris shoes," he says, sifting pocket change through his fingers.

She starts to get him a plate of beans and tortilla.

"Open the box," he urges, annoyed, needing a drink.

She takes the lid off the box and puts the shoes aside and strokes the tissue. "It's good for altar matting." She's almost blind from cataracts and stares blankly at him as she rubs the paper with her fingers.

There's a mystery about him, his dark crumpled suit, starched white shirt, his worried features. I want to go to him and hug him but I'm afraid. Drawn by the scents of whiskey, cheap woman's perfume, and cologne, I step into the kitchen and stand in the corner, anxious and excited at the same time. His gold ring, watch, and cuff links flash, hinting at the gambler's life he leads. His eyes have a weary sadness, from drinking and remorse, and as he sees me he hesitates, caught off guard; then he opens his hands toward me and I run past the woodstove and arched doorway into the small room with the kitchen table and bury my face in his suit jacket, holding him tight. Maybe everything will be okay again? He lifts me on his lap and pulls a deck of cards from his breast pocket. He flushes and fantails the cards on the table, tells me to pick one, and guesses the suit and number. We spar a little, because he likes boxing so much and wants me to be a prizefighter.

"One day you'll be on the Gillette card!" He levels his hand to measure my height. "You're getting big and strong."

"I'm going to be like Grandpa," I say. "I can beat up Mocoso!" I say this to impress him but it's not true. Mocoso and I don't even argue.

"You're not supposed to fight," Uncle Carlos says, on entering. He has an annoying trait when he is nervous—he sucks his tongue and makes clicking sounds. Aunt Jesse comes in behind him. The tension in the kitchen rises.

"Don't tell my son what to do," Father tells him, and then, to me, "Get lower, elbows against ribs, dodge and slip. Protect the chin."

"It's a disgrace," Jesse murmurs, as she sits at the table and crosses her arms.

"Get your clothes on," my father says. "We're going. Don't wake your brother and sister." I hurry because I'm afraid my father's going to fight with Carlos, and I'm relieved when we leave. I'm nervous too, because I hope my father doesn't take me on one of his long night drives. We go to the community center, a clapboard barrack with rows of ranch trucks and old cars parked in front. The full moon gives enough light to distinguish the well-worn dirt path leading to the entrance. A woodstove to the right of the door heats the place. My father buys a beer and a soda for me. People see us, and I know by their looks that they know about my father's drinking and my mom's running off with a gringo.

A violin, guitar, and accordion play polkas and *corridos*. I am amazed how couples dance smoothly through so many difficult maneuvers. The priest hurries outside and then scurries inside, urging the young men to pray for blessings, good health and a long life. He fails, however, to dispel their traditional disputes, inflamed by drinking, and by the end of the night they will invariably fight, young Chicanos from one village against young Chicanos from another village, to prove who's the best. Instead of going outside to play like I usually do, tonight I stay close to my father. I sense something bad in the atmosphere.

"Have you seen her?" Damacio asks Frankie, a friend who comes up.

"She may come with her sister from Vaughn," Frankie says. "Her brothers are outside."

My father says nervously, "I just wanted to look in."

"Take care," Frankie advises, his eyes moving to the side with warning.

But instead of avoiding Mom's brothers, my father walks out and goes behind the building, where they're sitting on a truck tailgate. They're laughing with other cowboys. They're big and brutish, guffawing loudly until they see him.

"Is your sister here?"

Albert guzzles his beer and throws the empty can aside. "You better leave her alone. She don't want nothing to do with you, greaser."

Frankie and his friends approach from behind us. "Yeah? You making the rules now?" They are steely-eyed.

"What are you going to do about it?"

My father ignores them and goes to the parking lot and starts peering in from car to car. I don't know what he's doing but I follow. Behind me, I hear the cowboys and Frankie and his friends fighting.

From one of the cars at the end of a row, I'm surprised and scared to see Richard leap out and flee.

A woman grabs me. "Stay here," she warns, but I struggle to get away. I can't see who my father is talking to, but my heart is beating loudly because I think it's my mother.

"Dammit! Why the hell did you leave, huh? Why?" my father wails. The pain in his voice makes me flinch and I break free from the woman's clutch and go closer to hear better. My father cries out, like a man who just got shot, "*¡Hija de la chingada puta madre!*" He grabs my mother by the hair, drags her out of the car, and punches her.

She slaps and scratches back. "My brothers are going to kill you, bastard!"

"Why did you leave me? Sign the divorce papers! Call the police!" He pushes her to the ground and straddles her. His curses and her screams explode like bombs and create deep black craters in my mind and heart. I have trouble breathing, as if a rope is tightening around my neck.

"I am finished with you!" She bites him on the arm and runs off.

My father goes after her. I follow them to the railroad tracks by the warehouses, in an open field. He forces Mom to sit on a discarded couch. It is cold and each can see the other's face clearly in the moonlight.

I crouch in the weeds close enough to overhear them.

"You know"—my father starts, then breaks off—"I drink. I'm trying to stop. I love you, Cecilia."

"You belong over there, Damacio," she says, indicating the Blue Ribbon cantina at the corner. She looks at him with genuine compassion and pity for a moment.

"We belong together," he says. "We drove down that street so many times, holding hands and sitting next to each other. We promised we'd love each other forever. We used to stand over there in the morning and kiss in the sun."

"I'm remarried."

"You can leave him and come back to me," he says.

I am confused by my father's helplessness and by my mother's bluntness.

"I can't let you go. I dream it's possible, that we have a chance." He clenches a wad of dollars from his pocket and throws the money up in the air. "That's what you always wanted—money. And it was never enough. What I got in my front pockets is what my life is worth. When they're empty—I got nothing but the next pool game, the next card game." He sees the wedding ring he bought her and brightens. "You still have the ring?"

"Memories."

"You still love me," he says triumphantly.

She takes the ring off and throws it. "I don't need it."

As if something is burning in my father's throat or cutting him inside, he chokes out the next words. "Cecilia! You have to come back to me!"

"You're wrong," she replies. Her voice is soft, almost forgiving. She looks beautiful, her green eyes and black hair, her light skin. She's wearing a blue dress, with blood on it from my father's bleeding arm. "I got tired of your drinking, hitting me. Of being scared, wondering when you were going to come home, if you were going to be drunk. You're the most handsome man I ever met. I loved you then and I love you now, but I can never be with you. I'm too scared." She starts to sob and tries to stop.

My father turns his head away from her. He too is crying, looking up at the moon and stars. I start to weep, quietly, so they can't hear me.

She continues. "I'll tell you one thing so you know. When I left with Richard that night, we stayed at a motel. After he fell asleep, I went outside and started hitchhiking on the highway. I wanted to come back. It was cold and cars kept passing me, blowing me back. No one would stop. If one had stopped"—she's crying and wiping her nose and eyes—"I would have come back. But afterward, I went to the room—" She pauses to clear her throat and gain control of her crying. "Richard doesn't drink or hit me. That's why I'm with him, not because I love him."

A row of headlights jolts toward them across the field.

"—My brothers!" she gasps.

I watch two of the cowboys hold my father while another cowboy keeps hitting him until he crumples to the ground. My mother tries to stop them but they push her into the weeds. I am paralyzed. One second I am watching them beat my father, and the next instant I'm sprinting blindly into the night; my soul leaves, spins out of my body and flies into the street, the buildings, the trees. My body is a hollow dark shell floating without sensibility. I finally recognize where I am and hide in the shed for a long time. I can't come out. I think the world is ending and all of us are going to die. It's so dark. I hear my Uncle Santiago's voice beyond the dark, calling my name, *Jimmy, Jimmy, where are you?* Then my grandpa's voice calls me. The shed doors open. I can hear someone's footsteps nearing me. I'm under a fifty-gallon oil drum, in total darkness, and I push against the rusty sides, trying to come out to hug my grandpa. I push and push against the barrel but it won't budge. Then I hear a voice, but it's not my grandpa anymore. I keep pushing to lift the barrel and get out.

Are you okay, are you all right? Someone is shaking me, and I'm flailing to lift the barrel. . . .

◆

"Sonofabitch needs medication!" A voice said. I opened my eyes and focused on the guard's face, peering down through the swill slot. "Looked like you were fighting off the devil himself!"

My need to revisit the past was stronger than ever, and my memories were saving me from becoming a zombie in this place with no color, no stimulation, nothing to feed my senses. It unsettled me a bit to know I was in two different worlds, but I was elated by the things that were surfacing in me. I couldn't explain it. However, I knew that my imaginary life was reviving my defenses against the numbing effects of isolation time in the hole, which usually numbed a prisoner's desire to fight to stay human. Prison makes the prisoner gradually accept the sterile emptiness of prison life. I didn't want this to happen to me. On one level I understood this, but I had no real purpose in mind for diving into my past, beyond just simple enjoyment. To kill dead time, I filled the void by entrusting myself to my memories. My body felt young, my heart appeased, my soul vital with renewed determination. I couldn't wait to travel out over the prison walls again. I floated above myself and looked down and saw myself on the cot, then eased out into the world and events all occurred again as if for the first time, growing clearer, closer. I was living again as I had been, as I was.

◆

I am free, past the floodlights on the yard, gliding back to the same good feelings in memories, where I smell the familiar fragrances of cedar and alfalfa. Drifting on a strong wind over great distances. Everything below is tiny, minuscule, like lines on a map. I fly down into the canyons and hills, swooping over grasslands, fearing nothing, filled with joy.

I am five years old. I realize it's spring, time for the fiesta of Our Lady of Mount Carmel. The people cook *posole, menudo,* pinto beans, and tortillas. Musicians play accordions and fiddles. Our Lady of Mount Carmel is lofted along streets amid prayers, and a man behind the procession shoulders a cedar cross. The people arrive at a field outside the pueblo and set the cross upright and carpet the base with a mound of flowers.

At dusk, stone benches are set with food under the cottonwoods. Lanterns hang from branches, a makeshift board floor is set up for the dance area, and *vigas* with oil lanterns mark the corners of the dance floor. Musicians start up, drawing people away from the food to dance.

Mieyo and I are playing in a thin trail of water in an arroyo. After an hour I walk over to a tree where Emiliano is sitting on the ground telling a story. People sit around with children on their laps and listen.

"When La Virgen de Guadalupe tied the belt of her robe in a knot, it was to symbolize that two peoples would join, Spanish and Indian, and from those two were born El Mestizo, us, La Raza."

"How do you know this, Emiliano?" a man asks.

"It is written in the Mayan and Aztec codices that Our Lady would appear at a time when she was most needed."

"But what of the other gods?"

"They are mixed too." Emiliano raises his eyes to the moon. "La Virgen combined with Tonantzin. We combined our Indio gods with Christian ones to make them in our image."

A woman from one of the tables calls "*Antojitos*" and I follow children rushing from all directions to the woman. *Antojitos* are baked sweets—cookies, cakes, sweet breads. I start jumping up and down in line when I see that Juanovera is one of the women handing out the sweets. When it comes our turn, she gives me and Mieyo extra big pieces. I sit on the ground and watch the men around the fire. The flames howl at their faces. Old men toddle past to fill their cups with more homemade wine.

I go walking and see men parked in pickups, wearing work caps, bearded, drinking beer. "It was bad last year," one says. "My cattle were standing in the fields and when I came close to them I saw they were frozen stiff, standing up dead. Even my dog froze on the porch."

I walk to Our Lady of Mount Carmel's altar under a tree and notice the soft tissue paper from shoe boxes Father has brought Grandma cushioning the statue. There are boxes with small gifts in them to Our Lady. They remind me of my mother, of the terrible afternoon when, weeks after she left, a box arrived with our clothes and toys in it. She was not coming back. There was no language, no prayer, no medicine for the pain and loneliness. I stare at the boxes, notice the tiny specks sparkling like distant stars in the soft tissue, and say a prayer for my parents to come back.

My sadness dissipates as I look around and see Grandma sitting with the other women. She is humble and steadfast, aware that life is a gift, gratefulness in her smile. Gray hairs stick out from her chin, gnarled humps of toes bulge out of her scuffed shoes, and cataracts cloud her eyes.

"*¿Quieres algon 'pa comer mejito?*" a woman asks.

I shake my head that I am not hungry.

Drinking with his friend Felix the sheriff, Refugio is slurring. "Attaboy, sommagun, whoaaa, horsie." Grinning spittle, he waves his hand to shake someone else's but stumbles instead into the friend's arms. I go to the campfire where the old men are gathered around, sitting and smoking. Music gives them relief. Others are eating, men group together talking, Refugio and his friends are drinking, Emiliano is telling stories, kids play in the arroyo, dogs sniff around.

I am filled with a serene, communal sense of belonging. I notice how the men's hands are so thick and strong and heavy. Once they grab—at the iron, the tool, the earth—they never let go until matter is bent to their will.

I am looking into the fire when a strong gust comes down from the mountain and blows out the lanterns. There is a swirl of hectic activity, people rushing to their vehicles and wagons and horses with food trays, helping the elderly to safety, folding up tarps, and rushing for cover. I find shelter from the wind in the cracks between two huge boulders and watch people fleeing headlong.

◆

Had I been able to share my feelings that moment, I would have said what I was able to add years later, lying on my cot in an isolation cell in total darkness. I would have said I felt the many lives that had come before me, the wind carrying within the vast space of the range, and all that lived in the range—cows, grass, insects—but something deeper. Old women leaving their windows open so the breeze can pass through the rooms, blessing the walls, chasing away evil spirits, anointing floors, beds, and clothing with its tepid hand. The breeze excites larks to jackknife over the park pond, knocks on doors to ask people to remember their ancestors, peels paint off trucks and scrapes rust from windmill blades and withers young shoots of alfalfa, cleans what it touches and brings age and emptiness to dirt roads. This breeze blows on my brow sometimes when I'm on the prairie, and I feel immortal; it whispers, Better times will come, and I believe my dreams will come true. The breeze chases the young heels of children and pulls at little girls' ponytails, draws red happiness out from their hearts and pools it in their cold cheeks, scruffs youth up, tugs at old women's long-sleeved bereavement dresses, sweeps away veils and handkerchiefs and dries their tears. It roars up from canyons, whistles from caves, blows fountains of green leaves across the air, loosens shale from cliffs, tears cottonwood pods, and bursts them to release fluffy cotton that sails past puffs of chimney smoke.

I felt it all, the magic that Emiliano had urged me to feel and worship, to surrender to. The wild wind tossed itself on top of grass ends and nibbled seeds, danced with dust, took hold of the devil and swung him around a cactus, through sagebrush, to the music of a hundred insect wings vibrating and snakes hissing. It scurried on, laughing a chill down the spines of vaqueros on horseback, making their ponies lay their ears back, attentive to the spirits. It howled and thrashed in arroyos and launched itself in swoops, veering off sides of boulders and loose tin, creeping into the pueblo, scattering its ancient sandy prayers. The wind reclined in flame and swung itself to sleep, played with tumbleweeds, untwined itself like a slow-opening music box, and gave to the naked woman sleeping with her lover a threadbare love song, to the man meditating on life under a tree its lyrical wounds. The wind, the wind, the wind: ruffles curtains with its remorse, flings the child's weeping complaint over post fences, muffles grief in the graying hair of middle-aged women, thuds at back doors and windows, slaps broken lumber against hinges, makes dogs cower behind houses, destroys tender gardens, effaces names on cemetery headstones, and makes my heart ache as blowing sand buries a wedding ring in the field. I felt all my people, felt them deep in the hard work they did, in faint and delicate red-weed prairie flowers, in the arguments over right and wrong, in my people's irascible desire to live, which was mine as well. I felt their will was growing inside me and would ultimately let me be free as the wind.

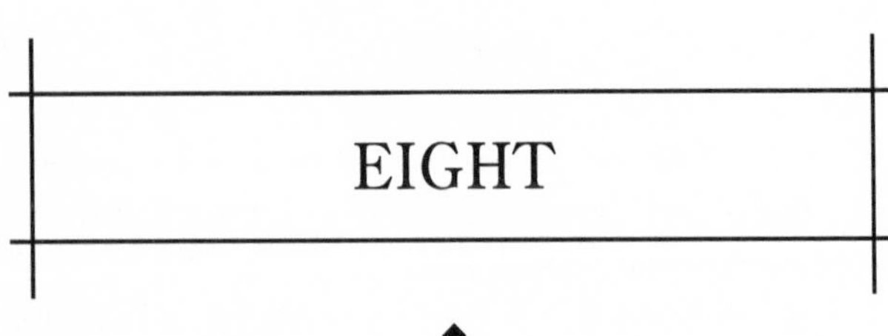

EIGHT

I was lost in the shifting phantoms of the past, and yet I still struggled to reach a present that seemed beyond my grasp. Time and space were jumbled in my mind. I had a hard time concentrating. And so when the door to my isolation cell unexpectedly opened, I squinted at the shadow in the doorway, wondering if my imagination was playing tricks on me.

When I began to search my mind to explore my memories of Estancia—bouncing in my uncle's truck through crisp cottonwood leaves around the pond, going to the foothills across a creek—suddenly a blade edge would glint and my knife would stick in the Mexican's stomach. The silver blade would chop the pastoral scene to pieces: the Mexican's face cringing in agony and shock, the cook fearfully crouching under the stainless steel table as oatmeal boiled over on the stove and mixed with blood trailing into the floor drain. I tried pushing the violent images away but it often didn't work, and I was relieved that a guard was really here to escort me.

As I dressed, my sense of smell was sharp and I could sense the morning air outside mixed with the stale inside odors of sweat, bad breath, rusty steel, and concrete. At first I felt morose and gloomy, but within minutes I started to feel the excitement of being released after a long time of isolation.

Skinnier, unshaven, blinking like a madman, I held my pants up with my hands as we descended the concrete stairway. The air grew lighter and cooler. It felt good to walk more than three paces at a time. I followed the guard down to the ground-floor tier, and then through several gates that divided segregated units on punitive lockdown. I kept telling myself everything was the same, but it wasn't. I was seeing things as if for the first time because something was different inside *me.*

I felt better than I had in months, almost lighthearted. Above and to my right were grimy windows unwashed for decades and welded shut with bars. The sun coming up through the bars was warm and beautiful. A few prisoners on death row to my left were writing letters. I wondered how they endured each day, inching toward the appointed hour. My escort unlocked the last gate. Guards moving in other parts of the cell block set off vague echoes. We passed the main guard station and went out on the landing that opened to the yard, where everything seemed wide open.

I looked around, taking everything in. It seemed I had been away for a long time. The main-yard walls and cell blocks and the main guard tower in the center loomed menacingly, in stark contrast to the freedom I was feeling. Yes, something had opened up in me and started a new stirring in my heart. I didn't need to explain it, just to enjoy it while it lasted.

All I wanted was a cigarette, a hot cup of coffee, and my own cell in the block. I wanted to get back to work, go to chow, and exercise. Newly arriving prisoners, carrying freshly starched prison blues and brogans to DC, glanced at me, pretending not to be afraid. I knew they were as scared as I had been, and I gave them a begrudging glare. They still had to prove themselves in here. Other cons marched in twos to work in the fields, passing the open-air shower stalls attached to a section of the main-yard wall by the gates. At the commissary window, cons lined up to buy cinnamon rolls, cigarettes, and coffee, envelopes, pencils, and writing pads, the cost deducted from money on the books earned at twelve cents an hour.

Wind whirled and clouds obscured the sun. The sky darkened with rolling thunderheads and lightning. Adrenaline rushed wildly through my twenty-two-year-old body. The air turned dusky, and spotlights flickered on above the razor wire on the walls. At the main gates, shift-change guards were turning over keys and clipboard rosters to the next shift. Above them, sparrows chirped excitedly, veering around the razor wire and the Wheelhouse, swooping over walls and away from the sullen-faced tower guards. It began to sprinkle; I lifted my face to the sky and closed my eyes to feel the rain on my skin. In isolation, how often I had dreamed of doing this very thing! Suddenly Big Foot was standing next to me. He yelled up at the Wheelhouse guard that we were going to the warden's.

Parked outside the door of the square cinder-block office was the white golf cart with a canvas canopy in which the warden rode around the yard with his guard-chauffeur.

It was a lot cooler inside. The concrete floor was waxed to a high dark gloss and the walls were painted flat gray. To my left was a light blue windbreaker and white cowboy hat; a leather shoulder holster hung on a steer-horn coat rack. A leaky swamp cooler hummed at the window and blew on Warden Howard, sitting at his desk. I watched him on the phone, his face mashed against the receiver as if he were trying to bite whoever was on the other end. He was clean-shaven, with heavy bags under his blue eyes, and he was fingering a religious medal on a chain beneath his shirt. A sunburned hat line ran around his forehead. He wore fancy brown boots, a blue pearl-button shirt with fancy threading, and Western dress jeans with pointed pockets.

Howard glanced at me, and I could feel the anger in his eyes. Just before I had rolled into prison, he'd come from Ohio, where he was a warden at a time when prisoners there had taken over his prison. He had driven a National Guard tank into the compound and blasted away at cell blocks, blowing up both cons and hostages. After he put the riot down, Arizona officials hired him for Florence, where there'd been a rash of gang killings and two guards murdered. He restored order by allowing guards to beat cons for any disciplinary infraction. Then he segregated the gang bangers. He ruled through intimidation, beatings, and lockdowns, and by taking away time served and imposing his own sentences. He could not be sued for breaking laws, so, being immune from punishment, he did what he wanted and flaunted his authority.

He exhaled through flared nostrils and jerked his husky shoulders to get the tightness out of them. Still on the phone, he stood and stared out the window at the yard. The swamp cooler lapsed, then surged to its normal speed. Accustomed to convicts listening to him without interrupting, he now listened, his ruddy faced flushed, his lips grim. Impatiently, he swiped at his thinning brown hair and snapped a string of curses into the phone about how his wife was upset because the plants were delivered dead. He demanded live ones and slammed the phone down.

Big Foot tapped my shoulder with his nightstick, and I sat. There was an odd silence as I watched the warden flip through my folder—not the kind of silence in isolation but a forced, taut silence that made his presence more menacing. On top of the steel filing cabinet and on the wall behind his desk were law-enforcement distinctions: seniority plaques, service duty awards, police academy diplomas. I couldn't imagine who would give such a man a ribboned basket of fruit or the decorative silver inkwell and pen set on his desk.

He finally looked at me. "My job is to run this prison, give citizens a good night's sleep, so they can go about their business without fear." His cold blue eyes drilled into me. My facial muscles tightened as he came around the desk, stocky as a tree stump, broad-shouldered, carrying himself as if ready to fight, his jaw rigid. Shoving his face in mine, he shouted, *"You understand that?"*

The force of his voice made me flinch, but I managed to stare straight ahead and avoid showing I was scared. As flecks of spittle sprayed my face, his tongue moved back and forth in his mouth.

"Since you rolled in you been nothing but a pain in the ass. A malingerer. A troublemaking malingering sonofabitch!"

I didn't know what *malingerer* meant. I was trying to be agreeable, but my voice shook slightly as I said, "I'm not trying to cause trouble."

After what seemed a long silence, he said, "I run this place. I own your ass. You understand *that*? You fuck with me"—he stuck his pissed-off face in mine again—"and you don't know what I can put you through." His coffee breath and the doughnut sprinkles melting in the crevices of his teeth almost made me gag.

"You're a gang member," he claimed.

"In a gang?" I said, surprised. "Never. I've never—" I started to protest but didn't. I had often been approached by gangs to join, but I always turned them down.

"Don't play stupid! You want to collect the contract on Rick because Rick snitched, and a dealer laid two grand to take him out! You're no slicker than the rest of the scumbags I've nailed. I'm taking away your good time and you're starting your sentence over."

"But I didn't—it wasn't—" I stopped short of saying anything more. And looked straight ahead.

He pointed his finger right in my face. "There's a craziness in you," he said, and walked back to his desk.

Maybe there *was* a craziness in me. If so, it came from the fact that the contrast between the innocent boy in Estancia and the terrified man wielding the cleaver was too hard for me to comprehend, much less explain. He had already decided I was in a gang. But if he was right about my craziness, part of it came from being in the hole sixty days and from my nightmares of the Mexican's guts pouring out of his belly, of him holding his intestines in his hands.

"I don't need proof. What I believe is enough," he said sharply.

My neck trembled and my eyes itched. I hardened myself, waiting for another outburst.

"Get in line or I'll hand you your balls," he said. "You gang bangers can kill each other, but if anything happens to Rick, I'll bury your ass. No one breaches security in my prison. No one." He paused and turned toward the window and the overcast sky. "I don't want to hear from you again. Now get out of here."

"Yes, sir," I replied weakly.

◆

For the next few months, snug in my blue denim coat and beanie cap, I went out at 4:30 A.M. with the kitchen workers and lined up in the yard for head count. Then we marched to work. These were the finest moments, before the world woke up, when the moon was so bright it bathed the prison grounds in beautiful haunting shadows, light and stillness. I could smell prairie herbs. The Wheelhouse tower guard, the stars in the dark sky, the razor wire and walls—my past all seemed mere reflections of a bad dream that would pass when I woke up. The beauty of the desert dawns also strengthened my determination not to be a corpse carted out of the cell block on a gurney, covered in a sheet, toe-tagged, and buried behind the prison. I would never forget that half a mile from here the road I came in on led back to Albuquerque. I was going to be on it one day, heading home, or die trying.

After scrubbing pots and pans, I'd go back to my cell on the second tier. CB2 was constantly noisy with the racket of clanging gates, stereos blasting, cons shouting, and guards yelling out orders. After my cell gate closed behind me, sliding on a greasy tow chain, I'd sit on my bunk and roll State Issue smokes from the stringy bad-tasting tobacco they gave out for free. I'd rest my arms on the bars, smoking a cigarette, watching runners drop off drugs or other stuff.

Once a week I stripped my cot and tucked in fresh sheets, folding the coarse blanket at the foot of the bunk, stacking my freshly washed prison blues on the top bunk, lining my toothbrush, paste, comb, and shaver on a hanky next to my clothes. During showers when the cells were opened, the gangs waited until last to shower because they were gossiping about who was going to get who. I'd do push-ups and sit-ups, pace, and stare out the bars until lights were turned off at nine. In the darkness, cons bluffed in a game of one-up, cutting each other down to see who could come up with the worst insult to tire themselves out so they could sleep. Curled up under my blanket, wearing my pants and T-shirt and beanie cap because of the night cold, I'd think how we all had our places where we once felt happy—even gang soldiers had their own Estancias, forgotten over time, just as mine was slowly fading since getting out of the hole.

But while these memories did fade, my routine never did. Each day I shaved off another sliver of time. The conflict with La eMe was a fact of life; my enemy walked next to me in line, celled next to me, ate at the next table, exercised with me on the field. In the cell-block foyer, solemn-faced mafia soldiers hunkered in a circle and gave me contemptuous stares. Brujo's mafiosos mad-dogged me and I remained ready, knowing they were waiting for their chance to get me. Entering and exiting the block, looking up at the cells, I saw them watching me. Sooner or later, for a left-over heroin cotton or spoon residue, one would try.

It happened one afternoon when I got off work early and the cell block was almost empty. Porters were carrying bundles of dirty laundry out, yard crews were shuffling off, trusties were running errands, and I had just stepped out of the shower when two soldiers came at me. I saw them heading my way and was ready to jump down two floors when I saw a mop bucket outside the shower, one of those heavy old-fashioned steel ones with the roller on it. I picked it up and went for them. They did a quick U-turn down the stairwell. From that point, I never took a shower without my shank in reach.

Wedo gave me the latest on who was paying protection, who was extorting who, and what the current rumors were. He was one of those who couldn't do his own time and he was always yelling at some con he was going to beat up on the field. He was freelancing in the strong-arm business, collecting poker debts and interest payments on drug fronts, and he and his two crime partners, Can Do and Gamboa, tried to get me selling drugs. I kept out of trouble, though, and even took on extra jobs. After general population ate and I finished scrubbing the pots, I'd load the chow cart and follow the guard to each of the three cell blocks to feed cons in the isolation cells. Depending on who the guard was, I'd smuggle tobacco, papers, and matches between slices of toast or under cereal boxes.

I counted the months until my reclass hearing day finally came. It was a wonderful spring day, and here and there in the hard-packed dirt of the yard sprouted little blossoms. I was feeling strong and hopeful and optimistic because everything had been going well for me. I went into DC through the scanners and handed my slip to the bull in the guard station. He motioned me to sit with others on a bench down the left-wing hall in front of the hearing room. The guys were talking about court appeals, writing chicks, or getting drugs from girlfriends on visiting day. The block speakers thundered out numbers, making my first weeks in prison come back to me. I wondered how Macaron was doing. I'd heard he was a minimum-security trusty, outside the walls. They got a lot of privileges—nice white khakis instead of blues, conjugal time with their girlfriends, better food, and more visits, and they got to walk around freely. If I could persuade the committee to let me go to school, it would be a start toward making my way out there. Cons were going in and coming out pretty quickly, getting classified to a lesser-security status and better jobs.

My number was called and I went in.

The room was small and painted all white, bright enough to blind me momentarily and make my eyes water. Five committee members sat behind a long folding table, with a recorder on it, serious as a high crimes tribunal. Under the overhead fluorescent tubing, their starched beige uniforms, brass badges, rank stripes on sleeves, and name tags gave them a forbidding formality: Captain (Mad Dog) Madril, Captain (Five Hundred) Smith, Lieutenant (Big Foot) Naya, a black sergeant, and the counselor, the last wearing casual sports wear. They opened my prison folder.

Mad Dog Madril punched the black portable recorder button and started, "Three-two-five-eight-one?"

"Yes, sir," I replied.

"Says you want to attend school," Five Hundred mumbled to himself, looking down, reading. He was a big blond guard. His son, Smitty, was in prison in the same block I was in. It was weird seeing him lock his son up. Smitty was a tough guy who was always fighting cons who ridiculed him because of his father.

"You've had problems adjusting," the counselor said.

"I'm adjusting," I said, searching his face for a hint of alliance. Now and then, over the past few months, he'd stopped at my cell to tell me how good I was doing.

Captain Five Hundred said, "You been in—sixteen months."

"Commendable job performance," the black sergeant added.

"I haven't missed a day, sir," I said proudly.

"You in a gang?" Mad Dog Madril asked.

"No, sir, never. Gang members have to get tattoos to be in, and I don't have any." I was wearing my T-shirt, and they could see for themselves.

"You think it's time you took responsibility for your actions?" The counselor's voice was accusatory.

"Yes, sir, when it's mine—"

Before I could go on, the black sergeant pitched in. "You're in for a violent crime. You're a menace to society. An FBI agent was shot; you escaped. Don't tell me your record isn't bad."

"Because you don't have a long rap sheet only means you've gotten away with a lot of things," the counselor stated.

I was confused. What could I say or do to convince them I was earnestly trying to do as they wanted, when every time I tried they put me back two steps? Why were they doing this? Had someone told them something? Had they had made up their minds before I walked in? Was it because a FBI agent had been shot during the drug bust? Had Rick said something to them? Had the warden given orders? I wanted to scream that I just wanted to get on with my time, but I sat there, stunned.

Mad Dog Madril glanced at the others. "Anything else?"

"Probationary period six months," Big Foot said, and wrote it down in my file.

Mad Dog Madril lowered his voice into the recorder for closing comments.

"This committee cannot in good faith recommend school at the present time. Prisoner is assigned field duty for six months. Request for schooling will be considered at that point." He shut the recorder off.

I was almost on the verge of begging them to reconsider. Feeling a great emptiness overwhelm me, I raised my eyes to the counselor and blurted, "You promised—you stood in front of my cell telling me how great I was doing!" I felt my whole body swell with an explosion of rage.

He leaned forward. "It's a fucking prison and don't you forget it. You're here to be punished."

"But the fights; I had to do what I did. You know what's going on. I was defending myself!"

Mad Dog Madril snarled, "Three-two-five-eight-one, you're dismissed."

I couldn't move. I wanted to start the whole proceeding over and ask them what I had done wrong. I would have apologized and even admitted I was guilty of whatever they wanted me to be guilty of, but in each committee member's face there was only contempt and hostile disinterest. Despair and pain were mounting rapidly toward eruption, and I was afraid I was going to black out. I was trying to control myself, but my hands and legs had no feeling in them. An overwhelming sadness swept through me, an all-consuming sense of helplessness that ate through my face and hands and legs, burning me down to nothing, to the end of my life in this room, my whole aching soul and heart hating them.

"*Dismissed!*" Mad Dog Madril commanded.

I don't know where it came from, my sudden inability to move. It wasn't courage or defiance. I just sat there until Mad Dog Madril and Five Hundred came around the table and grabbed me and stood me up.

I can still see myself. I've gone over and over it. All I remember is hearing myself yell, "I know what I was! But I'm trying to change! I'm just asking for a fucking chance!" But the simple truth was, from the warden on down to the guards, they had the power of life and death over me. And I truly thought they were going to keep me in prison forever.

◆

I tried not to think about what had happened in the hearing room. But after a while, with nothing to occupy my thoughts, I had to. I wasn't the same after my hearing, and the next day I stayed in my cell, snacking on sweet rolls and candy bars. I didn't shower, I didn't speak, I just lay on my back and stared at the underside of the top bunk, deciphering the graffiti and trying to explain my behavior. I tried to look at it from different ways, feeling the greatest desolation and hoping to understand why I just sat there. When the intercom crackled out my number at dawn for work, the cell opened but I didn't fall out. I felt removed from everything. I had already blown my opportunity to go to school and I didn't even have a clue as to why. I had always been able to endure anything, take it in stride, and move on; always the bad shit with the good because life always offered small clearings in the gloom in which I felt blessed and happy. What was wrong? I had no answers then, but looking back today, I know what happened: I knew in my soul that if I had gone along with their classifying me as they wished, simply ignoring my request for school, that I would still be in prison today.

Flaco and Chacho yelled up from the landing, but I told them I wasn't going and motioned them on. They understood I was doing what I had to do. I'd already gotten two disciplinary write-ups for not going to work, and the situation was becoming a standoff. But going into the second week, they began to worry. I felt guilty when I saw my homeboys worrying about me. I saw them murmuring among themselves and then their voices shot up.

"Come on, *carnal,* let's go," Icy urged.

"What's up, homeboy?" Choo-Choo asked.

"Let's kick it, *vato,*" Zero said.

"*¡No andas chafiando!*" Gamboa growled. Don't be kidding like this.

To this day I still feel bad when I remember looking at them behind my cell bars. I knew what really counted with them was respect and loyalty. We were solid partners; they watched my back and I theirs. I also remember they were willing to give their lives for me and how it hurt me in my soul not to be able to be with them as I usually was, laughing and horsing around. Most of my acquaintances knew I wanted to do good; we'd talked about going to GED school together when we walked around the field, and they hadn't seen this side of me. How could I have told them I hadn't expected it either? I didn't know why I didn't get up out of the chair. Coming from the very depths of my soul, it was beyond my control. Sure, I had had enough of the hole, but my defiance was going beyond casual noncompliance to serious opposition.

I worried about not only what was going on with me but also with everybody else. I knew they thought maybe I had a problem with someone, and I might be afraid to confront the guy. To their minds, it was impossible. Wasn't I the guy who kicked ass, who strapped down against La eMe, who spent so much time in isolation? My defiance had strengthened them, fortified their resolve to confront anyone. And now, *"¿Qué estaba pasando con el vato?"* they asked themselves. What was happening with him? They went to the chow hall without me, dismayed that they didn't understand and couldn't help me through my dilemma.

Over the next week I quit making my bunk and cleaning my cell. As usual, every time the bull came down the tier, he placed a write-up on the bars for breaking institutional rules. When I looked at the pile of pink slips, I had the feeling I was fucking everything up. I also knew that by simply refusing to take them off the bars, I was deflating the importance of what they represented. For the next few days, when the tier guard stood in front of my cell with his clipboard at count time and barked out my number and I'd turn my back to him like he wasn't there, he'd place another write-up on the bars and move on. The cons wondered when I might get up and stand for count time, but I never did.

To this day, it still amazes me how taking myself out of the system and refusing to work had everybody in an upheaval, from my friends to the guards. The more I did nothing, the more aggravated everyone became. It was the first time I felt I was accomplishing something, even though I couldn't see why. Regardless of what little my life meant in the larger scheme of things, at least for the moment it was mine and not the warden's, despite what he had shouted at me. It didn't belong to the state, the judge, the guards, or the cons either. They'd told me all my life what to do, and I had obeyed. But I couldn't take it anymore.

Before my reclass hearing, I was getting it together. I had friends and respect. I was starting to believe I was going to make it. Who knew that not working would take me out of my life as I lived it into a whole new chaotic and unrecognizable reality?

It started with my homies. At first they extended their hands and hearts to help me with whatever might be disturbing me. They would stop at my cell and exchange a few words. Now they avoided me. They avoided my eyes or, if they did look, it was a quick side view that meant they now suspected me of being a coward, of betraying their trust, of letting them down. I could sense the peer pressure boiling over, the secret accusations in their blood, the hard core stone-cold glares, and finally I heard the words I dreaded.

"Maybe he's a snitch?"

"He's a punk."

"He's afraid."

"Es puto, no vale verga, no tiene corazón, chale con aquel vato." He's a sissy, he ain't worth it, doesn't have heart, forget that dude.

Guards on every shift routinely came to my cell and, raking a baton across the bars, called my number. When I just stared back, they checked my number off on a clipboard and placed another write-up slip on the others.

The counselor came up on the third week. "What the hell you trying to pull?" He stood away from the bars.

"Fuck you, liar," I said, and turned my back on him and faced the sink. I spooned coffee in my plastic cup and filled it with hot water from the tap and stirred it. I turned and stared at him. Behind him other cons across the way were watching. I drank the coffee and felt it warm and bitter in my stomach. The whole time I was glaring at him I was thinking how he had set me up. My look must have frightened him, because he left without saying anything.

Later, when everyone had come in from work and was showering and getting ready for supper, five guards stormed through the front of the block into the landing with riot-gear helmets, shields, and batons. In the lead, Mad Dog Madril yelled at the tier guard to rack my cell as the goons clomped up the shaking stairwell.

"Shake it down!" Mad Dog was seething. He pushed me out on the tier in my boxers, without shirt or shoes or pants. Cons stuck their mirrors out through bars and I could see their confused faces, questioning eyes. The goons ripped the mattress apart, squeezed out the toothpaste tube, emptied my tobacco bag, searching my cell for a shank or drugs. They found a small packet of sugar from the kitchen.

"Add contraband to the charges!" Mad Dog commanded. Five Hundred jabbed me with his stick and marched me down into the landing in the middle of the block. Cons stood at the bars as one voice and then another and another cursed in a deafening roar. They shook the bars, yelping like hyenas snarling over fresh kill. Their eyes were hard and glassy. I tried to tell myself they were cursing the guards, but it was me they were condemning.

I remember the humiliation of seeing them grip the bars and push their angry faces forward as they screamed. They had revealed their secrets to me, and believing I had turned on them made me no different from all the perpetrators who had killed their spirits. I was the friend they had embraced and who then had stabbed them in the back.

That was one of the worst and strangest days of my life. Their rage and censure were forcing me to find something out about myself which didn't exist yet but which I felt struggling to come out. Stripped of everything I believed in—pride, friends, my reputation for being a solid con were all gone now—I felt as if I was on the verge of discovering something beyond what I knew about myself in the world.

I was facing the tiers toward my cell when a cup of scalding water hit me in the shoulder from behind. I turned and someone else threw urine and then someone else a Styrofoam cup of feces. It was as if I was standing outside myself and watching this. I told myself it had nothing to do with me. I wiped my face with my hands. The yelling caught on and the whole block was cursing me from both sides.

When I go back to that night now, I think I felt at the time that I was insane. That it would only be a matter of time before I swirled into a black pit of disintegration. With wide eyes, I watched the ones who didn't scream watch me with detached pity. *They* certainly thought I was crazy. If it happened to me, they thought, it could happen to anyone. Even them. Anyone could break. A link in the chain had snapped, and for that their repugnance stormed down on me, shaking tiers and trembling concrete. I stood quietly taking it all in, pretending to myself that someone else was standing there.

Mad Dog Madril came down and chained me around the waist, hands, and wrists. Then he and his goons marched me out of the block.

Outside, going across the yard, I knew that, despite this loathing, by standing up for myself I had done something completely new. I might have lost the respect of my peers, but I was feeling a sense of my own worth that I had never felt before. I knew I was no longer a twenty-two-year-old illiterate brown man, not just another con with a number who was going to submit to degradation. Something had altered in me. I felt tremendous pride in having taken this one little step. I now knew I had wanted to take it for a long time.

◆

This isolation cell was much smaller than the others I had been in. It was my third time in the hole, but no matter how many times you go in, you never get used to it. I tried to review the events that had put me here again, but I couldn't concentrate. Adrenaline was pulsing so strong in me that I could feel my blood pounding away in my bare feet, my arms, my hands. I listened to the noises of the prison, thinking about the tons of steel and granite that surrounded me and feeling them pushing in like a vise to squeeze the life out of me. I got up and took three steps to the rusty sink, pushed the button, cupped my left palm under the spout, and rinsed myself with cold water. Then I sat down on the floor, drew up my legs, crossed my arms on my knees, and rested my head on my arms. I could still feel myself trembling. I shook my hands out, massaged my arms, and tried to calm my breathing, inhaling and exhaling slowly. I rubbed my face with my hands, trying to shake off my confusion.

I began to question how I might have handled it differently. But there were no answers, just a growing explosion in me, like a deep cry to have a life, or at least a chance at having one. I thought how even as a kid I'd had no options except to take the hurt that came my way. As I grew a little older, I learned to strike back. It had been the quickest way to get rid of the pain, a way to show people I was alive. Until now. This time I didn't lash out, which short-circuited everyone's expectation of how a con was supposed to act. Despite the guilt of letting a lot of solid convicts down, not doing what everyone expected turned out to be the most powerful thing I ever did.

Behind my closed eyelids, I wanted to lose myself in a sweet memory, and my thoughts wandered off to the wind's blowing dust so that my mother and I snugged newspapers and rags in window crevices and doorjambs to keep the prairie grit from entering. I saw images of my peaceful village, the chimney stacks with woodstove smoke, the calm fields between adobe houses, and I'm holding Grandma's hand, standing next to my sister and brother in the bright sunny yard. In anguish my legs shake with fear and I pee my pants. Mother is telling Grandma she'll be back, but I see Richard's beet-red face. She's lying. She's leaving. I run and hide in La Casita's crawl space where no one can see me or find me. I clench my fingers tight to create pain, bending my fingers until they hurt. I'm pissed off and I start kicking and it's cramped and isolated and dark under the shack.

Alongside this memory, I realize I'm not under the shack, I'm in this cell, but then I'm thrown back to Estancia, where my Grandpa cannot get out of bed. With my Grandpa near me, I was certain that life would always be happy. But when Grandpa had a heart attack while scrubbing floors at school, everything changed for me. The shaman Emiliano, a friend of Grandpa's, came over and spent the entire morning praying and giving him herbal liquids. He did healing ceremonies, but they didn't dissipate the menacing pall that hung over Grandma's house.

"Two spoons sugar and cream," I had said to Grandpa, full of delight that morning, thinking coffee would surely get him out of bed. He had always risen before dawn, but it had been two weeks and Grandpa was still in bed.

"'Sta . . . bien," Grandpa had whispered, forcing a smile and nodding to the chair.

I said, "Get dressed, Grandpa. I'll walk with you to school."

He opened his eyes, as if reading my mind, and said, "*Jugamos mañana, mejito.*" We will play tomorrow. Then he closed his eyes. He was weak and breathing with labor. The wrinkles on his face were no longer smile creases but death claws, slowly raking my Grandpa away from me. I went outside and ran. I watched a hawk drifting backwards and watched it glide sideways, wings stiff against the breeze. For a moment the hawk whirled off balance, then it regained its poise. I took it as a sign that the hawk was my Grandpa, fighting against death. I watched it fighting the wind, trying to assume an aerial stance, but the wind kept buffeting it back and down, and then with startling grace it regained its glide and flew toward the Manzano peaks until it was a mere speck.

It was late in the afternoon when I went back to Grandma's. Trucks and cars were parked around the house. I made my way through adults weeping in the kitchen, and in the back room I peeked in to see Grandpa sleeping in bed. I was curious about the candles in the room and the group of old women with black veils praying, my Grandma among them, each with a rosary in her hand.

Uncle Julian grabbed me and forced me through the crowd and back out into the yard. He took me to the shed and smacked me across my head and shoulders, ordering me to stay there until morning. He kept saying, "It's your fault! It's your fault! All the worry you cause!"

"My fault?" I asked, not understanding.

He glared. "Grandpa died! And you're to blame, always worrying him!"

I yelled back, "I didn't do it! I didn't do it!"

Julian locked the shed and left. I peeked at him through the board cracks and looked around, expecting Grandpa to come out of the shadows. The evening light cast a sadness over the warped rafters, broken hoes, old hammers and shovels. He had worked hard and lived humbly. He prayed to live one more sunrise, to hear another song from the dove, to go to the woodpile and chop a log and put it in the stove and feel the heat on his palms, to savor one more plate of *huevos rancheros* and drink one more cup of coffee with milk and sugar.

He loved going to the community center on fiesta days, greeting his old friends under the colored string bulbs and listening to the fiddlers, accordion players, and guitarists. The women set out beans, squash, frijoles, tortillas, *empanaditas, bizcochitos, chile verde,* enchiladas, burritos, and tacos. The young men cried out and kicked up scuffed boots, cowboy hats cocked back, guffawing loudly and carelessly, lifting partners off the floor and twirling them. Men patted each other on the back, sharing stories about work.

He was hired as janitor for the first school in Estancia, a two-story building with windows brought in from Kansas and red flagstone brought in on wagons from surrounding red cliffs. The job came at a good time. He was having trouble breathing because of chemicals sprayed on plants in the fields where he had always worked. His joints hurt with arthritis, his knees burned, and his back ached. He read from the Bible and prayed the rosary each night. To him the most important tools in life were a good pair of work boots, a pair of gloves, denim overalls, and long johns. Putting on his secondhand suit coat and fedora at dawn, he'd say, "I think I'll chop wood." When he came back into the kitchen, carrying an armful of wood, he smelled of cedar shavings, and he'd sprinkle some on the hot woodstove top to fill the house with their fragrance. He would tell me stories on the way to school, about how he drove to the salt flats to load his wagon and trade the salt to Indians for fish, deerskins, and herbs. The simple times had changed, he said, and I knew what he meant. He saw what was happening to his family: Refugio and Damacio drinking every day, my mother leaving us, newcomers stealing our land and calling it homesteading. Ruined ranchers and farmers came and went through Grandma's kitchen, grieving the loss of their land because of new tax laws they didn't understand. To make a living, they left for Chicago or LA and never came back. One by one, families were disappearing, and life as Grandpa had known it was changing, and he died of a broken heart. His absence had always been a hurting I carried in my heart without recourse to God.

I had wanted to escape into sweet memories, but now I was thrashing like a leaf in a prairie duststorm and thinking one couldn't have had a worse life than mine. Suddenly I understood, not with my mind but with my body. I was sweating and the heat was unbearable in the isolation cell. Even as I gritted my teeth trying to stop the images, I saw a freeway and I remembered raising my face to the wind.

◆

I feel cold wind blowing my thick black hair. Mieyo and I are in the back of my uncle's truck, heading into Albuquerque. We're dropped off at Saint Anthony's Boys' Home. For weeks after that I weep under the massive summer branches of a huge cottonwood by the outside pool. I wait every Sunday by the gate next to the grotto of our Sacred Mother. From the gate I see arriving families getting out of cars, carrying bags of clothes and candy for kids they've come to visit. Every Sunday I wait there for my mother to appear. Children's names are called over the loudspeakers, and after their visits I see them coming out of the main building to my left, smiling and carrying gifts. My name is never called, but I wait until dusk and the last cars drive off into the evening before I go in.

The orphanage evenings are despairing, but one early Sunday morning, when I'm watching visitors arrive, I think I recognize my mother climbing out of a car. My heart leaps up in my throat and I can't wait to see her. I sneak out of the dining room and head up to the second floor to the Blue Room, where visitors wait for kids. Sister Anna Louise, coming down the stairs, catches me and orders me back to the dining room. She says I am not to go roaming the halls. But nothing can stop me from seeing my mother. She's here to take me home with her. I *knew* she would come back! Back in the dining room, when I think I've given Sister Anna Louise time to go about her business, I take off again, down the hallway, dashing around the corner to go up the stairs to the second floor and into the Blue Room where relatives meet their kids. As I turn the corner at a full gallop, a hand shoots out and grabs my shirt and throws me on the floor on my back. Sister Anna Louise is over me, screaming that she told me not to leave the dining room. She slaps me until my cheeks go numb, saliva forming at her thin lips, her eyes narrowed with rage. But even after the beating, when she drags me back to the dining room and leaves, I cut out again. This time I use a different route. I go around the front of the building, up the stairs, into the Blue Room—and the lady in the chair is not my mother.

A few years pass, and it has now been a long time that my parents have been away. I'm older and bigger when I'm called to

Sister Superior's office. She says that since I'm thirteen she's going to send me to Boys' Town. Attempts at placing me in a foster home have failed. When prospective parents come, my brother and I are never chosen. Our hair, our color, our speech—everything is wrong about us. She asks me how I feel and other personal questions, and I respond with shrugs, not really caring about anything. I already know what I'm going to do. That night I sneak out of my dorm and meet my brother by the fence. He promises he'll follow me as I take off down the ditch under the stars, crossing the alfalfa fields until I stop at the place we're supposed to meet. He never comes. Later the cops arrest me for running away. After several runaways I'm finally taken to the Detention Center for Boys and put behind bars. In the end, as always, a cell is the only place they have for kids without families.

◆

I tried to prevent these memories from surfacing, but they refused to be repressed anymore. I wasn't dreaming, it was all happening in my head as I lay awake. I wanted to run like I did as a kid but I was in this cell. I had nothing. Martina and Mieyo had each other. Uncle Refugio, the bottle, drinking every day. Father, fighting and drunkenly searching for Mother. Uncle Santiago, respect from his friends and love and work with his ranch animals. Grandpa and Grandma had God and each other. Uncle Carlos and Aunt Jesse, money and power. All of them knew where they were going, knew that upon waking up in the morning their shoes would be under the bed where they placed them the night before. I didn't know anything about the crazy world. I didn't know where trains came from, how windows are made, if trees are like humans and have minds and hearts. I didn't know. I lay down, pretending my cell floor was the dirt under the small shack beside Grandma's house. I didn't move but hugged my knees, feeling the coldest I'd ever felt, loathing myself, regretting being born. A sickly despair made me want to throw up. I squeezed my eyelids to push the hurting memories out, but all that did was make me weep out all my pent-up anxiety and frustration.

I wept with an overwhelming fear about what was happening to me and what I was doing. I felt like a little boy again, staggering in the fields, just knocked off his horse by a blow to the head, unaware of where he is or where's he's going, where to place the next foot, and what lies in front of him.

The cell-block speakers blared out supper and I tried to compose myself, to center myself, but I began to cry uncontrollably. I groaned aloud, biting my lips, on the floor in a fetal position, my body racked with a weeping seizure, purging out every lie, all the hurt streaming out of my eyes. I heard the chow wagon nearing and guards coming up the stairs. The swill slot opened. A porter shoved a tray through and I grabbed it. I sat on the floor, eating, my hands trembling as I lifted the spoon to my mouth, tears and blood from my lips mixing with the food. It was at that moment, in the dark, in my isolation cell, that a revelation struck me, the way lightning strikes ground in the night and reddens it. I knew why I couldn't get out of the chair, why I refused to work, why I stayed in my cell—in every muscle and bone of my body a tortured voice cried out that I could never again tolerate the betrayals that had marked my life, stretching back to my earliest years.

NINE

Letting me out after a month in isolation, Mad Dog Madril escorted me to the warden. I had done two years in prison already and had passed my twenty-third birthday in isolation. I found myself sitting before the warden as he yelled how I had failed to heed his warning about not getting into trouble. I needed a lesson. Insubordination before a Reclassification Committee and refusing to work were serious institutional infractions. No lecture, no conversation—he was tired of wasting his time. He didn't even say what the punishment was going to be. Mad Dog Madril didn't say anything either as he marched me across the yard.

The dungeon was a dark subterranean sewer under CB3, the highest level of security detention, with warring gang soldiers and death row on the east side and rival gangs on the west side. Running down the middle behind the cells was a narrow section with electrical and plumbing pipes. Convicts in the dungeon were almost never let out.

At the first security checkpoint, a huge guard with one arm opened a gate and we advanced deeper. The light grew weaker. Nerves made my stomach tight as banded steel. We kept going, farther down, all the way to the back, through four more gates, passing still more tiers of administrative segregation prisoners. Some gang soldiers yelled, recognizing me from when I'd portered the temporary lockdowns. It was almost dark now and lightbulbs encased in iron brackets burned to illuminate the short tier beyond the last gate. The usual cacophony that stunned the sensibilities in general-population blocks was absent.

Mad Dog Madril uncuffed me in the landing off to the side. I stripped down. Another guard stood behind me. I handed him my clothing and brogans and, wearing only my boxers, I went through the gate barefoot. I felt scared.

The air was humid with stagnant human odors. The short run of cells to my left, ten of them, were ancient relics, quite different from the cells in other cell blocks. The cells were smaller units, constructed of black angle iron and green-painted concrete. The dark, the sweat stink, the quietness, and the furtive glances of the cons reminded me of zoo animals that lived mostly at the back of their cages in the shadows. A dim haze from outside glowed from barred windows to the right. The last gate's hinges creaked. I stood in a small box cage and the guard told me to pull my boxers down. I turned around, bent over, and then pulled my boxers up. The guard checked my armpits, the bottoms of my feet, under my testicles, and my mouth. My body felt drained of blood, and I felt weak and limp. Mad Dog Madril led me through into the small landing, locked the gate behind me, and left.

A tall thin Chicano/Indio con with long black hair raking across his face stood at the first cell to my left in his boxers and shower thongs, silently staring at me from behind the bars. It was eerily quiet as hands and mirrors came out of the bars to see who I was.

"Psst! Pssst! What cell you going to?" the man to my left asked. I met his eyes. He had been down here for so long that his skin pallor was a sickly yellow, and his eyes had a paranoid frenzy in them.

"C-Four," I answered.

"You got your own cell." He gave me a clenched fist sign, meaning that Chicanos watch out for each other and having my own cell was good.

"Stand in front of your cell!" An old wrinkled guard at the manual control cage at the end of the tier cranked a handle that opened my cell gate. As I went in, I noticed a stocky black dude celling to the right and, to the left, a huge red-haired white guy, a mountain of a man with tattoos over his entire body. I felt more distant from the world than ever.

There was an uneasiness about the forced calmness that lay heavily over the block. The rusty scrap-iron cell was drab green. When I positioned myself in the center, I could touch both walls with my arms. The toilet and sink were ancient salvage-yard steel, operated by pushing a button embedded in the wall. I unrolled the rancid mattress over the welded sheet-metal cot with its angle-iron legs buried in concrete.

Beyond my cell in the ceiling corridor, lightbulbs that burned day and night in thick chicken-wire mesh cases were caked with dirt lint and gave off a weak glow. Against the wall ran a row of windows facing the yard, where, several feet above our heads, silhouettes of cons in long dark columns marched to the dining room or to the fields. I stood in my boxers at the bars, looking out at the walking shadows in the yard.

After a while, I lay down, listening to whispers about whether they knew me or which gang I was in. They worried that maybe I had been sent down here to kill one of them.

My neighbor, the black dude to the right, asked from the corner where our cell wall met the bars, "Whatcha down for?"

"Refusing to work," I said.

"What?" he asked incredulously.

"Refusing to work," I repeated.

My neighbor to the left, the big giant, asked with a gruff voice, "Did I hear right, Bonafide, not wanting to work?"

Someone else added, "He's bullshitting you, Texas Red."

Another con grumbled, "Muthafucker lying!"

I kept quiet.

A voice came from the end of the tier to the left by the guard cage. "Yeah, man, who are you? Who you click with?"

Another voice asked, "What the fuck you down here for?"

Again, I answered. "Not working."

Bonafide stuck his mirror into view from the side in front of my bars. I could see his eyes and he could see me sitting on my bunk, staring at the wall.

"What they really slam you down for?" he asked.

"Refusing to work," I answered.

Bonafide laughed. "Thought you made that shit up."

"Gotta be more than that," one guy snorted.

"What's your number?" another asked, to determine when I had come into the joint. His voice hissed like a rattler's tail.

Their questions were interrupted by the supper cart rumbling down the tier, taking a long time to get to us. I could hear gates open and close, echoing, and keys clashing closer, guard boots on the concrete louder until it arrived. Our trays were slid under the bars into our cells, and while we ate the cons talked back and forth about betting on games, appealing criminal cases to higher courts, and writing chicks on the streets. I took my time savoring the corn and peas, mashed potatoes and pork chops, bread and butter. I chewed each spoonful until the food almost dissolved in my mouth. Later, a porter came and swept and mopped the tier where the guys had kicked trays out, crashing them against the wall and spilling leftovers all over the floor and wall.

After supper, they still wanted to know the "real" reason I was down here. The guessing stopped when the tier guard's craggy voice rasped, "Piss and shit before water's off." Everyone brushed their teeth, urinated, and defecated. After a while the lights flickered, signaling bedtime, and went off a few minutes later.

I lay back on my bunk. It was a rule to keep one's head exposed and every thirty minutes when the count guards approached my cell I closed my eyes as the flashlight swept my face. I stayed awake late, listening to the guards bullshit with the cons every time they came through on count time. I stared at the ground-level windows, illuminated by spotlights. I kept thinking about the kind of person I was back in the streets, how my life had been, and how in a million years I could've never imagined myself in here. I thought that although my actions alienated and infuriated others, my reasons for not working had become stronger as a result of my revelation in the isolation cell.

We were awakened at 6 A.M. by the guards and porters handing out our breakfast trays. No one talked. They spit, pissed, and coughed. I made my bunk, grabbed my breakfast tray from the floor, and, after eating my Cream of Wheat, toast, and coffee, I paced, watching the faint dawn haze the windows. Now and then a shadow from the waist down would pass. The guard let us out one at a time for showers. As each con passed my cell he glanced at me. I paced back and forth. I put my face against the bars, feeling the iron digging in my cheekbones. I studied the mesh screen over the windows, caked with spattered blood and bits of dried grime, dead insects, and matter that had hardened to rock-hard dirt. I'd never felt so hopeless.

I could hear Texas Red moving around, punching the water button, making heavy noises on the toilet, bumping into the bunk, sitting down and sighing deeply. When he came out for a shower, I saw he was a giant of a man, his tattooed arms like mountainsides with rock pictographs. He was so wide that standing up at the bars his shoulders almost went the width of the cell. Bonafide's movements were more hushed, and I felt a disquieting menace about him. When he heard me ask the guard for State Issue paper and pencil, toothpaste, and shaver, his hand shot around the bars with a small pen and a few sheets of brown paper, the kind kindergartners draw on. I was going to draw the way I remembered Theresa looking, thinking it might help me get rid of my fear and loneliness.

Life was stripped down to essentials in the dungeon. I lived naked except for my boxer shorts. No head games went on down here—no threatening or cutting each other down, no selling wolf tickets, no running off at the mouth, no prying into personal stuff about childhood or families. Anytime any of the cons were taken out of the dungeon for visits or security status reviews, they towed chains on their legs, wrists, neck, and waist and were escorted by two armed guards.

It was an event whenever we heard tier gates racking in the distance, because it meant maybe one of us was getting out, going to the yard, and like the rest I came to my cell bars each time and looked down the tier with a mirror to see who it was. Life in the dungeon never hurried or slowed. Its routine tread was the same every day: wake up, have breakfast, take a nap, listen to music, write or read; then lunch and rap to others on the tier. In the afternoon we'd stand at the bars staring at the windows ten feet beyond, tracking the day's hours through the movements of shadows and light. At times each day an odd boredom fell over the dungeon, as if we were feeling what a waste our lives were and realizing in unison how long away we were from getting out. The silence was dismal.

Most of the cons in the dungeon were big-time shot-callers. They had a lot of soldiers under their power, and they could set up a hit anywhere in the country simply by sending out a kite or a word to the porter or guard. JJ was the godfather of La eMe in this prison, but second in command to the main godfather in California. Snake, his celly, was his bodyguard. JJ and Snake were on the list for Marion, a prison in Illinois, where officials supposedly experimented with brain surgery to modify prisoners' behavior. JJ and Snake were considered future candidates for lobotomies because they had recently killed a guard. JJ was short and Snake was tall; both had pale skin from being in the dungeon too long. Their eyes gleamed furtively and bristled with deception. Their blade-lean bodies, arctic stares, and, gaunt faces made them a lethal threat to anyone they looked at. Warlock was one of the leaders of the Aryan skinheads and Bubba was the head of the blacks. Indio and Bonafide were lone wolves, not belonging to any group but extremely dangerous and never allowed in general population.

We were let out for an hour, twice a week, in two separate groups, in the enclosed exercise cage out back. We looked forward to getting together under the hot sun, pacing, lifting weights, and shadow-sparring. Mondays and Wednesdays were my exercise days. We ignored the guard sitting on a steel folding chair outside the cage, clutching his high-powered rifle, and the other guards on the yard wall catwalk. We exercised and talked until our hour was up, then a guard patted us down and we went back in to shower and eat.

During our gatherings, I learned that Indio, the Chicano who'd spoken to me first when I came in, was doing four lives because he'd killed that many rednecks. I'd spot Texas Red as he bench-pressed over three hundred pounds. Because he didn't think he'd had enough visiting time with his wife, he once took the visiting-room guards hostage and initiated his own visiting hours. Bonafide, five foot seven, stocky and muscled, was feared and respected. He had arms and legs the size of telephone poles, a ballerina's waist, and a leopard's litheness. Bonafide huddled in the corner with Indio telling funny crime stories. Bubba and Bones practiced a form of karate, in slow motion only, against each other. Their bitches, Black Beauty and Jelly Roll, giggled girlishly as they watched and did each other's hair in cornrows. Luis and Benito celled with each other, their tattooed bodies mural tapestries of Chicano history, La Virgen de Guadalupe and Christ's Head with Crown of Thorns. In the other group there was Warlock, JJ and Snake, and Lucas, a white dude from Florida and Oklahoma, an ex–recon man from Vietnam who was still at war in his head.

◆

Letters made a big difference by breaking up the day's monotonous tedium, and the guys waited anxiously at the bars when mail call came. Though I knew she'd never write, hearing them talking on the tier about people writing them made me think of Theresa. Wouldn't it be wonderful to receive a love letter from her? With her perfume and lipstick kisses on the envelope, photos inside of her smiling in a pretty dress that showed her shapely figure, news on what she was doing, her classes at the university, what kind of job she had, how she missed me and was staying true to me? I secretly longed for such a letter and was positively thrilled one afternoon when the guard called out my number and placed a letter on my bars.

Aside from my sister, or maybe Lonnie, I hadn't a clue as to who would be writing me. It was a one-page letter written on a church notepad sheet, and I spent days trying to decipher the cursive writing, tracing words to understand which alphabets they were, figuring slowly by sounds what the sentence was. It was in English but the writing was shaky, which made it even harder to read.

The last time I had anything to do with words was reading a little out of that girl's stolen book in the county jail in Albuquerque. Before that was when I was seventeen and locked up in Albuquerque on suspicion of murder; I had punched out my windshield when Theresa broke up with me. To pass the time while awaiting arraignment, the guys there read books aloud to those of us who couldn't read for ourselves. The stories had affected me deeply. I couldn't tell you what a noun or verb was, or a subject and an object, or anything about punctuation, but that didn't take away from the magic of the stories. I could have shared in the hero's courageous achievements and felt the villain's remorse for his actions.

Sitting in prison years later, unable to read my letter, I regretted not having learned to read. After hours of frustration, I finally understood that the man's name was Harry, he was from Phoenix, and he had picked my name during a Christmas mass from a church list of inmates who had no family and no one writing them. I was eager to communicate with someone to alleviate the boredom of the dungeon. The state paid for stamps, envelopes, and paper; I borrowed a pencil. I started writing in the morning, and almost all my attempts ended in crumpled paper wads on the floor. But by dinnertime I'd managed to put together a page.

(11–14–75).
Dear Harry
Hello Mr. Harry, my name is Jimmy Santiago Baca I'm in prison. Well your probably thinking who thise person is. Well everything started like thise. See I been here for two year or more. I didn't gravateted from high school. I am triendy to get my [GED] but I cuudent. I like it a lot. That's why I'm asking for some advies how can I get good at it. Study a lot or keep reeding book's. See write now I have a lot of time in prison. Some day I hope I cuuld write. Im twenty-three year's old and I hoping if you give me some addvices.

Thank you,
sincerlly yours
Jimmy Santiago Baca.

It saddened me to realize that I had been in prison a little over two years. But I was hopeful too. I only had two and a half years left, and I felt I could make it. One of the guys showed me how to address my letter and where to put the stamp. Then, feeling flushed with achievement, I set it on the bars for the guard to pick up.

I pictured myself as a man in those black-and-white movies, an important man writing letters with business to do, plans to fulfill. Writing letters added an exciting dimension to my lackluster days and gave me a sense of self-esteem. My grammar was so deplorable that when a reply came, a few days later, accompanying Harry's letter was a new paperback dictionary. He mentioned that I really needed to use it. His second letter was longer, and filled with missionary zeal.

Using the dictionary, I figured out that Harry was confined to a wheelchair from a World War II PT boat explosion. He was now a volunteer at a Samaritan house in Phoenix, ladling out soup to the homeless in the morning and sandwiches in the afternoon. His letter, friendly but polite, was expansive in its faith and religious fervor, exhorting me to welcome God's love in my life. It took tremendous concentration to get through his letters. I'd study a word in connection to another word, and the longer I studied the more meanings it took on and the more subtle variations I could take from it.

I would set my dictionary next to me, prop my paper on my knees, sharpen my pencil with my teeth, and begin my reply. I would try to write the thoughts going through my mind, but they didn't come out right. They lacked reality. A stream of ideas flowed through me, but they lost their strength as soon as I put them down. I erased so often and so hard I made holes in the paper. After hours of plodding word by word to write a clear sentence, I would read it and it didn't even come close to what I'd meant to say. After a day of looking up words and writing, I'd be exhausted, as if I had run ten miles. I can't describe how words electrified me. I could smell and taste and see their images vividly. I found myself waking up at 4 A.M. to reread a word or copy a definition.

One day the guard placed a package on the bars along with a letter. I tore it open, eager as a child for a Christmas present. It contained some spiral notebooks and several bilingual pamphlets by Mary Baker Eddy, each chapter headed with a devotional sketch of a family in prayer. One page was in Spanish and the facing page in English. I now read a little in English, and if I didn't get it I could remember enough Spanish from when my Grandpa used to read the Spanish Bible to me each evening. Harry sent more religious pamphlets, and over time I slowly learned to read with more comprehension.

I found myself copying the pamphlet's religious dogma in the spiral notebooks to practice writing sentences. Then I did the same with words and definitions. Sometimes I'd pick a word and string nonsense words after it to see what kind of meaning came from the random arrangement. Then a particular word would catch my attention and ignite memories. I would try to recall the memory vividly in language, spending hours crossing out and rewriting until I got so overwhelmed by all the word choices that I had to confine myself to describing the dungeon windows embedded with chicken wire.

I had to ground myself in small things or my thoughts scattered everywhere. The days went by unnoticed. My letters to Harry grew longer, until I was writing three pages. How he read through them was beyond me, but he was kind, never criticizing my pitiful confessionals but patiently laboring through the misspellings and bad grammar, responding always with friendly sympathy.

Although replete with religious principles, his letters conveyed not only empathy for my situation but also an optimistic faith that I could make a better human being of myself. Nobody else had ever believed in me or accepted me unconditionally. I began to record my memories and dreams in the notebooks Harry sent me. Every time I received a letter from him, I'd stay up at night pacing and sounding out words and rereading them to make sure they made sense. With writing, it seemed, if you opened one faucet of words, a hundred more would come on. I'd stay awake with my head filled with things I'd forgotten to add, things I wanted to say but couldn't put my finger on exactly. It could go on and on and was simultaneously wonderful and awful.

If there wasn't an actual person receiving what I was writing at the other end, it made writing harder. Writing for me was my connection to the streets, to someone out there. And although Theresa wasn't my girlfriend anymore, it helped me to imagine she was going to read what I wrote. When I finally finished my first poem, I read it to Bonafide. It went:

There He stands Looking for the Dream that he lost.
She walked Away knowing little what it really cost.
He thought She was Really all his own.
But then he Looked around that had once been his happy home.
She had left and taken his Dream.
Yes she was so so keen.
But In time Someone will shatter her Dream.

She wears a pretty yellow bow in her hair.
She Also has a halo and skin so fair.

She walks so perfect like a doe prancing
Look at the stars and they may be dancing.
For my lovely Theresa walks very near
She so very kind she'd shed a tear
For the poor one.
Her eyes so lashing like moonlight on a lake
Her lips the m—

It was still too painful to finish. After seven years, the memory of her face was as clear in my mind as if I had just taken a Polaroid photograph of her in front of her white stucco house in her jeans and red shirt. And when I looked at the mental pictures, there was always an aching sadness.

Harry mentioned that my daily letters were overwhelming him and described how calm his days were. At sunrise he routinely opened the soup kitchen and cooked oatmeal with other Samaritan brothers to feed the homeless. Then he'd attend church services, and then go to his room and read the Bible until it was time to make and hand out bologna sandwiches. After cleaning up, he'd spend the rest of the evening in his room reading the Bible.

I was more interested in his life than in God, but since I could no longer dismiss his religious talk I took it on. Harry kept avoiding my experiences, denying that injustice existed at all. I told him God hadn't done a thing for me. That God sat back while I lost my family and everything that went with having a family. That justice was abused by the rich; as proof, this prison had 90 percent poor Chicanos in it. I went on about poverty, violence, murder, abuse, and greed. We had been having a good correspondence until he wrote that my letters were troubling him. I told him I didn't want to hurt his feelings or disparage his piety, just express my opinions.

His response a few days later was not what I expected. I'd thought he'd be mad or tell me off, but instead he wrote that we were all in one cage or another, him in a wheelchair, me in a cell, but the most serious cages were sins. Obeying God's will, even though his body was in a wheelchair, allowed his spirit to soar.

And even though I was in prison, I too could share in God's grace and soar. He gave biblical examples of how other saints and martyrs had suffered and encouraged me to surrender my will to God. His explanations seemed to imply that I was a sinner and should repent, but I wasn't going for that. He also hinted that there was nothing I could do to change my life; it was all in God's hands, and there was a divine purpose behind these atrocities I experienced. Things had to work as they did for a reason beyond human understanding. I wrote him right away, and again I poured out all my doubts in a stream. I ended by saying that, to me, God was nature, the mountains, streams, rocks, and trees, the sun and moon and stars. That was my God and always would be.

Harry's letters grew even more perplexed. His kindness was beginning to fray. I sensed that his tolerance was being taxed but I couldn't help myself. Compelled as I was by having someone listen to me for the first time in my life, and take me and my views seriously, I kept writing every day. A little voice in my head was finally talking about what I had known all my life. With every word I was gulping fresh air and filling my lungs. I felt I was writing for my life.

I began to jot down external observations. Small things: describing the quiet of the tier; the way the sun at dawn slowly lit the dungeon, creeping along the floor, reaching the cells like a timid snow leopard prowling up the bars. Fragments, one-line thoughts, and paragraphs of memories stirred up emotions in me that forced my hurt to the surface. Opening old wounds was not my intent, it just seemed to be one of the side effects of writing, and it often left me reeling in anger or self-pity. Too much self-absorption was dangerous. I knew that cons who got too deep into themselves usually ended up on Nut Run, the tier for the wackos.

God had come between Harry and me, and after months of writing, Harry still couldn't accept the reality of my life. His letters came less often. He didn't like my questioning God. We'd been writing for about seven months when he wrote me one last letter, saying he would not write again. Ours was not an acrimonious parting, but one based on respect despite our differences. He had made me feel like my opinions meant something, and to this day I feel a great sense of gratitude to him.

I had lost a compassionate friend because of my growing convictions. The bleakness I felt after alienating Harry made me wonder whether writing was worth it. Maybe I should have just played along and kept things to myself. In hindsight, I think Harry understood how the world was opening up to me through writing and reading. He also knew how impulsive I was, at twenty-four years of age, how I had to question everything and was contrary to a fault, someone he couldn't convince wasn't already in hell.

◆

I began to compose sentimental poems. I discovered that good and bad experiences had hibernated in me, and when they awoke they did so without warning and with the velocity of a sniper bullet, making me shake and choke up. In return for cigarettes and coffee, I'd write chicks for the cons in the dungeon. Bonafide was my steady client. Getting the chicks to write and send nude photos was the goal. He'd get their addresses from porn magazines. As we'd sit on the floor against the wall separating our cells and hold mirrors out the bars so we could see each other's faces, he told me what he wanted to say.

"You're not really going to say you're a lawyer and own an Arabian ranch in Malibu, are you?" I asked.

"Naw, put that I'm a Colombian drug lord."

"And why not add you're a born-again Christian?" I kidded.

He grinned. "Anything to get that perfumed letter and a picture of her naked ass."

Because of our frequent collaboration, I thought I knew Bonafide as well as one could. I could tell he was not the psycho that everybody claimed he was. I looked up to Bonafide, thinking he was right about how he lived.

Then one morning after breakfast a new face showed up on the tier, a black dude carrying his carton box containing personal items: clothes, books, toiletries, stationery. He stood in front of Bonafide's cell. He was built like a heavyweight boxer, at least a foot taller than Bonafide. The cell opened and closed. I was sitting on my bunk reading when I heard a muffled violence. It sounded like a ferocious tiger tearing apart a small dog. I paused in my writing—actually, I stopped cold—when I heard another voice come out of Bonafide, not his normal one but one filled with a murderous rage to kill.

"Fucking bitch!" Bonafide roared, with such power and velocity that it stunned the whole tier into silence.

And then I heard squeals and whimpers and repeated blows to the body, anguished groans, and teeth-gritting yelps of pain. Bonafide was raping the man, pulverizing him to nothing but a crumpled and bloody writhing heap of meat without mind or soul. The guards came and carried the man away. I couldn't believe that lurking within Bonafide was a monster that had just devoured a human being. This totally bowled me off the track, to think that this whole time I thought I knew him, and there was another man inside him totally alien to me.

◆

Being almost naked all the time didn't alleviate the 100-degree-plus summer heat in the dungeon. I can't remember much happening except a relentless tedium. I occupied my time reading and writing and exercising twice a week. During those long hot days, I found myself comparing Bonafide and Harry. After that rape, and even though I knew he had no choice, I realized that Bonafide's approach to things was not what I wanted for myself. Had he not done what he did, it would have been done to him. The guys on the tier would have thought he was weak. Still, it filled me with bitter awareness that being in prison could turn a man into a monster.

Somewhere deep inside myself I knew that, put in the wrong place at the wrong time, Bonafide would have tried to rape me. The rage that came out of him was the kind of rage that transcends friendship. It's the kind of rage that can only be created in prison. The seeds of that rage are nourished by prison brutality and fertilized by fear and the law of survival of the fittest. It grows and grows, hidden deep in souls that have died from too many beatings, too many jail cells, and bottomless despair, contained like a ticking bomb. And this kind of firestorm wrath crushed even the divine rules of Harry's God, because once a man has it in him, the man, when the rage comes out, becomes god.

The way Harry was, if the same thing had happened to him, he would have given up the cell and lost his manhood. A guy like Harry would be killed in this place. Bonafide upheld the convict code as much as Harry followed the Ten Commandments. Bonafide had passion and no God; he took life to survive, while Harry's excessive piety respected life and drained it of passion.

Bonafide's attack on the guy brought prison reality back to me with full force. A month or so later, something else happened that really disturbed me. A new tough kid was brought in, and while the guard went to the other side of the block to get the bull to open one of the empty cells, the kid waited out on the tier. JJ and Snake were out for a shower, and when they saw the kid standing there all alone, they ripped his throat out with a homemade meat hook.

After this, I wanted to find refuge in something, or at least find a place where I felt safe and could believe the world wasn't crazy all the time. Maybe faith and reverence for human life were the answers. I would have liked to preach and believe in a doctrine of peace, but I knew prison wouldn't allow that. Harry's world had nothing to do with me. But neither did Bonafide's.

At the time, I didn't believe in anything or anyone. I drifted between choices, between hoping for freedom and resigning myself to being a convict. I didn't want anyone preaching to me or anyone messing with me. I ate in silence, read and wrote in my journals, exercised in my cell, and went to bed. I wouldn't talk to anyone. I kept a low profile and existed almost invisibly. But I know now that even if I couldn't actually touch or see the insidious process that criminalizes a man and makes him more violent, the process was taking place in me. Spilled blood and real death and choices that sometimes had to be made in here kept us alive but often stripped us of humanity. The man who backed down still lost his soul— and in a humiliating way, which was the worst way. It was a no-win situation. And all the books in the world and all the poetry ever written couldn't help you get out, because this was prison, and prison had its own bizarre and cruel codes.

◆

On a cold February morning I was called back to the Reclassification Committee, held in a corridor two gates out of the dungeon in a small landing. I was escorted in chains by two guards before a small folding table with three officers sitting behind it on steel chairs: Mad Dog Madril, the counselor, and the black sergeant.

"Three-two-five-eight-one, you're ordered to work detail—" Mad Dog Madril began irritably.

I cut in. "I refuse, unless I'm allowed to—"

"Put his ass back," Mad Dog ordered, and closed my folder.

I had never been able to reach an agreement with the prison administration. Their impression of me was that I was nothing more than a troublemaker. For the time being, though, I wasn't so much disappointed as relieved. Even though I missed the sunshine and going out to the exercise field, I had the feeling that I was doing the right thing. Yes, I missed being in general population and the freedom that went with it. But in the dungeon I had my own cell, and I enjoyed my privacy and the time I had to write and read. Because of drastic overpopulation, few cons in the prison had their own cells, and hundreds were sleeping on the floor in dormitories.

This time, no sooner had I entered my cell and settled in to read than a con showed up carrying his box. His escort barked my cell number to the cage guard and left him standing in front of the bars.

"Yeah, man, I don't want anybody celling with me," I told him.

"I'm just doing what the warden told me to do," he said.

"Why do you have to do what the warden says? Just refuse to move in. Stick with the cons, not the warden."

Instinctively, I followed Bonafide's example, but not to his extreme. When the guard racked my cell, I leaped out and hit the guy. The guards must have been expecting it, because as the inmate was picking himself off the floor, Mad Dog Madril and some guards rushed through the gate and hauled me off to the hole.

The warden's purpose in sending him down was to move me out. For the next five weeks, I'd go from Reclass to my cell, fight, then to the hole for a day, then back in the dungeon and back to Reclass. But it wasn't bad; the hole was more like a meditation place for me now. Each time I came back into the dungeon, the tier would hoot and jive me in a friendly manner, telling me I was crazy and encouraging me to never give up.

The only thing that really bothered me was when the guards tore up all my journals and confiscated my books. However, the cons on death row on the other side of the block heard about what was happening and began to send me good books. I started training myself to remember poems, so that in the hole I could study and go over them. I remembered lines and stanzas from Neruda, Emily Dickinson, and Rilke. I'd go over plots, characters, styles, and descriptions of landscapes in novels by Hemingway and Faulkner. I grew into the habit of lying down on my back and putting a towel over my eyes and crossing my arms over the towel so I was in pitch blackness. I would recount what I'd read, hear the rhyme or see the line, and mesmerize myself by repeating the words until I was asleep.

◆

Every Saturday morning Bonafide and I played chess. We set the board and pieces outside the bars and crouched against the wall between our cells and played and talked, smoked cigarettes, and drank coffee. One morning, a guard pushing the meds cart and handing out pill packets stopped in front of my cell.

Let's go, "Three-two-five-eight-one! Visit!"

Bonafide said, "You got the wrong number. He never gets visits."

He was right. In three years I'd never had a visit. I didn't expect one either. Other cons hollered that the guard was wrong, but he insisted I get dressed and rack out.

"I don't give a shit. It says here he's got a visit."

Even if it was a mix-up, it would be nice to go out on the yard for a walk. I put on my pants, shirt, and brogans, which felt strange because I almost never wore them. Mad Dog Madril arrived, chained me up, and we made the long walk through the various sections of the basement lockups.

Outside, the bright sunshine made me squint. The open space was breathtaking. Maybe it didn't interest others, or maybe they were indifferent to it, but being in the dungeon so long I could taste and smell it like a ripe desert fruit. Passionate blue air swallowed me up. I could see motes of dust floating an inch above the ground. My heart was beating wildly and for an instant I felt revitalized, light as the sparrows and prairie doves that gracefully scaled the walls and played back and forth on their razor-wire perches.

At the visiting room by the main gates, Mad Dog Madril unchained me and left. Two guards, standing opposite each other, scanned the cons. Surrounded with lovers, wives, and families, I felt anxious, disconnected, like a monk who has spent too long in a cell. Not knowing what gestures to give people, what to say or do, I just took it all in with my senses—the colors, the perfumes, the women. I sat down at a long table, visitors on one side and convicts on the other side. I was sweating and chewing my fingernails, picking at my skin, looking around at visitors engaged in a steady low hum of conversation. I sat and waited, wondering who I would see.

There was a child about four years old who kept leaping up trying to get a drink of water at the fountain. He pressed the button, the stream of water curled up, he jumped up to drink, and the water went down. His father and mother were busy talking. I got up and walked over and lifted him and he drank. His father immediately came over and pushed me aside, eyeing me with a hostile glare. I took a drink and went back to my chair, and just as I sat down my brother walked in with a woman.

With a tense smile he introduced her as Lori, his girlfriend. He held himself stiffly, his black hair combed back, his body muscular and tanned, looking every inch the playboy he wanted to be in his trendy jeans and red cowboy shirt. She was elegant and gentle and a bit tentative. I wanted to make them feel comfortable but that was impossible; this was a maximum-security state prison. I wanted to give them the impression that I was doing fine and tried to smile, but I could tell, as I remained staring at them from my chair, that they were worried by my gauntness. My appearance brought a worried look to Mieyo's face, and he shot a sharp glance at the guard behind me and murmured curses.

Lori broke the stiff silence. "They allowed us only an hour."

"Did you come from New Mexico?"

"Yeah, we're on our way to San Francisco, to visit her parents. You okay?"

"I'm writing," I said, which seemed a stupid thing to say to them.

"Are you reading anyone?" Lori asked.

It was strange to be talking about this stuff. I didn't want to talk about reading or writing but about Mieyo, my brother, whom I missed and loved. But it was like we had no words. At some point as kids, physical movement, competitive sports and partying and getting high, had replaced talking to each other, and now, when we couldn't do any of that, we had to look silently into each other's eyes, speechless.

Mieyo said vehemently, “I’m going to get you out of this place! I’ll get you a good lawyer, pay off the judge—do it one way or another.”

He had good intentions but didn’t fulfill them. How was I to tell him that I was a ghost of the brother he had known? That I had left broken fragments of the previous Jimmy on the floor in the isolation hole, while other pieces of my former self were scattered on the ground where I smashed the black guy’s head and still other parts were dripping in the drain in the kitchen where I cut the other guy?

He asked about my release date, and I told him I had a little over two years left. To change the subject, I asked, “Are you engaged?” I gave Lori a warm look as she innocently clutched Mieyo’s hand. I took it to mean yes. I asked what he was doing these days.

“I’m a housing contractor. I’m going to be rich, Jim, rich.”

Since he’d been a child he always said he was going to be rich. It didn’t mean much, but I guess it reassured him in some way. He always dressed in fine clothes, tall and handsome, and usually he had a great smile. Now it was strained as he pretended things were fine.

“So, how you doing in here, Jim? How you doing?”

I reflected a second on the dungeon and thought how he could never imagine it. He must have sensed some sadness in me.

He smiled. “Martina had another baby—her third. She bought another new house.”

I didn’t ask about our mother and father, because I knew he didn’t want to talk about them.

“You okay?” he asked again.

“Yeah, I’m fine.” I hid the hurt of sensing how much distance was really between us. I was different, harder, and Mieyo could see it.

Our conversation started and stopped as we awkwardly probed, not wanting to say the wrong thing, touch on a wound.

He asked, “You need anything?”

I kidded. “Yeah, an old secondhand typewriter.”

The guard leaned in to us and said, "Visit's over."

Mieyo's eyes grew dark with anger and Lori pulled him back. She trembled, on the verge of weeping in sympathy. I was forbidden to reach over and embrace them. It was a tough moment that wrenched my heart. Without endearments, I rose and turned and offered my arms to Mad Dog Madril as he came in. I went one way and they went the other. But before they left, I turned and called out, "Get ahold of Theresa! Ask her to come visit me!"

"I will! I promise!" Mieyo yelled back.

A couple of weeks later an old Royal manual typewriter arrived, along with an acoustic guitar, radio, lamp, and a letter from Lori, saying she hoped the gifts would help me pass the time. I later found out my personal account was credited with fifty dollars she had sent. But I never saw either of them again for the rest of the time I was in prison.

I don't remember how much time passed after that. All I did was type and play the guitar. I was in heaven. Poetry and music blocked out all other life. I was in my own world, swirling in the magic of language and imagination. Days, weeks, and months went by, but I hardly recognized them. Only my writing marked the passage of time.

Then my number was called for another visit. When I entered and saw Theresa I remained standing but then finally sat down, trembling and embarrassed to have her see me like this. She was tanned very dark, shimmering with lotion. She wore jean shorts cut high to her crotch, halter-top yellow blouse, red fingernails, red lipstick, necklace, and jewels, and when she took off her sunglasses I could see her eyes were glazed with drugs. She was high. She looked gaudy, worn, and drugged, angular from lack of nourishment; I could smell her cheap hair spray and perfume. Despite it all, she was beautiful.

I was nervously trying to think of something to say, and I finally asked, "How's your mother?" But not waiting for her answer, I blurted out, "I still love you!"

She said nothing, just stared at me as if disappointed and frustrated. Her dark hair had been gathered up in a sexy bunch at the back, and she let it loose to fall erotically around her bare shoulders.

"I only want you," I said, which brought a grimace to her lips. My heart sank.

"Live your life, Jimmy. For heaven's sake, live your life. Quit screwing around."

"I left Albuquerque because I love you so much. I just couldn't stand to see you with other guys."

She became defensive. "Don't blame me that you're in here. It's not my fault. The warden says you're making things worse for yourself! Why do you have to be your own worst enemy?"

"I know," I said. "I know. It's my fault."

She went on. "Maybe this place will do you good, help you get your life straightened out. And then when you get out, you'll find somebody who will love you the way you want. I can't do it. I'm not the woman for you."

I said, "I dream of you. I had to go away to California, you know, after we broke up."

She said, "I saw other people. I was partying and having fun."

It was as if she said it to hurt me. I wanted to tell her how much I had learned. I knew how to love her now.

She gave me another hard stare and sighed impatiently. "It won't work! Jimmy, you can't even get along *here.*"

As she spoke I wanted to tell her about my poetry and how I had so many memories I wanted to share with her.

She asked, "What do you think you're doing?"

I was caught off guard by her anger.

"What you mean?" I asked.

"The warden says you refuse to follow the rules. How do you ever expect to get out of here if you don't follow the rules?"

I wanted to tell her that we could still live together, love each other, make plans for the future when I got out, talk about us getting back together, but it was all turning out terribly wrong.

She repeated sarcastically, “Don’t you ever want to get out? You better work if you want to get out. I just don’t understand you—at all! You’ll never change, will you?”

“I’m trying,” I said.

She leaned forward. “I come all this way to help you and you haven’t even been trying to do right? You sit there not saying a word, wanting me like always to read your mind, do things just for you! Expecting me to feel sorry for you! You’re not the only one in the world.” She stood to leave.

“Please don’t,” I pleaded. “Just sit down and I’ll try to explain why I’m doing what I am. It’s hard, sitting here, when you tell me everything I’m doing is wrong.”

But she said good-bye and was gone. I sat there as the visiting-room guard called in his walkie-talkie for Mad Dog Madril to escort me back to my cell.

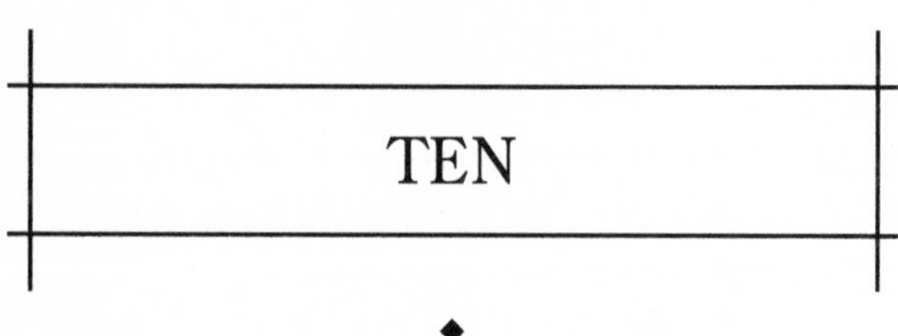

TEN

I'd just written a journal entry on the last page on my second spiral notebook when a guard came by and placed a letter on the bars. It was from Lori, informing me that Mieyo, after the visit, had gone on a wild drunk and ruined their plans for visiting her parents in San Francisco. Though she still loved Mieyo, it had destroyed their relationship, and they weren't seeing each other anymore. The news was difficult to accept. I wanted Mieyo to have someone love him, but he knew nothing about love and sustaining a relationship, or about honesty and commitment. He was motivated by one dream—to be rich. He would talk about how he was going to buy race cars and a mansion, but he never talked about what he felt about the past or our parents. Since becoming a drunk at the age of nine, he had developed lots of secrets, and he was good at keeping them.

Mieyo, like me, had been taught it was better to live a lie than tell the truth. To live with guilt rather than do something about it. Disappointed at himself, he lived quietly in isolation, never trusting to convey to anyone what he really felt, drinking himself into oblivion. I couldn't say why my anger at him had been replaced, while doing time in prison, by a feeling of sadness. Lori's departure was going to be hard for him, and I found myself writing, trying to understand his suffering, my words shaped by my heart as a little brother, not as a person who had moved ahead and become a stranger to him.

I wrote until my fingers cramped, pouring all my frustration into my journal. Thinking of him as I sat on my bunk, I remembered how meticulous he was in his carpentry work. He would have known every hairline crack in my cell's concrete floor; by looking at the swirl of the mason's trowel on the wall, he would have known the competency of the mason. I studied the oxidation on the bars, where the welder put too much or not enough flame, the chips in the thick lead-based paint, how sweaty hands had rubbed off the paint in places by gripping them. Coffee, blood, and urine stained the ripped mattress cloth; the section of concrete directly below the cot where men rose in the morning and set their bare feet had a lighter discoloration; the small rounded dents where a man vented his rage and beat his fist against the steel cot surface; the grooves in the mattress where a man masturbated in the same position every night for years. Mieyo, like myself, would have been sick of the male stench of prison bodies, the vile odor of men living in cages, the noise of slamming iron gates; nauseated by confining walls, the graffiti of despair and vengeance, cockroaches on the cell bars, contentious cons, arrogant guards, gun towers, and razor wire. At heart, Mieyo and I were both decent men, famished for affection and eager to live in a decent manner. And while I was slowly rebuilding my life with books and writing, Mieyo, on the other hand, was casting himself out into deeper and deeper isolation, into a place where I could not help him as I once did as a kid brother.

◆

Early one morning we were pulled out of our cells and ordered to stand down the tier against a wall before a cardboard Christmas tree for a holiday photo to send home. I glared at the camera. I hadn't looked at myself in years, and when the photographer handed me the Polaroid I hardly recognized myself. I was almost twenty-five years old, and the three-plus years I had done in prison showed on my features—I had an impenetrable indifference, an impudent disdain. My brown eyes were antagonistic, my stance confrontational. I couldn't send it to anyone—it was too disturbing. You could see the anger in my face. But it would serve as a reminder to me to fight against what prison was doing.

Around this time, Harry sent me a Christmas card, along with a note that he had passed my name along to the director of a writers' group in Phoenix. She had written in turn to a poet, asking if he'd write me, and Harry had enclosed a copy of her letter. It read:

12–30–76.
Dear Norman—
A day off work—holiday—I've been taking it easy, except for talking with a couple of estimators re some roof work. Someday I will get this house "cocooned" and be able to relax.

Re the prisoner, he is Jimmy Santiago Baca, Box B 32581, Arizona State Prison, Florence, AZ 85232. Do mention my name when you write to him. Harry, a friend, asked me to find a writer for him to write to. I plan to write to him that I have given you his address, but I will not give him your address unless you want me to. You can write to him directly on whatever basis you prefer.

I don't know his age, crime, etc. I do know that he is doing hard time, on the Ad Seg unit in the dungeon. I don't know whether you understand the terminology, but I gather that he is trouble. I think he has a few years remaining on his sentence, which I believe he feels was unfair. I have not tried to pry with Harry, so I report only in general what he has confided in me. Thank you for being willing to write him. Harry says he has pleaded for friendship and appreciates any correspondence. (I sent him a clipping of poems—some by prison poets—in the New Times *campus paper, and it was labeled as contraband.) Apparently, his condition seems non-rehabilitative. Be careful. Keep in touch, and Happy New Year.*

Gertrude Halpren

At the end of January 1977, I received a letter from Norman, who was writing me while driving from New York to Berkeley in a beat-up '56 Chevy. His letters were abbreviated scribbles on motel stationery, café napkins, and grocery bags. We began our correspondence, averaging a letter a week. I sent him a sampling of early and later poems so he could measure my progress.

3 JANUARY 1977
Thought
is the vibrating cane
of the blind,
poking there
and feeling here
for the flower.

9 JANUARY 1977
A leaf blew in my cell
through the bars
and the veins on the leaves
          were like the cheekbones
          of very old people.

11 JANUARY 1977
How desires to love her
turn this night
into salt water
and my loneliness a wound.

12 JANUARY 1977
Addicts
lay
on beds
in soft black rooms,
And the tapered flames of life
fingering your heart
do not awe
                    your round warm mouths
                              anymore.

13 JANUARY 1977

My words
sound
like rusty siding
on a country chicken coop,
flapping, rattling, clattering.
Solitude walks
in the sand-blowing wind and weeds,
roaming the ghost town of my heart,
digging up bones of the past.

Other than Norman's exciting letters about his bohemian poet's life in California, time went by in a continuous ream of uneventful days that fell away in dreary routine, until one day when a con came up and dropped his carton before my cell. He was Chicano, solid and muscled, with a tattoo on his forearm that read *Boxer.* I shook my head at him, meaning that no one was going to cell with me. He went down the tier, and then JJ called out.

"Let him in, Cyclone—for a day. He's with us. Just for now. We'll get back with you—cigarettes, coffee." They had given me the nickname Cyclone because when I fought I'd jump in and wreak havoc without uttering a word.

"Can't do it. I don't want anybody in my cell," I said.

Boxer kept reassuring me. "I'm here for a day, nothing more. I won't bug you. Just business and I'm gone."

As soon as he came in, he said the typing bothered him and told me to stop. Then he changed the channel on my little radio to his station, and that evening he said he couldn't sleep and wanted me to turn off my reading lamp. He stood at the bars talking in Chicano code slang to JJ and Snake about drugs and money. My life had been pretty calm, and I wanted to keep it that way. When he was let out for a shower, I crouched in the corner by the bars on my haunches to talk to Bonafide.

"What do I do?" I asked.

Bonafide said, "He's an eMe shot-caller, with a crew of fifty soldiers."

"I don't care how many are in his posse, I want him out of my cell," I said.

"Bring it to him then. Don't let him shine you on. Bring it. Bring it or get off the fucking tier!" I could see Bonafide's square face in the shaving mirror he was holding outside the bars, and he could see my face. "I'll watch your back. No one's gonna blindside you. You just do what you gotta do—bring it to him and keep bringing it."

The next day was hot and sunny. We were out in the exercise cage behind the block. A guard sat just outside by the fence gate, and two bulls on the catwalk never took their eyes off us. Boxer was in the corner doing his warm-ups, his arms out in front of him as he squatted up and down; then he dropped and pumped off push-ups and then back up, squatting up and down.

Bonafide grouped the cons at the opposite corner and was entertaining them with one of his crime stories, and I was pacing back and forth, trying to get the courage to tell Boxer to get out of my cell.

I stopped in front of him, to his right, and asked, "Can I talk to you?"

"What do you want?" he asked, exhaling without pausing his squats.

"I want you out of my cell," I said, wishing immediately I had said it with more conviction.

"Go fuck your mother," he said.

I repeated, "I want you out of my cell."

He cursed me again. When he said he wanted me out of my own cell, a firestorm of fury detonated in my brain and rage rushed through me. My eyes filled with bright flashes. When he went down for a squat again, my fist caught him under the ear on the right side. In a split second I followed with a left hook to the opposite side, then another right. I hit him with every ounce of strength I had, and it was doubled in force by my surging adrenaline. He went down, staggered to his knees, and fell back. He was partially unconscious, stunned, bleeding from a cracked cheekbone. He took out a shank he'd hidden beneath his sock and I grabbed it. I was standing over him, my feet planted on each side of his shoulders. In that moment, all I could see was his face, the blood pouring out from a wound in his cheek where a bone was exposed. In that moment, everything seemed so calm and quiet. I gripped the shank to stab him. For a second, every horrible thing that had happened to me in my life exploded to the surface as if had been building up to this moment. The blade in my hand, my legs spread over his chest, I loomed over him, staring into his eyes and then at his heart. While the desire to murder him was strong, so were the voices of Neruda and Lorca that passed through my mind, praising life as sacred and challenging me: How can you kill and still be a poet? How can you ever write another poem if you disrespect life in this manner? Do you know you will forever be changed by this act? It will haunt you to your dying breath.

Whistles. A gunshot from the catwalk crackled the air. Someone was pulling me back up from the avalanche of fire that had blinded me. I slowly emerged back into a conscious place and time and dropped the knife.

I heard Bonafide. "They're going to shoot you!"

I followed his eyes up to the two catwalk guards—their rifles were aimed at me.

"Move and you're dead!" one yelled.

Meanwhile, Boxer had gotten up woozy and pulled another shank, from his jockstrap. He lunged, saying with a startled voice, "Why did you hit me, why did you hit me!" Dazed, he kept trying to get at me, sweeping the knife, missing, stabbing the air, stumbling forward and coming at me again.

I backed off, kicked his wrist, and the shank flew out of his hand. I moved away, dancing sideways, keeping away from his lurches. I slipped and almost fell in his blood, trying to keep away from him. Two more shots stung the air.

The guard by the gate yelled, "Back off!"

I looked up. Two other guards on the wall had me in their sights.

Across the main yard, a security alarm sounded its siren. Led by Mad Dog Madril and Five Hundred, a half dozen visor-helmeted, shield-wielding riot goons dashed in swinging lead-filled batons. They drove me against the back of the cage with their batons. I balled up on the concrete floor with Mad Dog Madril choking me, Five Hundred shoving his weight on me with his knees.

Boxer was rushed away to Maricopa County Hospital, still screaming, "Why did you hit me? Why did you hit me?"

I was let up, drenched in blood. One of the goons asked, "Where are you stabbed?"

"I'm not," I said.

I was ordered to strip. The other cons stripped down too, and then we were marched naked into the dungeon. When I passed Snake and JJ's cell, Snake was trying to retrieve a pistol from a hole in the wall behind his locker.

"Bring it," I said, still angry. More than angry, I was feeling powerful and fearless. I had felt something in me, standing over Boxer, something that took my fear away and moved me closer to not caring about anything.

JJ was saying, "You're dead—you're fucking dead!"

Before Snake could get the pistol out, just as the expression on his face told me he had touched it, I moved on. The guard racked my cell. I jammed the gate with the guy's mattress to keep it from closing and gave Bonafide and Texas Red the guy's watch, cologne, anything of value that belonged to him; then I threw his mattress on the tier and announced for everyone to hear, "I don't want anyone in my cell!" Shivering from nerves, my legs feeling like I might crumple any moment, I splashed water all over me to wash the guy's blood off and then lay down.

In another section of the block, members of La Familia, another heavy-duty gang from Califas, were shaking the bars violently. Because of the goons marching down the tier, they believed a riot had started and wanted out. The cell block was vibrating. The atmosphere was volatile, dangerously unpredictable. About an hour later, JJ and Snake sent Texas Red a vial of Napa, a flammable liquid chemical, that guards sold to the gangs. When it was tossed into a cell and a match thrown in, the liquid exploded, charring the flesh instantly.

Texas Red called out, "JJ, Snake, I can't do it. He's straight up. He took the dude toe-to-toe. And he ain't no snitch." Texas Red passed it back, hand to hand, down the cells.

A while later JJ yelled to Bonafide, "Bony, here comes a package." Bonafide extended his cell broom out the bars and as the package came sliding down the tier, he stopped it. I saw it go by, a small towel-wrapped item.

A minute later he whispered me to the bars, "Cyclone, check it out."

I positioned my mirror and saw a .22-caliber pistol in his hand. I stared into his dark eyes, which were almost laughing at me.

"I'm not," he said, "but they're going to. Take as many with you as you can." Then he called JJ. "I can't play the hand. He's square up. I'm chilling."

As my hands trembled it seemed that the only thing that made sense anymore was poetry. I sat down and reread the poem I was sending Norman. I found myself wishing I still had time to change some words.

23 APRIL 1977
It seems
prison confines and destroys—
it does, I know, no need to argue
the point, just look at these
infamous edifices thrashing out,
consuming
human beings like bait sardines,
but I cannot stand on this.

Yes, the great iron hand of prison
crushes all in its grasp,
the mind and soul become
feeble sacks
filled with rotten fruits,
a gunnysack crumpled in a dark cell.
But to control your mind and soul
is to become a stronger hand,
embanking gently the loose clods
of a ravaged and confused past
so the river of your heart
and clear streams of your soul
may pass,
full and freely, into rich fallow beds
of freedom, waiting for you
even in prison,
even in prison; many will not understand this,
but I will say that we can
overcome,
not today, tomorrow, or next month,
but at the very moment
one decides upon it.

I kept reading the poem until I heard the faint rumble coming. I stuffed the poem in an envelope, and as the goons marched down the tier, gate after gate, to the dungeon, I handed the letter to Texas Red to mail for me and then I sat and waited.

Mad Dog Madril stood before my cell and yelled at the tier guard, "Rack it!" He ordered me to pack my stuff and follow him. "Everything to the property room," Madril instructed one of the guards.

As Mad Dog Madril marched me out of the dungeon, I kept thinking about the fight. He was down and I towered over him like an animal with a survival instinct to kill. In that one jeweled moment I felt I was God, deciding whether he would live or die. That feeling of power nearly compensated for everything that had gone wrong in my life. But as intoxicating as it was, something stopped my hand, poised above his heart, prepared to drive the shank in his chest. In that instant of indecision, standing over him and staring into his bloody face, I saw a man with a mother and father, siblings, a human being with dreams and feelings and loves. Thankful that I had not killed him, shocked I had even considered it for one shining moment, I was relieved to be leaving. If I had stayed longer in the dungeon, who knows what kind of person I might have become.

◆

I wasn't taken to isolation, as expected, but to DC, where I was locked up on Nut Run, which was reserved for severely medicated cases—cons that had flipped out or were there for presentencing court observation. Maybe the warden thought I was going crazy and moved me for security reasons. Still, to my mind, these reasons didn't justify assigning me to Nut Run. It seemed obvious to me that the warden was classifying me as a mental case just for harassment.

The two tiers below Nut Run were reserved for cons who had committed minor infractions and were on lockdown for a short period, from a day to a week. It wasn't as dark as the dungeon, nor did it reek, like places that hadn't had fresh air or sunshine in a long time. Nut Run was quiet, except when the zombies occasionally freaked. Intermittent shrieks crackled throughout the night, trailing off into the throbbing silence. My first night there I tossed and turned and couldn't sleep. About one in the morning, I overheard two cons talking on the first tier below about the contract on my head. Contrary to my expectations, they both stated it had been a stand-up fight and admitted that no one was going to collect on it. Besides, one said to the other, the guy's a nut.

The next morning, let out for a shower, I walked past the cells of disheveled cons staring at me with blank expressions.

Some wore white pajamas and paced in their cells, and the hems of their pajama bottoms were caked black with dirt from dragging on the concrete. Others sat on their bunks and stared at the wall. They had an air of decrepit infancy, a benign, paranoid frailty. They glanced at me with terrified eyes. They required little attention. When the meds cart rolled through three times a day, they stood at the cell bars, seeming to achieve serenity only when the medic handed each one a small manila packet of pills. All day, every day, they waited for the meds cart and, hearing it, became excited, picking at their flesh, scratching their faces, biting their lips, and clasping and unclasping their hands. I could almost hear them give a collective sigh as they swallowed their pills and reclined on bunks or shuffled back and forth in bare feet in a forlorn daze, in another world far away from prison.

Those guys didn't know what day it was or how much time they had served. They had forgotten the streets; their minds blurred and detached, they floated freely and had little if any association with their previous selves. The tier smelled like a hospital ward full of patients who haven't washed for months. The zombies only stirred when the meds cart was coming or when a white-coated intern would show up to recruit subjects for some new drug or shock therapy. All of them were blank-eyed, seldom out of their cells, and they never combed or washed unless told to do it.

The prison psychologist wore Bermuda shorts and a Bahama shirt, brown polished penny loafers, and wire-rim eyeglasses. He had bird-thin legs, wide hips, and a big butt; he was balding on top but had enough hair at the sides for a graying ponytail. Obviously believing his patients were monsters deserving of punishment, he put his career ahead of treating them, even if this contradicted the healing goals of psychology.

"Uh—how are you? Uh—my name's Dr. Reese. Uh—how would you like to come in and talk to me?"

He had an irritating habit of pausing when he talked, as if preoccupied with other matters. I knew that the warden used his diagnoses to assess our security status. I also knew he'd be out of a job if he found me sane. To keep his job he would label me psychotic, manic-depressive, violent malcontent, or schizophrenic.

"Leave me alone," I said. "You know nothing about me."

"Uh—I'll leave this here for the medic to pick up. It's a prescription. You'd like some Valiums, uh?" He smiled.

I approached the bars and took the paper and crumpled it and threw it at him. "I'm not playing your bullshit game."

He appraised me with an impatience that had more mockery than medical concern. "You—uh—need a psychological exam. Uh—your refusal will go on record, in your jacket, and you'll get a write-up. It won't look good to the Parole Board."

"I don't go before the Parole Board. I'm doing day for day. Flat time."

"Yes, I know. Uh—of course, but medication can help," he said, and rubbed his chin and left.

During the day, in the rest of the main block, the clamor was sustained at a steady buzzing level, and above the din were the always incessant guards, crackling out numbers on the intercom and slamming gates. *Rack A-Five, shower! Four-five-six-two-one, visit. Let's go, Jack, up and center! Now!*

Mad Dog Madril patrolled the tier every morning, and behind him, always, scurried his goons. They had enough hardware dangling from them—Mace cans, keys, billy clubs, handcuffs—that they resembled Western chuckwagons hung with pots and pans jangling over prairie potholes. Mad Dog Madril enjoyed scaring the paranoid cons, threatening them, telling them someone was coming to get them, and creating a state of terror in the zombies, who sometimes begged for him to stop. He had a face like a jowled pit bull, snapping, banging bars with his billy club as he picked out a cell and shook it down. He knew they had no contraband; they were conditioned to submit and would do anything asked of them, including what Mad Dog Madril made them do—drink toilet water, kiss his hands, sometimes even suck his dick through the bars. He ran Nut Run with impunity, a tyrant accountable to no one.

There were the slashers who cut their arms and wrists; a black dude in a waking coma, who didn't know his name; Hilda, who thought she was living an upscale hooker's life in the French Quarter in New Orleans; PeeWee, a redheaded Puerto Rican, who fancied himself a fisherman in Puerto Rico. Then there were Max and Wilbur, brooding darkly with sullen shoulders drooped and arms hanging between their knees, always looking down at the concrete floor in their cells. Meanwhile, my neighbor in the next cell, Richie, was Elvis, and all day he combed his black duck-tailed greased hair into a wave, singing and humming the King's songs.

As I watched these Nut Run cons over the course of three months, neither their sullen expressions nor their disturbed silence changed much. Every day they shuffled back and forth in their cells and took their pills and existed in disarming tranquillity.

One morning, however, after Elvis repeatedly complained about a toothache, his cheek and jaw swollen, Mad Dog Madril came by flanked by two of his flunkies.

"You got a toothache, Elvis?" Mad Dog Madril leered.

"Sure feels like it."

"Sing us a song, and I'll help you," Mad Dog Madril mocked.

"'Oh, baby, don't step on my blue suede shoes.'" Elvis raised his eyes and put his mouth close to the mike and swiveled his hips and sang.

"All right, all right," Mad Dog Madril said, "come here . . . closer to the bars, put your head here, gotta see what the problem is."

I was sitting on my bunk, and I could see Mad Dog Madril standing at the bars. He pulled pliers from his back pocket. Then I heard a crack. And while Elvis moaned in excruciating pain, Mad Dog howled with laughter and stepped to my cell.

"Here's the crazy one," he said.

I cursed him beneath my breath.

"Oh, the psycho's upset—in time, in time," he scoffed, the threat lingering palpably in his words.

◆

Reading books became my line of defense against the madness. I began writing poems for cons in exchange for books; one of those books was Anne Sexton's poetry. She too had gone to an asylum, but her poetry was inaccessible to me—too staged with academic technique and not spontaneous and from the heart. I started reading Ezra Pound and working with metaphors. The common language employed by William Carlos Williams also appealed to me, and Whitman's long adventurous lines fit my sense of what a poem could be—strong and large like life.

I would get up every morning and write for a few hours after breakfast. Then I would read for an hour, take a nap, have lunch, and read some more. For no apparent reason, I started getting very tired. I attributed my fatigue to the July heat. I increased my exercise routine in my cell to build up strength and stamina, but my fatigue worsened. I was having difficulty getting out of bed in the morning. After making my bunk, I lay back and covered my face with my arms. I stayed in my bunk with my eyes closed for a long time. My thinking had become cloudy and feeble, and stationary objects wavered as if they were being shaken. I heard myself talking to Elvis but seconds later couldn't recall what I had said. I stuck my mirror through the bars and looked into his cell. He'd be combing his hair back, cuffing his blue denim sleeves above the wrists, arching his collar, saying he was going to marry Priscilla and live in Memphis with her. My mirror crashed on the tier. I'd lie back down on my bunk in a mental swirl; my hands felt like they were slipping away from me. I had trouble controlling my body. When my meal tray was slid under the bars, I had trouble controlling my arms. They seemed to be moving on their own, leaving a trail of other arms in their movements. I barely had the strength to lift the tray, to get my throat muscles to cooperate and swallow the tasteless stuff.

A lull came over me as days followed days, and I felt an unfamiliar kind of peace as I grew weaker and weaker. I started to hallucinate. The walls moved, the ceiling wavered, disembodied faces of strange ascetics of Asian descent appeared in the ceiling corner of my cell, smiling. Days and nights came and went, with an opaque thickness, as if I were standing behind warped mirrors, and the cons on the tier looked as if they were moving behind milky panes. I ate my food with my fingers because I couldn't hold the spoon. I felt food crud on my chin and cheeks. I would find myself at the bars, standing in my pajamas. I didn't know what day it was or what I was doing or what was going on. I lay on my bunk and slept; from time to time I'd wake, stare at the ceiling, and go back to sleep again.

One day my cell gate drew back and two guards entered. One of them said, "Come on, fleabag, time to get fresh air and sunshine."

Obediently, I went outside with the rest, shuffling like an invalid old man to the main exercise field. It had been so long. I sat on the bleachers in the sunshine, my saliva dripping down my chin, my mouth feeling filled with lead as if I had just returned from the dentist and he had given me a mouth-numbing shot. It was bright; the sun was far away. Was I in my cell, imagining all this? Guys were running around the field. Others played handball or baseball or were boxing. It was hard to focus. A few cons came up to me. I saw their mouths moving but I couldn't hear or understand what they were saying. One was Macaron, my old buddy from years ago, who seemed like he was hollering. He looked worried. I felt myself trying to talk, thinking I needed to talk. Talk, I told myself, but I couldn't say the words. He motioned me no, no with his hands but I wasn't doing anything wrong. I was trying to speak to him.

He was yelling, "Take care of yourself, brother, *carnal,* take care of yourself!"

A small voice the size of a necklace bead of light radiated through my body with its own disembodied voice, struggling to get words out of my mouth.

"I am fine, brother; they are not breaking me; they can't, they won't, I am okay, I'm fine."

But I couldn't hear my words. Why couldn't I hear my words? I tried harder and harder to get the words out. I didn't know what was wrong, something . . . something . . . a con was pointing to his tongue, shaking his head no-no-no.

Macaron suddenly put his arms in a headlock around my face, which forced my eyes down, and I saw blood all over my shirt. I was trying to talk. I put my finger in my mouth, feeling for something stuck in it. I realized I had chewed my tongue and it was bleeding profusely. Chicanos surrounded me, pushed me at a run toward the exit gate on the field. Then the guards took me away.

I don't know when or how, but I was taken to the infirmary. When I regained consciousness, I was in my cell, my face wrapped in gauze. A leather strap kept me from opening my mouth. For a couple of weeks my tongue felt like a towel, stuffed in my mouth. I quit eating and, in my haze, sat all day on my bunk, listening to Elvis standing at the bars singing rock-and-roll. When, three weeks later, they finally forced an intravenous tube in my arm, I was so weak I couldn't even shout, let alone resist. Hooked to the I.V., I began to get clearer. I could hardly move my tongue. I tried to eat oatmeal and managed to swallow a little, but I was still afraid to chew. I got so tired of not being able to talk or chew my food that I tore off the leather strap and gauze.

Elvis told me they were putting medication in my food to make me lethargic. He said he'd seen them do it before, so that prisoners would go along with the program.

Unable to think clearly, had they continued, I probably would have gone along with anything they wanted. I would have been a good prisoner, had it not been for my need to speak.

ELEVEN

◆

It was late summer 1977, and I was twenty-five years old and had less than a year to do. Because of mandatory laws for drug possession, many more young prisoners were coming in with longer sentences, and the prison population had exploded, doubling in the last couple of years and far exceeding prison capacity. Nobody was single-celling. Overcrowding was so bad that Nut Run was moved from DC to CB1 because there were no cells for incoming convicts. With no more Nut Run, half the mentally ill cons had been dumped in Ad Seg on both sides of the block, and the rest were sleeping between the bunks in dorms under the cell blocks in general population.

Even I had a cell mate now. It had been almost five months since they had moved us here. There wasn't enough room for Tom and me, so I bunked on top, staying up there plucking my guitar and writing poems. Every time Tom used the toilet, his intestines came out of his anus and he bled profusely. I couldn't bear the smell or the sight of him standing there scooping his intestines into the bloody cloth he used to wrap around his crotch and waist to hold his guts in. I was no doctor but I knew it was bad, but he wasn't in the infirmary because the prison doctor didn't think so. Tom was in his late forties, weighed three hundred and fifty pounds, and slept on the floor because he was too big for the bunk. He'd been a pro wrestler, a fall guy in gangster-run clubs, and his cauliflower ears, mashed flat face, crushed nose, scarred arms, huge stomach, and bull shoulders testified to it. His brain, too, was damaged. His smile was crooked, his blue eyes dull, his speech slurred, but given all this he had the innocent candor of a likable adolescent. We lived together as best we could until one day, after I had returned from the exercise field, he was gone. He had had complications with his intestines and died. I felt sorry for him because his job in life had been to make a fool of himself, to lose, and his reward was only the mindless crowds screaming for his destruction.

I often thought of Tom when I heard the cooing pigeons and prairie doves roosting in the cell-block rafters. They awoke and chirped wildly when the lights came on in the morning. They had forgotten what a real sunrise and sunset was. They lived under industrial corrugated metal and creosote rafters and awoke to a fluorescent sunrise.

While most guys classified on Ad Seg were there for fighting or contraband, I was still refusing to work. So many cons were on lockup that there was a shortage of help, and instead of feeding us in our cells, we got to go to the mess hall to eat. After the evening meal, at mail call the guard left letters on my bars. I was corresponding with a woman, named Virginia, introduced to me by Norman, who was also still writing and sending me books from publishers, small poetry magazines, and other periodicals. The one letter I never expected to get, though, was from my *tia,* Jesusita, my father's sister.

◆

She'd always been quiet, almost invisible and very religious. The last time I'd seen her was in Estancia when I was a teenager. Mieyo had given my address to my sister and she'd given it to my *tia.* I still had conflicting emotions about Julian, her husband, who had forced us to go to the orphanage. In her letter she said she was still in touch with the Saint Anthony nuns. The orphanage had closed and been converted into a Job Corps office, and the Franciscan nuns were relocated to Indian pueblos around New Mexico. I wrote her with a message for Sister Anna Louise—that beating kids was not the way to handle misbehavior. I also asked for any information about my parents. Had she heard from them? Where did they live? What were they doing? When Aunt Jesusita wrote back with my dad's address in San Francisco, there was no mention of my mother. That was no surprise, because she'd never forgiven her for leaving.

I had a million questions. But as I sat down to start a letter to my father, every memory I had was a sad one: anger, drunkenness, violence. I couldn't think of a single time when we were happy together. I finally just kept the letter short and cordial. I was afraid I might make him back off. I had changed from the son he had scarcely known but as I wrote on wide-lined paper, choosing the simplest words, so he could understand, I became a little boy again, hoping for love and affection. I apologized for being in prison but assured him I was fine and getting out soon and I loved him very much. I kept it short because he was illiterate. Writing him gave me hope, and I dreamed of leaving prison and living with him someday.

I waited anxiously for weeks and no reply came. I wrote my *tia* to confirm the address. She wrote that he had been admitted to a detox center. That was good. I was reconnecting with my father and my *tia,* I was writing and had friends who were poets, and we were finally being allowed to go to the big exercise yard. Three times a week, after getting scanned at the checkpoint, I'd cut briskly to the right from the column of cons heading to the courts and bleachers on the left and start running around the circular dirt field. Fifteen times around made three miles, and I'd used up every minute of my time outside.

Sprinting hard for a long time, I'd fall into running reveries, my mind soaring above the prison, basketball courts, over the heads of sparring boxers on the field, gliding across the expanse of grass and the baseball field and beyond the rows of cons bending with short hoes in the vegetable rows as guards cradled carbines on horses behind them. My reveries always concluded with seeing my father and me together, living in a small apartment, taking evening strolls, and spending at least two months traveling in Mexico.

I came back from the field one day to find a letter from my father on the bars. It was written on a hospital pad with a unit nurse's name on it from the detox center. I was very careful with the envelope—his fingers had touched the paper, and mine touched where he had touched. I didn't want to tear it, so I heated some water with an electric tong used to boil water for instant coffee and unsealed it. It was just a few lines conveying his love and the news that he would be leaving the detox center soon. His handwriting was shaky, the simplest words misspelled, the tone apologetic.

After lights went off in my cell and the cell block quieted down, I would imagine my father in San Francisco as the evening bus deposited him at the corner. I concentrated hard in the dark to imagine him walking up and down the rolling sidewalk, carrying a paper grocery bag under his arm containing a loaf of bread, a package of bologna, and a fifth of Seagram's. I imagined him in a small room with a bed and dresser, rented by the week. The bottle would be empty, he's passed out, and then in the morning after shaving he would slap Old Spice on his face. In my mind, I followed him back to the bus stop and accompanied him downtown to another day of selling shoes. I thought how all his life he'd been a loner, and he was more alone now than ever, with no friends or social life, desperately existing on the threadbare hope of accidentally running into my mother. It never happened, though, and his life would always revolve around work, liquor store, and boarding room. And as the guard swept his flashlight across my face on his hourly head count, I imagined myself waiting for my father on his building doorstep. I imagined so many times that we would sit in a house and talk like father and son, and all I imagined myself doing was listening to him, hearing him talk about his growing up as a boy in Estancia, and asking him for tips on shooting pool.

◆

After running one day, I stopped in a circle with others watching two fighters in a ring. The black guy was good, but the gringo was blocking and counterpunching, ducking, jabbing, sliding in and out. He finally connected with a solid uppercut and laid the black guy out. The gringo then entertained us with hand speed on the bags, sweating in the sun, shinier than a new nickel, his gloves blurring against the body bag, grunting as he smashed blow after blow into it.

He grinned. "Any of you feel lucky, wanna try the roulette wheel?" He slapped his gloves, challenging us.

Without warning, a Chicano gangster standing next to me nudged me enough to make me step forward a foot to gain my balance. I stepped back immediately, but I had already caught the gringo's eye. He turned like a snow leopard responding to a slight movement in the grass.

"You want some?"

"Yeah, he wants some, you clown," retorted Chelo, the gangster who had "accidentally" shoved me. He started pep-talking as my impromptu manager. "Kill that meth-fed crackbrain sonofabitch." Chelo took the gloves from the black guy, pushed them on my hands, and laced them.

"I got a carton on this homie. I'll go two for one! Baby, jot 'em down." As Chelo's girlfriend started taking bets, he said to me, "Let him clown around, do his little three-ring-circus bit, and then roundhouse him. ¡*Snapeate,* bro! Get in there and take care of business. Do the drive-by and quit o-zoning!"

Caston, the black trainer, a nationally ranked light-heavy boxer, hit the bell. The gringo's hips, arms, head, feet all moved in different directions. He bobbed, weaved, slid in and out. I covered my ribs with my elbows and my jaw with my gloves to minimize the damage. To impress and entertain the cons with his speed, he came at me with a machine-gun succession of jabs, glancing off my gloves but still jarring me. He had style but no slugging power. I measured him through an opening in my gloves, waiting, anticipating. Flaunting his footwork, he dropped his hands at his sides and shook his gloves, showboating for the fans that he didn't even have to guard himself. I stepped in and bombed him with a left, a right, and another left. I moved through him with each punch, and he went down.

Caston leaped off the bench in the equipment dugout. "Man, what a left! Where'd you learn that shit?"

I declined Caston's offer to join his crew of boxers. I didn't need to have every young buck who came through the main gates wanting to take me on to get a reputation. I was content with the couple of cigarette cartons Chelo had given me after the fight.

◆

I didn't know Chelo before that, but I'd seen him and I didn't trust him. I'd heard he'd been one of the Inner Circle mafia bosses but was now their enemy. He was short but stocky and muscular, in his mid-thirties, with slicked-back black hair, blue oval sunglasses he never took off, not even when he went to bed, and a contrary demeanor that had helped him survive doing time at Marion, San Quentin, Folsom, Huntsville, and now Florence. He was a heroin addict and sported the baddest gangster walk, talk, and attitude. Not only were his back, chest, and arms covered with tattoos but tattooed teardrops dripped down his cheeks beneath both eyes. Meticulously cuffed and pressed blue jeans edged over the shoelaces of Stacy street shoes that glimmered with a spit-shine polish; his shirt was always perfectly creased; not a strand of hair was ever out of place. He had money on the books and cardboard shelves brimming with candy, cigarettes, doughnuts, and sweet rolls. He hustled everything and everyone, his stereo blasting Chicano songs and his color TV booming out sports games. His "girl," a long-limbed blond-haired darling called Tish, was always at his side. A foot taller than he, in tight jeans, high heels, and implants, she had had a contract put on her by the inner circle of La eMe for stealing drugs. They had ordered Chelo to make the hit. He had stabbed her with an ice pick close to the heart, enough to get her to the hospital but not kill her. He'd hoped the attempt would fulfill his obligation but it didn't. They put a contract on him. After count time at night, they'd carry on like teenage lovers, squealing and giggling; at other times they argued and fought like an old married couple.

As our friendship grew, he'd say, "Don't be so serious. Smile once in a while, let go and be happy."

After jogging, I would usually walk with Chelo. He began teaching me Chicano slang, Mexican/Indian words originating from Mayans, Olmecs, Aztecs. When combined, these words created our own distinct Chicano language, a language truer to expressing and describing my experience. In his early juvie days he had learned from older cons how to tattoo, and he'd done it for more than twenty years. His tattoos were like a walking library. He explained the significance of the turquoise Quetzal bird with expanding wings on his right shoulder, its feathers radiating red and blue rays in all directions. It was an Aztec sacred bird, its feathers more honored and valuable than gold or jewels. They were worn in priest headdresses and warrior shields. The jaguar, he said, lifting his arm to reveal a jaguar whose legs and head moved when Chelo flexed and unflexed his muscles, was a sacred animal. Holding class while we walked around the field, he shared with me the legends and folklore passed down to him from "pintos," Chicano prisoners.

I knew almost nothing about my culture and I was surprised by the extent of his knowledge. From history to language to politics, he had opinions on everything, and when he spoke he did so with a flair—his expression intense, his words passionate, his hands pointing or pounding or waving with conviction. He told me one day that to outsiders his tattoos symbolized criminality and rebellion. But it was not so, he said. "I wear my culture on my skin. They want to make me forget who I am, the beauty of my people and my heritage, but to do it they got to peel my skin off. And if they ever do that, they'll kill me doing it—and that's good, because once they make you forget the language and history, they've killed you anyway. I'm alive and free, no matter how many bars they put me behind."

Chelo's stories made me think a lot. I couldn't answer him when he asked if I knew the primary cause of death among our people. "Broken heart," he said. The more I thought about it, the more it made me wonder whether my grandfather hadn't died of a broken heart. Certainly my father drank because of a broken heart. When their dreams had been crushed, when their prayers seemed never to be answered, when life seemed to cheat them out of every glimmer of happiness, their hearts broke. And then alcoholism and despair set in.

I guessed it was from thousands of broken hearts, and an attempt to mend them, that gangs started. Chelo had said prison gangs had originated in the early fifties with a guy named Cheyenne from Los Angeles. He established a group of Chicanos in Chino, a facility for young offenders, to study, educate themselves, stick together for protection, and help every young Chicano coming through the gates. He raised money to build small satellite educational sites throughout California where cons could meet and learn. The State of California labeled the meetings as gang gatherings and shut them down. They took to meeting in prison yards, mess halls, and barbershops, on tiers and in churches. Hundreds and hundreds of new Chicanos were signing up every month, and within a few years, ten to fifteen thousand Chicano inmates were part of self-help groups designed to help each one succeed in life.

"Drugs, *compadre,* drugs," Chelo had said. "Every time. I seen guys kill their brothers for a fucking gram. That ain't a man, that's a spread-legged junkie bitch with a dick. Twenty-five years I been doing time, and instead of getting together we kill our own. It was some rival gang that took Cheyenne out because he wouldn't have anything to do with drugs."

Every Monday, Wednesday, and Friday, after our discussions, I managed to fill my journals with ideas and sort out the information Chelo was sharing with me. I wanted to put some of it in my poems, use my time and energy to explore how it tied into my own family, and save it for later, when I was free to go to a library and do research. I'd grown up in an American society filled with stereotypical labels that discredited my people as inferior and lesser in moral character. Chelo went back to the beginnings, telling me that our people, the indigenous people of this continent, the Mayans, Olmecs, and Mexican tribes, were hundreds of years ahead of the Europeans in mathematics, agriculture, astronomy, literature, medicine, engineering, and aqueduct systems. Little by little, from our conversations, I began to see who I was in a new context, with a deeper sense of responsibility and love for my people. I wrote these poems during this time:

6 AUGUST 1977
Healing Earthquakes
Through little garden plots I was enchanted by
Nuns cultured at the orphanage,
Through streets torn and twisted like gnawed bark
I lived on like an insect,
Through all the writers and artists of America
Who never wrote my story,
Through all the stately documents deceiving my ancestors,

Quietly by itself are the Healing Earthquakes,
From sides it comes
Through the black-knotted drunkenness of my father,
Through the cold deep bowels of hope,
Through the trowels of sombrero'd bricklayers
And wall-builders spreading the moist mortar,
Through all the Chicanos in work T-shirts,

To the snarling guards that broke loose from their chains,
To the crumbling houses of the poor,
Through the scorpion-tailed magnums and carbines
Held at their heads by death squads,
Healing Earthquakes comes up from the debris and rubble,

Splitting its own body and heart
Into a million voices and faces,
Mumbling below in its own discontinued winds,

Threading slowly my torn soul in a grip of fury,
To the eye of its mark it leans undaunted.
I am Healing Earthquakes
Not in the swirling commotion upward of the atom bomb,
Nor the blast and heraldic upshoot of a rocket,
A lesser man by all the lawbooks,
A man awakening to the day with a place to stand
And ground to defend.

14 AUGUST 1977
When that force
          shrieks out of me my chains rattle
like a great footstep on brittle cornstalks,
                              my soul came forth
to me like cold water upon my sleepy face,
and ivory words turned dark in my breath
like a fountain of such ancient rock wet with dew
and a few trickles crackling the silence
and round and hovering thick uncasual branches
with leaves dropping swaying softly
round my toes,
                    this was a thirsty man's pleasure
                    to bathe in my soul's cool water
                    and sleep in its shade
                    and hear its motions
                    silver water drop
                    contently to measure time
                    extend a day into a dream.

That's how it came to me, loosened from its sorrow
like nails plucked from its shoulders and knees

it withdrew its sorrow of silent spikes
and with them penned a poem across my heart
and sang that song that silent tears silenced
such silent tears such storms
that washed and pounded and hurled out and up every single thing
and left me standing with a song, the long hush
of waves destroying and rising to swallow up my life,
gave my voice a sing, and snapped those chains. . . .
My soul came forth,
dripping wet and cool and vibrant
a handful of butterflies let loose
to flutter like harmonica notes
on blue-jeaned breeze
worn at the knees and buttocks, sliding down hills
while a band of whirling butterflies
unfolded rose-twirled wings
my soul came forth.
It came
flute music footsteps and its touch a simple happiness,
felt through my feelings
to see them different than others had
their fullness stuffed, now before it starved,
cleaned, revived, emptied, and drought-mouthed,
It came then.
It came
strong and warm to my eye, then deeper to my soul,
became part of me, with its great force
like an earthquake, tornado, or erupting volcano,
Wake up!

For months cons had been talking about a riot. Guards were using five-point hold-downs, harassment shakedowns, classifying people as gang members and locking them down, cutting time on family visits, and writing up cons for minor bullshit infractions. Then one day my sessions with Chelo were interrupted when a guard was killed in CB1. The guard, who went out of his way to harass cons, had been walking the third tier on count time when, for no perceptible reason, he collapsed and died. I found out later that a con had moistened magazine pages and rolled them tight into a hard cone that would act as a dart blower, about three feet long. He scraped a bobby pin to a needle and melted the end to a plastic Bic cap. He molded the Bic cap so it fit perfectly down the dart blower chamber. The guard came on the tier screaming at cons because their toilets were flooding over. The whole tier had jammed towels along the floor and bars so the water couldn't run into the tier. When the guard came to the dart blower's cell, he puffed and the pin went through the guard's beige uniform shirt, into his heart, and out his back. The blue plastic Bic end of the dart pin came off on impact and fell on the tier. It was washed away when the towels and blankets were taken out and flood waters rinsed the blood and floated the corpse down the middle of the tier to the entrance of the stairwell. The paper blowgun was burned and flushed.

The cell block erupted in high-pitched staccato yelps of victory, and an hour later it went up in smoke. Reserve units and off-duty reinforcements gathered in the main yard, putting on gas masks, carrying shields, clubs, and pistols, preparing to storm the cell blocks, but they held off. Cons were burning and ransacking cells. Smoke billowed from the windows and the whole prison was on level-five security lockdown. Electricity was turned off, water shut down.

All of us got swept into the violent hysteria. We burned mattresses, blankets, beat the bars, hammered, and shook the iron cage gates, trying to get out of our cells. Somebody finally succeeded and opened the control cage on two tiers and then racked open the cells. Chelo came by and gave me an ax, the blade a piece of porcelain cracked off from a toilet tied to a cell broom handle with a torn strip of sheet. I cut holes in my bedsheet, soaked it in water because of the fire heat and smoke, and wrapped it around my face. I threw my blanket over my shoulders as a serape to deflect any shanks that came my way, and then I stepped out on the tier in ankle-deep sewage and billowing smoke.

Some of my friends took control of the back half of the tier. There was Clifford, Skunk, Wedo, Luis, Wizard, Gumbo, Ray Ray, Spray Can, and Snoopy, my celly.

Wedo and others were ripping off the mesh screens that enclosed the tier. Some cons were dragging out suspected child molesters or snitches and stabbing them. Others grouped in packs on the tier, ready to defend themselves. Across the landing cons were chiseling at bars on cell gates with angle iron, hammering with prison brogans. I thought it was impossible for them to cut through reinforced iron, but over the next eight hours they had cut through the bars, squirmed out, and opened more cells. Twenty-four hours after the takeover, the National Guard and prison officers attacked with fire hoses, shields, rifles, and tear gas—and took the block back.

They had us lined up naked against the wall on the ground floor, as they stood with rifles aimed behind us. On the tiers above us, goons went cell to cell, hurling down TVs, stereos, and anything else they found. National Guard officers ordered us not to move, but Ray Ray turned and they shot him. His blood spattered over my arm and the side of my face, but I couldn't move to wipe it off. I couldn't help him. I wanted to scream that this was madness. I wanted to scream that this shouldn't be happening. With my arms above my head against the wall, I put my head down and saw the officer kick what Ray Ray was going for. "Check the frame for drugs," he said to another guard. Through the corner of my eye, I saw it was a shattered family portrait of Ray Ray with his wife and kids. Later, I dealt with Ray Ray's murder the only way I could. I wrote a poem for him and sent it to his family.

Following the riots, politicians promised in the media to do something about the overcrowding and inhumane conditions. It was ironic that Mad Dog Madril was one of the guards who escorted legislators through the blocks. They were so fearful they were visibly stiff and could hardly do anything but look straight ahead and mutter *oh yes, oh yes* as Mad Dog explained the cells, tiers, and the way the block worked. They couldn't wait to get out to the parking lot again. Sweating in their nice clothes, they looked up, around, and down, with an air of important resolution. They were instructed not to talk to the convicts. When they came down my tier, most of the cons were telling them to do something. I don't know why, perhaps partly from shame or anger, but I turned my back to them. I didn't want them to see me like a caged animal behind bars. They had only come to get votes to get reelected or out of perverse curiosity to see human beings who had become animals. Nothing would change.

We were put on indefinite lockdown. The block sounded strange with no TVs or stereos blaring. My guitar and typewriter were trashed and I was back to writing on paper with pencil. I'd study every day, past midnight, with cons yelling back and forth in the block, the dark giving anonymity to voices cursing, joking, talking trash, and greasing the rumor mill. You couldn't see their faces, just hear voices.

"I am the spirit of Malcolm X, I am the spirit of Malcolm X," one con repeated over and over again until somebody replied.

"I got your number, punk, you better strap down on the yard 'cause you gotta see the devil tomorrow!"

"Quit putting your business on the tier, bitch!"

"Got any coffee, Louey?"

"I need some soap to wash my clothes."

"Let's go to the canteen tomorrow."

"Yo momma, I'm gonna fuck you, punk!"

"Quit sand-bagging, bitch!"

"Yeah, Cyclone, what you doing? Is that all you ever do is fucking read?"

My lamplight on, pacing back and forth in my cell with a grammar book in my hand, I called back to the con, teasing him. "Studying you, Felipe."

"What do you mean, studying me?"

"Yeah," I'd say. "Studying you in this book."

"What do you mean in that book? What kind of book is that—better not be my court transcripts!"

"Says here in the book that you are a human being."

Felipe asked, "Does it got me in it?"

"Says," I would continue, "you're a noun."

"Don't fuck with me," Felipe threatened.

"I'm not. A noun is a person, place, or thing. You are a person. A human being. And you, Flaco, you are a verb, fastest thing on two legs, all action, brother. And García, you're an adjective: flair, pizzazz, and color." It was my way to visualize grammatical abstractions. I could remember them by applying the grammatical terms to cons who personified the elements of grammar. Picturing certain cons in my mind helped me recall what a verb or noun or adjective was.

"Cyclone, read us one of your poems," Chelo called out.

I read one about the legislators coming through the block.

They Only Came to See the Zoo

Our muscles warped and scarr'd
Wrap around our skeletons
Like hot winds
That sweep the desert floor
In search of shade,
Sleeping each night
In the hollow of petrified
Skulls.
And from our mouths
Words of love would come
If we let them,
Like molten stones shrieking
From the belly of a volcano.
But standing at these bars
We watched you leave
And only wondered. . . .

You looked up at us with passion
As we stood at the bars.
A vacuum swelled and our hands
Went pale, our fingers cold.
The gray pity of our lot
Made you turn away.
But our spirits met that moment
Faraway in the land of Justice
And we whispered with our eyes,
"Come closer,"
But you did not.
It's been so long now
Since you left.
Did you tell them
Hell is not a dream
And that you've been there?
Did you tell them?

After the block quieted and cons gradually dozed off, I'd stay up reading, enjoying the calm, until one or two in the morning. I tried to sleep but, behind my eyelids, memories would light up the faces of my brother and sister and how our lives had moved so far apart we were all but strangers now. It was as if a curse hung over our family. I had less than nine months to do, and I was twenty-five years old. After my release I wanted to see us all together—aunts and uncles, mother and father—but it was wishful thinking. No one got along, my mother living in fear that my father might find her, my father still haunted by his delusions of winning her back. I ached in my heart to turn back time and change the way things had been.

◆

Not long after the guard was killed, Mad Dog Madril escorted me one morning to the warden. I'd been expecting it. Convict after convict had been pulled out of his cell and interrogated about the guard's murder. I was dreading the possibility that the warden might try to implicate me or blame me for the stabbing and beatings that happened to cons alleged to have been snitches or child molesters. When I walked in I told myself to remain calm, answer his questions, and keep my responses short.

I stood before him and showed no emotion. I expected him to get worked up, but he didn't look upset or aggravated; in fact, he was relaxed and easygoing.

"Hot weather, ain't it?"

I didn't answer, caught off guard by his statement.

"Listen, I've got something to tell you. Your father passed away."

He was trying to get me to react and by chance get me to admit that I knew something about the murders.

"Your father passed away," he repeated.

I could feel my face blanch with a crushing sense of shocked helplessness. Stunned by this unexpected news, I detached myself from the person receiving it. The warden wasn't speaking to me but to someone else.

"You don't care? Just as well, because your family doesn't want you to attend the funeral services. It's our policy to allow you and we're willing to do so, but"—he paused—"not even your family wants you."

He had nothing more to say. As I walked back across the main yard toward the block, it was as if I were a little kid again, holding my mother's hand, walking down that county jail corridor in Santa Fe to see my father. Except it was *I* who was now screaming inside for *him* not to leave. Instead of his voice pleading for me to return and save him, I heard my own voice begging for him to return. As a child, visiting him in jail, I was terrified of the dark gloom that inhabited those cells, haunted by those hopeless eyes that stared so bleakly at me. The jail he was in stank of suffering and despair, but I had grown up and was not afraid of shadows anymore. I was now joined to my father through the misery and oppression we had both endured. I may have been a criminal in society's eyes, but privately, to honor my father's memory, I vowed never to let them break me. To honor his memory, I would never let them take my pride from me, never give them the pleasure of seeing me beg for mercy.

We could have lived together, walked along the Rio Grande river trails, laughed and watched football games, read the Sunday paper, worked on the roof, planted a garden, loaded wood in the mountains, gone piñon picking, roasted and peeled green chile, traveled, but none of this was going to happen. When a tide of grief welled up in me, I closed it off. When I almost cried, I held back the tears. When I felt myself wanting to get into a fight, I turned away.

My writing became the receptacle for my sorrow. I wrote even when I didn't want to, because I knew that, if I didn't, my sorrow would come out in violence. I wasn't able to express my grief. It felt as if my heart was bound like a kidnapped hostage. I silenced its voice, but the more I wrote in my journal, the more I felt deserted by everyone. My family's not letting me attend the funeral only added to the pain. I kept to myself, afraid of the growing emptiness in me.

I sincerely wanted to mourn him. He deserved at least that, at least one person on earth to forgive him for all his unfulfilled promises, all the expectations never achieved, for a life littered with broken bottles and lies, tears, outbreaks of rage and violence. I crouched in my cell, trying to weep, but I couldn't. I was mad at myself for not crying for my father, and I butted my head against the sink, repeating, "Cry, cry, cry!" I knocked my forehead against the cell wall. I kicked my bare foot against the steel bed leg, trying to create enough pain for tears, but I couldn't. I paced back and forth, slamming my fist into my open hand, commanding myself to weep, but I couldn't. I hit the steel toilet with my fist until the flesh around my knuckles split to reveal chipped bones. And then a calm coldness came over me. A chill fury exploded in my heart and became the numbing determination to beat up a guard. I was anesthetized with a wrath that even God could not quell. I felt prepared to destroy my life in a frenzy of violence. Because, even as I looked at my reflection in the stainless steel, I saw no tears. Life in prison had killed a part of me.

I received a letter from my sister, explaining the real reason why I couldn't attend the funeral. Julian, Aunt Jesusita's husband, had called the warden and said I had threatened him, and it was best for the family if I stayed away. It didn't make sense to me. What I didn't know at the time was that my father had left me a twenty-thousand-dollar insurance policy, with instructions to use it to hire a good lawyer. Julian, however, convinced my Uncle Santiago, who has the same name as mine, to fly with him to San Francisco and sign the insurance check over to him so he could use it—ostensibly for paying a lawyer to get me out. Of course, he never intended to do that. After the money was deposited in Carlos and Julian's account, it was used to buy a liquor license or some such thing and never mentioned again, but I didn't find out about any of this until I had left prison.

TWELVE

◆

CB1 had been thoroughly trashed during the riot, and civilian construction workers were brought in to repair the damage. Prisoners were reassigned to different blocks and during all hours of the day guards would yell, "Pack it! You're moving! Up an' at 'em! Hubba-hubba!"

Sometime in November 1977, Mad Dog Madril called our numbers, and about a dozen of us packed and were escorted out of the block. We crossed the main yard, and went out the security gates at the west end toward the field, and turned left. Beyond the two rows of fencing was the minimum-security area, with a cluster of gray block barracks. Cons in white khakis carried books and moved easily along the complex sidewalks; some were probably attending GED classes. We went down a narrow road, enclosed with coils of razor-wire across the gravel and above, creating a tunnel of thorny spikes. At the end was a small new two-story cell block.

The ground floor housed convicts, and the upper level was a cafeteria. The entrance faced north and a single hallway ran east–west for the entire length of the block, with cells on each wing facing one another. A guard in a cage at a control panel operated the opening and closing of all the cell doors. Behind the guard cage on each side were steel shower stalls. It was devoid of the clamor that pervaded the main-yard blocks. Each cell had a steel slab door with a shatterproof port window, and behind the windows cons faced other cons, using hand gestures to communicate. As I passed each cell I recognized some of the gang bangers, Nut Run prisoners, and Ad Seg lockdowns. Mad Dog Madril led me down the corridor. The guard at the controls punched his panel buttons, and a loud pop sounded, hurting my ears.

I walked in and the door closed behind me automatically, with another pop that grated on my nerves. I looked out the port window in the door at the faces looking at me. I figured there were about fifty new cells, freshly painted gray, each with a stainless steel toilet and sink, a sheet-steel bunk with angle-iron legs bolted to the concrete, and a single recessed light with protective screen. The one significant addition to the cell was a window. For years, all I had seen were the main-yard walls. Everything stopped there. I stood at the window gazing out at the weight pit and the basketball half court and the convicts moving around the educational barracks and felt like I was the most fortunate guy in the world.

All I did for the first month was stand at the window, smoking and studying sparrows bathing in the dust. We went out each morning for a couple of hours to exercise. I lounged in the sun, against the wall, my thoughts on poetry. Afterward, we washed up and went upstairs for lunch. Meals were the ordinary institutional grub, no worse or better than boot-camp chow. After lunch it was back down to the cells, where I napped, read, and wrote until shower time and supper. The only interruption to this calm routine were the electronic door latches. They locked and unlocked with a deafening report that ripped through the nerves and made me jump every time. Despite this, I wrote contentedly, trying to describe the rising sun, the sky, the clouds, dirt, weeds, moon, and stars.

During this time I met a prisoner named Nick, who was in his late forties and wrote for newspapers. He was short, thin, and small-boned, with thick black-framed reading glasses, and he leaned in when listening to someone. He was generally quiet, thinking about what he was writing. At TV time every evening we gathered in the hallway, and he would appear in a silk gentleman's jacket, smoking a Cuban cigar. When I told him I wanted to be a poet, he gave me Russian novels to read. I especially loved the landscape portraits of Turgenev and Chekhov's stories. Nick's success made a huge impression on me. It was clear that even in prison it was possible to be a writer.

I was still writing Virginia, Norman's friend in North Carolina. She had sent me history and poetry books. I couldn't get enough of Mexican history, Aztec poetry, and Mayan religion. The more I read about my ancestors, the more significant I felt. I was making their history mine as well; I began to feel myself fused to thousands of years of culture. It was as if this new knowledge was peeling off layers of wax paper from my eyes. I had a clarity of thought and feeling I'd never experienced.

I gazed out my window at the swatch of oily grass hugging the base of a telephone pole. I wondered how the grass survived, wondered what it felt when the sun entered its pores and fed it the glowing food that made it grow. I wondered if the grass had a mind, a soul, what it felt about the prison, how it transcended the bitterness of the environment and imbued itself with the sheer joy of living. I closed my eyes and, for hours, focused strictly on the grass at the utility pole base, and I felt my soul grafting with the grass blades. I seemed to be able to feel what it felt: the golden warmth of sun, the dancing breeze waving with light beads in my blood, the earth in my body roots.

One day, looking up from my journal to stare absentmindedly at the cell wall, I experienced a revelation. In the wall—in the sand and mortar and stones and iron and trowel sweeps—were the life experiences and sweat of my people. It contained a mural of my people's toil, their aspirations, their pain and workmanship. I imagined my grandfather's hand smoothing out the concrete. I saw my Uncle Santiago stepping out of his truck, laughing, and I could hear him talking in his good-natured way to his friends.

The iron that made the bars came from a mill in Silver City; the workers who had built the mill came from little villages on the plains. The dirt that mixed with the cement, before it was scooped up and trucked and delivered to make this wall, had been prairie soil where families camped and a woman had lain and gave birth to a child. In my mind's eye, a bonfire raged and people ate deer meat. People had slept on this dirt, tilled it for their crops and gardens, built their adobe homes with it. It had given them shelter, kept out the howling winds, the rain, and the snow. I could smell the promise of the cornfields and see water from the Rio Grande irrigating the chile plants. Children played in the alfalfa. From all directions, people arrived to celebrate a birth, mourn a death, erect a hay shelter, round up stray livestock. Vaqueros slept in their bags on the ground, under the stars and the moon and the clouds, and from the darkness of the wall came light, and knowledge of how people lived in the way of the sun, rising with it, depending on it for their crops and for the health of their souls and hearts.

I too was flourishing, my body physically affected by my words. When I put paper and pencil down after a day of writing and lay back on my cot and closed my eyes, a sudden eruption of energy sizzled at my tailbone and went up my backbone like scalding water on a hot frying pan. It burned a fuse line up to the base of my skull and catapulted me forth through the top of my head and out of my body. Incredible as it sounds, I would find myself floating above my cot in my cell, looking down at my body lying peacefully below me. I did this deep meditation every day for months. It was the start of my out-of-body travels. A physical substance—call it soul or spirit—left my body, intact with sensibilities to feel, see, and hear. I visited Theresa's house. I'd sit in the rocking chair and watch her for hours, then go visit my brother and sister in her trailer. I could do whatever I chose, appearing anywhere, anytime. While these out-of-body flights were pleasant for me, I would always return to the cell, trying to make sense of the experience. I pulled my flights back because I had no way of understanding them. I feared that if I continued to leave my body I might not be able to return to it.

Language was opening me up in ways I couldn't explain and I assumed it was part of the apprenticeship of a poet. I culled poetry from odors, sounds, faces, and ordinary events occurring around me. Breezes bulged me as if I were cloth; sounds nicked their marks on my nerves; objects made impressions on my sight as if in clay. There, in the soft lightning of language, life centered and ground itself in me and I was flowing with the grain of the universe. Language placed my life experiences in a new context, freeing me for the moment to become with air as air, with clouds as clouds, from which new associations arose to engage me in present life in a more purposeful way.

To keep from isolating myself too much, I went outside to break away from my out-of-body travels. I welcomed the hot soothing sun on my face. I took off my shirt and lay on the ground. I was almost asleep, half in dream, half awake, when I heard my name called. I opened my eyes. At first I didn't recognize the convict in white khakis in the minimum-security area. He was standing against the fence, something we maximum-security cons couldn't do. When my eyes cleared, I saw Rick, dressed in sharply pressed white denims, carrying schoolbooks.

We looked at each other. I thought of Lonnie, my old girlfriend, and Carey. I'd heard she was a heroin addict, but I hadn't seen or heard anything recently about how Carey was doing. Rick looked like a college fullback, clean-shaven, sporting a crew cut, beaming with health, bulked up from lifting weights. When we first came to prison, who could have guessed I was going to become a poet? And my journey here had all started because Rick sold heroin to the narc that night. I knew from the way Rick was looking at me that he was thinking about what had happened to me. Maybe not that I was a poet, but I was sure that he'd heard how I had refused to work and spent my time on administrative lockup. On the surface, it appeared he had fared better than I. But I knew he'd snitched on us, and cowardice is hard to live with. I didn't envy him a bit. The day he signed papers agreeing to be a witness for the state, he signed away his dignity. And that was why, even though he appeared to be doing better and looked much better, it was he who looked away, who couldn't keep his eyes on mine, who moved away from the fence.

Seeing Rick brought back all the reasons we were in prison and made me reflect on the changes in me. I started having a series of strange visions that ended in something resembling a nervous breakdown. I had been hearing voices for quite some time. However, one morning when I lined up as usual for breakfast behind the cons upstairs—which I had done a hundred times—the cons began to age visibly, as if I were holding a remote control and had pressed FAST FORWARD. Their hair grayed, their features wrinkled, they hobbled forward in an old man's stooped shuffle, and then their clothes began to shred. Ragged strands clung to their emaciated limbs, and then their flesh fell off and I stared at a line of skeletons, collapsing into a heap of dusty ash. I left the line of skeletons and headed toward the coffee machines. All around me the kitchen crumbled and flames smoldered and I stepped through the debris and filled my cup with coffee and walked to where the tables were and sat down. I couldn't hold the cup. I tried to lift it to my lips but my hand shook uncontrollably. I tried both hands around it, but my head shook. I put the cup down and with my right hand I tried to hold my neck from behind and push my head down and hold the cup with my left and draw it up. But this failed too. I stood and walked out of the kitchen, certain I was having a nervous breakdown. I brooded for weeks without uttering a word, staring off into space and seeing waves of molecular light beads tidal-waving on the air. I saw with my eyes what you see with microscopes. I responded to everything with a gloomy stare, walking past, paying no attention at all.

During the next few months I tried to curtail my out-of-body traveling and to exercise more. I tried to focus more on practical writing exercises. Every morning I tried to sketch out the rising sun, to write down and describe the landscape's changing hues and shades and contrasts, how plants turned from blue to yellow in the dawning light. It was intended to improve my writing skills. I closed my eyes to nap but couldn't sleep. In the darkness of my alert mind, a white ivory horn curled from a wide base upward to a narrow tip. I was at the very top, the size of a small pinkie finger, and I slid down the horn, round and round to the bottom.

A few weeks later, upstairs in the cafeteria, I took a tray and followed the serving line. My head was always down, so when someone whistled, I don't know why, I assumed he was whistling at me, and with my tray half filled with food, I flung it at the con I suspected of whistling.

He looked at me angrily. "I wasn't whistling at you."

"I don't care. Don't whistle when I'm around."

It was totally out of character, but it happened, and no convict lets disrespect go unchallenged. When I finished my oatmeal, I went outside, and three of the kitchen servers were waiting for me. I had on my roomy blue prison coat with deep pockets, and I figured as I stood before them on the landing that they thought I had a shank in my pocket. It was a showdown. I stared at them and they stared at me. None of us moved. Suddenly, staring at them, I saw past their faces, past their flesh, into their hearts; I saw them as infants, their parents addicted to drugs, screaming and drinking. I wanted to tell them something of what I just saw of their childhood, but instead I walked down the stairwell and into my cell. After this incident, my nervous breakdown seemed to end as abruptly as it had started. The whole episode left me feeling timid and vulnerable.

At the end of December we were moved back to CB1, as they had fixed all the damage. Despite all the internal disruptions I had gone through, I felt good. I was becoming a better poet. I boxed my denim shirts and pants, underwear and socks, books and letters and stationery supplies. I was emotional. Leaving a cell was for me like leaving a house I grew up in and loved. My cell brimmed with my constant emotional transformations, insights into my experience that ignited in my breast and allowed me to experience emotions of joy and rage that had always struck fear in my heart. I hated the prison system and witnessed gruesome crimes against human beings, but I sometimes found myself astonished by the endurance of some cons, and my heart was gladdened by the humor they used to poke fun at adversity.

After packing, I waited on my bunk, thinking of my cell as a womb from which I was repeatedly born into a person with greater and deeper convictions. I reflected on the challenges in understanding certain poets, on how I loved Neruda's work more and more, and Whitman's expansive celebrations of the common person. Russian writers wrote under oppression and gave me hope. My cell was my monastic refuge. Instead of closing in on me, shutting me off from life, and cannibalizing me, my cell was the place where I experienced the most abject grief, in which I yearned to the point of screaming for physical freedom. Through the barred cell window I saw lightning and thunder and rain and wind and sun and stars and moon that mercifully offered me reprieve from my loneliness. There I dreamed and kept intact my desires for love and family and freedom.

But the moving box was troublesome—packed boxes had haunted me since childhood. Everywhere I went, I arrived and left with a box; it reminded me that I had no place in this world, that no one wanted me. It seemed there was always a box nearby, ready to be filled with my clothes and shoes. No matter how I tried to get rid of them, they were always with me, in view, never thrown away, the one concrete object I could count on to be there, when everyone had abandoned me. In the orphanage, boxes were stowed in the attic; so many sad kids came and went down the hallways with boxes in their arms. At the detention center in Albuquerque, each kid was given a box to be filled with clothing and set square under the bunk with all his photos and letters and court documents. In the county jail, prisoners who were sentenced carried their box with them out of the jail and went into prison carrying it.

The box reminded me how paltry my life was. Guys my age on the outside had jobs, girls, careers, futures, communities, children. I had well-thumbed and dog-eared journals. Being a con gave me an identity, a purpose, a reason to wake up. It was good to struggle, and I carried on with vigor, eager to challenge the enemy. But the boxes still gave me a feeling of failure. I stared at them with a nauseating anxiety, recalling the ride from Estancia to the orphanage, when I had been taken away from Grandpa and Grandma. Or at my Aunt Charlotte's when I ran away to her, hoping to have a normal life, and came home to find boxes in the truck bed and Aunt Charlotte saying they were taking me back to the detention center.

In this cell, meditative hours spent in solitary writing and reading broke old molds, leaving me distraught and empty and forcing me further out on the edge for answers to my questions and pain. Psychic wounds don't come in the form of knives, blades, guns, clubs; they arrive in the form of boxes—boxes in trucks, under beds, in my apartment when I could no longer pay the rent and had to move. Still, I was comforted by the thought that I was bigger than my box. I was what mattered, not the box. I lived *out* of a box, not in one. I was a witness, not a victim. I was a witness for those who for one reason or another would never have a place of their own, would never have the opportunity to make their lives stable enough because resources weren't available or because they just could not get it together. My job was to witness and record the "it" of their lives, to celebrate those who don't have a place in this world to stand and call home. For those people, my journals, poems, and writings are home. My pen and heart chronicle their hopes, doubts, regrets, loves, despairs, and dreams. I do this partly out of selfishness, because it helps to heal my own impermanence, my own despair. My role as witness is to give voice to the voiceless and hope to the hopeless, of which I am one.

I stood at the window one last time and gazed out on the weight pit, the half court, the place where I usually rested and remembered something the *curandero* from my childhood village had told me so many years ago. His sacred name was Piriwheendela, which means he was born with everything backwards. They said his heart was on the right side, not the left, that night was day to him, that he walked with eyes closed. He was one of my Grandma Baca's friends. He was old and stooped over and walked with a red-

and-yellow sacred cane. He loved to sip wine from a tin cup he carried in his sheepskin jacket pocket. Mumbling sacred phrases to himself, talking to spirits constantly, he would sit on the porch and listen to men and women sing *corridos* and play the violin and accordion. One day when I was racing through Grandma's kitchen after my brother, he stopped me by gripping my arm firmly and told me to close my eyes.

"Run your finger down the cane," his ancient voice instructed.

I slowly felt down the cane, over the gridwork of carved images, and then stopped my finger. I opened my eyes. It was the sun image.

He looked kindly into my eyes. "Ah. The sun will guide you in a special way. It will bless you with its power of vision."

I had no idea he meant it would be in a cell, where light that feeds the heart and soul is needed so much and where for the last few months, I had been gathering it like bundles of wheat in my arms and milling it into journal entries and poetry.

THIRTEEN

◆

As soon as I walked back into CB1, I shrank back from the noise. Convicts were everywhere, three tiers high on each side, in a crazy-chain reaction of showers steaming, numbers screamed over speakers, TVs and stereos blaring. After getting my cell in order and cleaning it, I stood at the bars on Baker Run (second tier). The same cells retained the same faces, and there were more new convicts just starting their sentences, coming in on the landing with rolled-up mattresses and starched prison blues.

It was the first I permitted myself to think about how much time I had left. When I went to the dungeon, poetry had come into my life and fully absorbed me. As long as I was writing or reading, time passed by quickly. When I first arrived, I vowed that I would not think about time because I knew keeping my mind inside the walls, in the present, was going to keep me alive. I didn't have a wristwatch or calendar to mark off days. I never thought about how much time I had done or how much I had left. After doing half my sentence, I should have felt like I was over the hump, but each day was as indistinguishable as the previous one. When I had first walked through the main gates, I had cut all ties to my past and connections to the outside. I didn't have to appear for parole release before the Parole Board. I never had pin-up *Playboy* centerfolds or photographs of girlfriends taped to my cell wall. I had five flat years to do, and from the beginning to the end I had resigned myself to doing them day for day. The days never hurried or slowed, they settled like heat waves at dawn that evaporated like mist at dusk. Whether it was Friday or Monday, March or December, one year or three, it didn't matter. But now, looking down at the new convicts, I realized that in a few months I was going to be free.

I had nothing out there, no one and nothing waiting for me. But freedom meant that I wouldn't be living in a six-by-nine cage and guards wouldn't have the freedom to order me about every minute of the day. Could I make it out there? I felt a mixture of trepidation and excitement stirring in my heart, a subdued anticipation beginning to take shape and growing with each day.

Back in the old cell block, my cell cleaned and in order, I spent my time standing at the bars on Baker Run and writing letters. Virginia and I had been corresponding for months. Her letters alleviated the tedium and, even more important, made me feel like a man again. She was a poet with three published books. At first our correspondence was literary in nature, but it had evolved into a passionate romance. Every day at mail call I waited for Captain Avenitti to deliver the mail. I liked officer Avenitti. I had written a poem for his daughter's First Communion, and he was so grateful he had smuggled in green chili for me. When I heard him coming down the tier, my heart would race and I'd stand at the bars. Virginia and I had given each other intimate nicknames—she was Mariposa, the butterfly, and I was Colibri, the hummingbird. Her letters were perfumed, and hummingbirds and butterflies were sketched on the envelopes with colored pencils. Sitting on my bunk, I'd inhale the perfume again and again, retrace every delightful line, and imagine making love to her. I imagined walking with her in the woods around her house in North Carolina or sitting on our bed after supper and reading poems to each other. I suggested to her, because of my previous disasters with Theresa and Lonnie, that she write a series of poems on what a woman needed, how a woman felt, what she dreamed, and what she wanted in a man. I, in turn, would write of a man's deepest secrets. Our letters, often two a week crisscrossing each other, grew from a page or two, to ten pages, to fifteen and twenty pages, each one filled with an erotic hunger for what we were going to do to each other when we finally met.

She described her place in the woods, and the rustic life appealed to me. Ponds and woods surrounded her cabin in the Piedmont foothills, and I could stay home and write all day if it pleased me. I could fish as I wanted and use her father's canoe to float around the pond behind his house, reading a book of poetry, my fishing line loosely floating on the water until a fish took the bait. Slowly, I'd mend the psychic ruptures incurred during my imprisonment.

She wrote ten- to twenty-page poem-letters, all about a woman's desires, her dreams, what parts of her body could be stimulated to give the woman different kinds of orgasm. She dove into the feminine depths, into the female soul and her many labyrinthine emerald lagoons and coves to reveal her jewels, fashioned by age-old tides of earth and moon cycles. Her poem-letters revealed exquisite mysteries of a woman's spirit and indulged equally in lusty debaucheries. I clung to each word like puppet silhouettes flitting behind a paper curtain, believing it to be her flesh. I was insatiable. I didn't want to waste time with park-bench talk and holding-hands romance. I was possessed with a deep hunger to understand womankind, to know a bit about the darkness of lust, the spiraling jettison of blind love so many talked about, about motherly sweetness and the wench's cruelty.

I was also doing other writing. Long after the rest of the cons in the block were sleeping, I'd be answering letters to Norman and my *Tia* Jesusita, trying to decide which poems to send to Timberline Press in Missouri or Rock Bottom Press in Santa Barbara. The two small presses had each asked for a small collection of poems to publish as a chapbook. This filled me with tremendous excitement and self-esteem. Most of the poems had grown out of my commissary needs: cigarettes, coffee, paper, and pencils. That is, I wrote special poems for prisoners in exchange for things I needed. I composed sentimental poems for cons missing family holidays, nostalgic regrets for being absent from a son's birthday, sweet affirmations for anniversaries, devout gratitude for Mother's Day, and other poems of personal significance to prisoners. Although they were written for others, the poems expressed my own dreams and fears. My intellectual and emotional growth was also evident in their increasing literacy and the deeper understanding of myself that they revealed.

Macaron had come back to prison and was celling in CB. Chelo also had managed to get a cell on Baker Run with Tish, and he turned me on to Aztec and Chicano poetry. He emphasized the importance of reading poems aloud, exhorting me to recite my poems through the bars to him as he stood listening intently, nodding his head when a verse line was good and wrinkling his brow when it was bad. He had a critic's instinct for knowing a good poem; this talent came from his motto, NEVER BACK UP. He had put his life on the line so many times that he had an uncanny sense of what's real and what's not. There was no room for academic foreplay or pretentiousness. His convictions came by standing his ground in the trenches, face-to-face, chest-to-chest, and eye-to-eye with the enemy. He said I was still too serious and to lighten up, and one day, to tease him, I wrote this fun poem, which gave him a big grin.

It was the night of Friday
And all through the town
Not a hooker was working,
No narcs were around.
The joints were all rolled
And put into stacks
In hopes that we'd soon be
Stoned to the max.
When all of a sudden
There came a loud knock
And everyone yelled
It's a cop! It's a cop!
We went to the door to
See who was there,
To see who it was
That gave us a scare.
And what to our glossy red eyes

Should appear
But a pound of Colombian
And two cases of beer.
The guy standing by
Was wearing a smile
So we invited him in
To party awhile.
He spoke not a word
But started to roll,
Opened a beer,
And lit up a bowl.
By two in the morning
All had gone well.
The people were happy
And screwed up as hell.
We heard that guy say
As he waved us good buy,
"Marijuana to all,
And to all a good high."

I wrote poems for convicts, and the poems belonged to them. However, in another notebook I kept poems for magazine submissions, and for a year now I had been writing established poets by submitting work to magazines. Norman Moser, editor and publisher of *Illuminations;* Denise Levertov, poetry editor for *Mother Jones;* Joseph Bruchac, editor and publisher of the *Greenfield Review;* and the Chapel Hill journal, *The Sun,* when it was little more than a handout; also *Seer's Catalogue* from Albuquerque and *Akwasasne Notes,* up in Canada. PEN in New York sent me poetry chapbooks and poetry newsletters. Richard Shelton had been (and still is) conducting a writing workshop for prisoners here in Florence, and since I wasn't allowed to attend I sent him my poetry and he read it and wrote me back with helpful suggestions. Another poet, Rex Veeder, helped me to improve by inspiring me with the confidence that I really could write poetry. They were all wonderful people and I could never have managed without their help.

◆

One morning, Baker Run was racked out and we all lined up in the landing in twos, to go to chow. We were marched out the back of the block and lined up single file at the back doors to the chow hall. At the doors I grabbed my tray and moved slowly forward with the line.

The chow hall was huge; besides the field, it was the only place where a crowd of cons could mingle loosely. Guards were stationed at various points. You couldn't see their eyes because even indoors they wore aviator sunglasses. I slid my tray on the stainless steel counter past the servers, offering it under a plastic divider to the kitchen help, who heaped it with mashed potatoes, pork chops, corn, and green beans. At the soft drink machine I was filling up my cup with Kool-Aid when someone behind me said, "Been a while."

I turned. It was Carey.

But he was different now. He had Aryan Nation tattoos on his arms, neck, and chest, where part of a big chest tattoo spread up to his pecks. He looked a lot older. We sat at an empty table with four seats. A guard moved close to our table, monitoring us because it wasn't that often that a Chicano and an Aryan skinhead shared a table.

"It's been a while," I said, lost for words. "You and Lonnie still together?"

"Yeah." He was stiff and cold. "How come you been locked up on Ad Seg all this time? You got problems with people? Can't you handle being on the yard?"

His question implied that I was a coward.

"I think it's bullshit," he said.

"The warden and me had a standoff, that's what happened. But what happened to you? I can't believe you joined the Aryans. We were fall partners, running dogs, and we can't even talk now."

"It happens," he said flatly.

The tables were immovable, the round steel seats welded to the table's center pole driven into concrete and bolted down. But I felt there was so much anger in Carey that, if he wished, he could have ripped the table apart.

"I just wanted to tell you that I think it's bullshit!"

I didn't remind him that four years ago my trouble started with saving Rick's life because he had asked me to.

"You're leaving soon, aren't you. I shot that FBI and saved your life and you're getting out while I've got a shitload of more years," he declared. "I'm glad, because if you weren't I'd probably have to kill you."

I didn't know how to respond. I didn't say anything as he got up and joined other Aryan skinheads at another table. I got my tray, deposited it at the wash window, and went out at the other end of the chow hall.

For days afterward, his words kept repeating themselves in my mind. *I shot that FBI for you, and you're getting out.* I felt ashamed and guilty. I was partly at fault for the destruction of his life. There was nothing I could do to make up for it. But at least he had Lonnie. She'd been released a year and a half ago, and she was probably living in Phoenix and coming up to visit him on weekends. I had no choice but to accept and live with his hatred for me.

Around this time, just after I saw Carey, it was growing harder to do time because I was counting down the days as my release date got closer and closer. Toward the end of February 1978, I received a notice to appear before the Parole Board. I tried to explain to the escort officer that I wasn't supposed to see the Parole Board, I was a flat-timer, doing day for day. He didn't know anything, just that I was wanted in the parole office. I went, thinking that, once there, I would explain to the committee that I had no parole.

When I entered the small room by the entrance to the main gates and sat down before the committee, I saw the warden standing behind them.

Before I could say anything, he began. "Three-two-five-eight-one has consistently broken every rule in the book and has conducted a campaign of disruption since his arrival."

The chairman looked at him. "I don't have his records here. I'm sorry." He motioned the guard to take me away.

I assumed they had the paperwork mixed up and had faith that they would straighten it out. I left it at that and, since I was so close to leaving, took myself out of my books and writing and resumed my running around the field. I ran under the sun, happy to be alive. I lay on the grass and stared up at the blue sky, inhaling the dirt smell and the sage and prairie scents that stimulated every nerve.

A week later, I was again called out. Again, the warden was present. The board was murmuring among themselves, with the warden whispering something about my refusal to work. With glum faces they ticked tongues and sighed and told me to leave. They still hadn't cleared up the paperwork. I reminded them that I was doing flat time, five years flat, and I was not supposed to have a parole hearing; my time was day for day, no good time, no two-days-for-one; that other cons were doing just day by day too and I was almost done. But all my explanation did was confirm their belief that I was a troublemaker.

April 17, my release date, finally arrived. I had my boxes packed, and I sat in my cell the whole day waiting for someone to come and get me, but nobody did. Then, toward the end of the day, a guard came to escort me to the Parole Board room. They had finally figured it out. But when I got to the door, the warden met me. Before I could walk in, he said it was the wrong day and ordered Mad Dog Madril to return me to my cell. Where the Parole Board usually sat, the seats were empty.

The warden was fucking with me. For days I said nothing, did nothing. I went to eat and then back to my cell. I was trying to hold myself together. I got another slip to appear before the Board for the following morning. All night I tossed, eyes wide open, staring into the cavernous cell-block space and wondering if I was ever going to get out.

This time, the parole hearing was conducted as if they were really considering my parole. They hardly asked me any questions at all. Sitting with the board members behind the desk, it was the warden who spoke, saying that my defiance was a personal affront not only to him but to the members of the Parole Board.

"Three-two-five-eight-one," he declared, "you have never worked, you have disobeyed the rules of this institution, ignored every regulation, and it is the decision of this esteemed committee to deny your parole—"

"I have no parole, I'm doing flat time!" I cried out, exasperated.

Mad Dog Madril grabbed me and took me out. I went willingly, without struggle. I didn't know what they were doing. I was supposed to be free. It was a mistake and I still clung desperately to the hope that they would find it and correct it.

I tried not to let it get to me, but my nerves were going. Then sometime in late April, at night, the shakedown goon squad came through the cell block late at night and took me out of my cell and made me stand in the dark corridor by the main guard cage at the entrance. I was scared to death that they were going to set me up with contraband and give me more time. But after an hour of waiting, I was returned to my cell.

On the field I ambled aimlessly around. I was falling deeper and deeper into melancholy. The warden has finally won, I thought; he has finally broken my spirit. I was thinking of things I wouldn't ordinarily entertain. There was a certain convict who had taken a baseball bat and beaten a Chicano over the head. I had been playing handball when I saw it happen at the far end of the field. After finishing the game with Macaron, I walked over to the convict and told him that if I didn't get out, I was coming for him.

About this time a beautiful boy by the name of Chiquita had come to my cell and asked if I would be her sugar daddy. I had never messed around with a guy, fearing that it might ruin the pleasure I found in being with women. But now, thinking I might never get out, I told her that if I didn't make my Board, we'd talk, and in the meantime, I'd keep her under my wing and make sure nobody raped her. I'd never talked to fags in prison. But as Chiquita began to sit at my table in the chow hall, and as I listened to her talk, for the first time in my life I realized that some men really had female spirits. When I spoke to her, I was speaking to a woman.

I was called to the Board again in May. When I appeared before them, they dismissed me within minutes, saying they were reviewing the warden's order superseding the court's sentence. I was shocked that it was under review. It made me lose all hope. I went to the cell block, borrowed a shank from Wedo, tied it to my inner thigh, and went out to the field to look for the guy.

He was not there.

I went to the cell block. He was not in his cell.

I went to the chow hall and there he was, sitting with his Aryan skinhead brothers. I walked past the tables with cons eating, staring directly at him. I was within a yard of reaching him, when at the corner of my eye I saw this friend of mine, Mascara (Mask because of his burned, disfigured face), get there first. I couldn't have been more than two feet away when Mascara stabbed the guy. I kept moving. Guards rushed Mascara and took him away.

Later, I sent a kite to Mascara asking him why he did what he did. He wrote me back a kite saying he was already doing life and wanted to spare me the same. He wrote that I didn't belong in prison, that I needed to be out there writing for people like him, telling the truth about the life that prisoners have to endure. Mascara would walk with me around the field and we would talk. He was short and tough, not someone to mess with. He had a brave heart. The apartment he and his sister and mother lived in had caught on fire. As the flames engulfed the house, he woke up and called for his mother, but she was dead on the couch. He was on fire, but he grabbed his little sister and dragged her out. She was dead too, from smoke inhalation. He blamed himself for her death. After he saved me, I wrote three poems dedicated to him.

By the beginning of June, I was cracking up. I had lost a lot of weight and I had sleeplessness circles under my eyes. I was belligerent and surly because I was supposed to be free but was still sitting in prison. I was already beginning to think that I might have to stay indefinitely or do my sentence over, when one night around 4 A.M. Captain Avenitti appeared at my cell. He startled me at first. To have a guard appear at your cell in the middle of the night usually meant you were being taken out to get beat up or worse. He had a flashlight and he shined it in my face. I blinked, still half asleep, not sure what I was hearing.

"You're going home. Get ready. I'll be back."

His footsteps echoed sharply in the silent cell block. When he finally reached the landing below, I got out of my bunk.

"Captain Avenitti," I whispered down to him, "what did you say?"

"You're going home."

"It's not a set-up? I'm really leaving?"

"You're really leaving, Jimmy. I'll be back."

I was going home. I scanned the dark and quiet cell block. I hadn't pictured myself leaving like this. His steps and keys in gate locks gradually faded away. I didn't dare believe it, not until I was outside the gates. Over the past month my emotions had been out of control, in free fall—one moment I was happy, and the next, brooding darkly with depression. I didn't allow myself hope. It was best to expect the worst. But as I got dressed and boxed up my poems and books, I felt a great loss at leaving my friends behind. I wanted to wake up some of the guys on the tier to say good-bye. They were closer to me than any family had ever been. But then suddenly the door creaked open and I looked out and saw the tier guard. I stepped out with my box and walked down the tier. I looked in the cells at my friends, all asleep; I felt for each of them. I wanted to take them all with me. All they needed was a little help. I felt again as I had felt at the orphanage when I ran away—a despairing, horrible sense of leaving so many human beings like myself with no resources to make their life better.

Outside, under the night sky, I felt myself solidly placed. In many respects I was not ready for freedom; I didn't know what to expect, how to live in the world. But as far as having changed, and being proud of what I had accomplished here, I was okay with it. I felt like a star in the sky, glowing, with darkness all around me.

At the property room, Captain Avenitti gave me twenty bucks for the road. He handed me a paper bag with the clothes I had worn when I was first arrested. The big spotlights illuminated the deserted main yard. The captain's black boots crunched on the hard-packed ground. Everything here had weight and substance, intended to silence, imprison, destroy. Yet somehow, I had transmuted the barb-wire thorns' hostile glint into a linguistic light that illuminated a new me. In a very real way, words had broken through the walls and set me free.

Avenitti led me to the main gates. He called up to the catwalk guards to lower the bucket. He handed me my release papers to sign, and I did. He put them in the bucket dangling at the end of the rope. The guard hoisted the bucket back up. He signaled the guard tower and the gate slowly slid sideways, letting us through. The stars flickered. The moon glowed in the sky. A prison bus was waiting, sputtering smoke out of its exhaust pipe. The sun was just coming over the horizon. It would be another hour before it emerged but I could smell the sage, the parched dust sucking the moisture of the night.

"I never thought you'd make it out alive," Captain Avenitti said. "Good luck."

I didn't say anything, I just nodded and walked to the bus. There were two other inmates aboard, a black dude and a white one—enemies of mine at one time, because of their skin color. They looked at me and I looked at them, a hard glare, and then we smiled, on the same side now. I sat down. I didn't dare look back as the bus drove us away. I was scared, vulnerable, believing at any moment we might turn back. I looked out the window, the inside bus light reflecting a stranger's twenty-six-year-old face off the glass.

EPILOGUE

◆

I was still a convict at heart. I didn't know, when I left Florence and went to live in North Carolina, that I was going to have such a difficult time being with people. Many times, standing in a corner at a cocktail party, or in the office of a magazine editor, or at a gathering of writers in Raleigh, I yearned to be back in prison. But the thought of going back made me grit my teeth in bed. I gritted my teeth loudly the whole time I was with Mariposa, not because of anything she was doing, but because of the nightmares I was having. I stayed with her for two years, and then, toward the end of 1980, I moved up to Blacksburg, Virginia.

In Virginia I picked some strawberries in the fields and loaded tobacco leaf in tractor trailers to earn enough money to buy myself a beat-up Harley, and here and there I managed to contract my services as a poet to community centers, art centers, and schools to feed myself. But I couldn't afford an apartment, so I slept in my sleeping bag by the nearest river I found myself. Then, since I had been thinking about Albuquerque almost every day, I decided to go back.

It was a long hard ride on that Harley, but I took it easy, stopping and camping out, eating free fruit from orchards and other vegetables from fields as I encountered them along the way. After I finally rolled in, tired, hungry, thinner, but happy, the first thing I did was look through the want ads. I managed to land my first job on the graveyard shift as a night watchman at a house for court-supervised adolescents.

In 1981 I met the woman I married. She was a counselor at the house, and one cold evening when I had come in on my Harley, freezing, wrapped in my jacket and mittens and scarf, carrying a backpack full of books, she asked me what I was reading. When I showed her all my poetry books, she smiled and invited me to her house for dinner. After that, we met on a regular basis and became good friends. One snowy morning she called me to say she was driving a kid to his village in the mountains and wouldn't be back until late. I told her the roads were dangerously icy up there and I would drive them. I knew the roads, she didn't.

Within a few months, she was pregnant. We moved in together. Shortly after that, we bought our first house with a thousand dollars down. It was an old, seriously wrecked fixer-upper. When I took a claw hammer and yanked the nails from the plywood covering the front doorframe, all these drug addicts who had passed out in the living room woke and stared at me, wondering if I was a narc. They'd been using it as their crash pad. When I told them I had bought the place, they laughed that anyone would be stupid enough to buy such a decaying heap. For a whole year, every day from dawn to dusk, I fixed the place up, rebuilt the entire house, and trucked more than fifty loads of trash in the backyard to the county dump.

After my first son, Antonio, was born in 1983, my mother came back into my life. I was thirty-one and I hadn't seen her since the brief encounter shortly before going to prison. I had friends always coming by to help out, and on this day I was up on scaffolding taping Sheetrock and smoothing stucco in the cracks in the cathedral ceiling, when she drove up in a new Lincoln Continental. No one knew she was my mother. She was quite a sight. In a short red dress, lush sandy hair curling over her ample cleavage, big diamonds on her fingers, and silver and gold bracelets on her wrists, her green eyes sparkling, she looked up and greeted me cheerfully.

"Hi, honey." She exuded health and optimism.

I climbed down the scaffold. "How'd you know where I lived?"

"Your sister told me," she said. "We're best of friends now."

My sister had tried to persuade me to see my mother, but I had declined. She had bought my sister a new house and Mieyo a new motorcycle and had given them both additional money as they needed it.

"I came to see my grandbaby," she declared, with a big smile.

"They're not here. They've gone shopping for food."

She left after visiting awhile, but after that she stopped by every day. When she came, I stopped working and we went outside and sat on a plank bench in the shade. She asked if I would teach her Spanish, and I told her she could hang out and pick up the language as we spoke it. She had not spoken Spanish in so long she had almost forgotten it. She started coming by a lot, hanging out for hours, mimicking our Chicano language, practicing her words against ours. We had a good time. She'd spoken Spanish as a child, and it came back to her. I guess to compensate for her guilt at leaving, she offered to buy me a house, give me money, help me out in any way she could, but I told her I was okay and didn't need anything. I was working on a book of poetry at the time and asked her if I could stop by sometime to interview her. I wanted to know more about her life growing up on the ranch in Willard and what her family was like, her childhood, and her life with my father.

It was a beautiful spring day when, with a recorder and legal tablet, I drove up to the affluent area where she lived. Her house was white brick, red shingle roof, impeccable lawn and garden, the perfect magazine cover for *Good Housekeeping*. She hugged me at the door and led me to the kitchen table. She was always busy and vibrant, on the go, planning this or that social event, shopping, receiving friends. Her life seemed perfect. She introduced me again to my stepsister and brother, in the same manner as she had introduced me years before, as her good friend. Richard, who had never liked me, greeted me in the kitchen, his cordiality overlaid with mistrust.

He left us alone, though, as we proceeded with the interview. At first she was all bubbly and eager to tell her story. But as the interview stretched over days and then weeks, she began to skirt certain questions I asked. Full of euphoria about how good times were growing up, she abruptly stopped and then burst out weeping. She tried to light a cigarette but her hands were shaking too much, so I lit it for her. She looked at me, tears streaming down her pretty face, and broke down, muttering through convulsive sobs that she had been raped and her brothers had made fun of her when she was young for being overweight. That was why she kept herself so attractive, because it was what men wanted. If you were pretty, she had learned, men would give you anything you wanted.

Then I asked about why she had hid her past and her identity from her children. She said her husband had forbid her to tell them. And his parents thought she was white. She exploded in telling me this—her teeth clenched, her fist slammed the table, spilling my coffee, and her face flushed red with rage.

"All my life I've had to hide who I am, because Richard's parents wouldn't let him marry a Hispanic. But I'm going to tell them. I'm going tell them everything and I'm going to tell my kids the truth too. I'm leaving him. I can't stand him, or the lies I'm living. I'm going to go out whether he likes it or not. I'm filing for divorce. I can't take it anymore." She reached into her purse, twisted off the cap, and swallowed some pills. "I can't live without drugs. Just to go home, I've got to be drugged!"

A few weeks later, while I was loading my truck with trash, she came by to tell me she had told her husband.

"And what'd he say?"

"He said if I tried, he'd kill me."

"Does he mean it?"

"He's said for a long time that he'll kill me if I leave him. But I can't lie anymore. I have to tell my children and his parents the truth. Only then can I start living my life."

Later in the week, she called to tell me she had told her children about Martina, Mieyo, and me. She also told her husband's parents that she was Hispanic. She planned on seeing a lawyer about a divorce and would call me back. I found out later that she was in her kitchen polishing her nails, preparing to go dancing, when Richard came into the kitchen and shot her in the face five times with a .45. Then he put the pistol to his temple and killed himself.

Mieyo never got over it. He plummeted into drinking and drugs. He lost all connections to reality and just wanted to find oblivion. He had loved her a great deal. He had always wanted a mother, wanted her love, and when she came back and they got together, he was happier than I'd ever seen him. After her death, he spiraled out of control, drank every day, and started using crack cocaine. When he called me once to come get him, saying he needed help, I went immediately. I hardly recognized him. He'd been beaten by several men with bats. He was six foot one, and normally weighed close to two hundred pounds. He was less than a hundred pounds, and because his arms had needle marks and because I wanted to make sure he didn't have AIDS and his skull wasn't cracked, I took him to see my doctor. After he checked out okay, he took a bus to Fort Lauderdale, Florida, to live with Martina, who had moved there after Mother's death.

Around this time Martina heard that Theresa had died from a drug overdose. She was not going to let the same thing happen to Mieyo, so everywhere Mieyo went she went with him. For the time being, he was happy and not using drugs. He was working and making a lot of money. He was exercising, riding his bicycle, lifting weights, and taking vitamins, and he weighed over two hundred, all muscle. I was happy to hear this, and once I even talked with him on the phone. He sounded great, saying how much he enjoyed fishing, how he loved Florida, that living there was like being on a permanent vacation. About six months went by. My sister had called me once during that time telling me Mieyo had gone back to drinking. She hadn't seen him. She was worried about him. Then she called again, weeping, scarcely able to get a word out until finally she said that someone had killed him. They had found him in an alley, a bloody galvanized pipe next to his crushed skull.

I went to the funeral, and, using every bit of strength I had, I went up to his coffin and looked into his face. I touched his hands, rough from the carpentry work he'd done most of his life. What went through my mind was how he had never been able to express himself. Like my father, he was shut down emotionally. And I didn't know even how to think about this, the three most important people in my life, with no linguistic skill to express themselves. They lived in shame. They lived with guilt. And then my father choked to death when he came out of a treatment center, my mother was shot to death when she was about to start living her life, and my brother, trying so hard to stay clean, relapsing, but always trying to stay clean, was bludgeoned to death in an alley. It has taken me a long time to understand how so much injustice could happen to such good people. Why had my family gone through so much tragedy? Why had they met with such horrible deaths? Why so much suffering? They were three people trying to regain their self-esteem, after being considered too brown, after being raped, after being abandoned. They kept trying to make a comeback and heal themselves. But they couldn't seem to get past the pain.

Months later, still struggling to understand my brother's death, I found myself one evening in Santa Fe, standing before Saint Francis cathedral. It was where I was baptized. I went in to see what it looked like. I didn't know what the event was, but a lot of people were in the pews. On one side were Indios, on the other side parishioners. A young priest was shaking the hands of the Indios. The Archbishop and scores of other priests milled around, talking to the people. Everyone seemed in good spirits. I asked this lady next to me what the special event was and she said the pope had proclaimed that this evening every Catholic church was formally to ask for forgiveness from the indigenous people, the Indios, for the atrocities perpetrated on them in the name of God by Catholics. In essence, the church was apologizing for its acts of genocide.

I was okay with that and decided to stay for the whole service. Then I saw this young couple approach the altar and stand in the center. He looked just like my father and she looked just like my mother when they were both young, in their late teens. They were holding a brown baby that looked just like me in the photographs my sister had shown me. They were my parents and I was the baby they were preparing to baptize. I saw them exactly as I must have been here once with my parents, innocent, my whole life ahead of me, they with their dreams still intact.

And suddenly I began to forgive them for what they had done or had not done. I forgave myself for all my mistakes and for all I had done to hurt others. I forgave the world for how it had treated us. As the priest stepped up to the fountain to begin the baptism, I had so much emotion welling up in me, with such violent force, that I knew I was going to cry and cry and cry. As the ceremonies began, I left the pew, genuflected, and walked out.

Outside, tourists were laughing in candlelit restaurants, others were drinking and carousing loudly in open-door bars, and the streets were wet from a light rain. I walked down a deserted street, wrapped in my coat, my head down, feeling an overwhelming relief from giving and accepting forgiveness. I felt it was a new beginning. That little baby was me, before my father became a drunk and died in the gutter, before my mother left and was murdered by Richard, before I was taken to the orphanage and the D-Home and then jail and prison, before Theresa overdosed, before my brother was murdered. I was innocent and pure. I was that child, free to begin life over and to make my life one they would all bless and be proud of. I was truly free at last. And as I thought this, it began to rain harder and the cathedral bells started ringing.